God the Eternal Contemporary

God the Eternal Contemporary
Trinity, Eternity, and Time in Karl Barth

ADRIAN LANGDON

WIPF & STOCK · Eugene, Oregon

GOD THE ETERNAL CONTEMPORARY
Trinity, Eternity, and Time in Karl Barth

Copyright © 2012 Adrian Langdon. All rights reserved. Except for brief quotations in critical publications or reviews, no part of this book may be reproduced in any manner without prior written permission from the publisher. Write: Permissions, Wipf and Stock Publishers, 199 W. 8th Ave., Suite 3, Eugene, OR 97401.

Chapter Four is an expanded version of "Our Contemporary from Now until Eternity: Christological Recapitulation of Time in Barth," *Princeton Theological Review* 17:1 (Fall 2011): 7—21. Permission has been granted by the editors of the journal to republish the article.

Wipf & Stock
An Imprint of Wipf and Stock Publishers
199 W. 8th Ave., Suite 3
Eugene, OR 97401

www.wipfandstock.com

ISBN 13: 978-1-61097-998-6

Manufactured in the U.S.A.

Contents

Acknowledgments vii

Introduction: Eternity, Narrative Time, and Analogy 1

PART I: Overcoming the Babylonian Captivity
One: Eternity as the dissolution of Time? 21
Two: Rethinking Eternity and Time 56

PART II: Barth's *Analogia Trinitaria Temporis*
Three: The Theatre of the Divine Glory: The Father and Time 85
Four: *Anticipatio et Recapitulatio*: Christology and Time 123
Five: The *Vinculum* of Contemporaneity: The Holy Spirit
   and the Time of the Community 159

Conclusion 187

Bibliography 207
Index of Names and Subjects 217

Acknowledgments

THERE ARE NUMEROUS PEOPLE to thank who helped bring this work to completion. The germination of the project began in a seminar on Barth with Prof. Douglas Farrow at McGill University. Subsequently, Prof. Farrow patiently guided my doctoral studies and the dissertation on which the book is based. His always-perceptive advice guided my murmurings and hunches into a more coherent and manageable exposition. His own work has not only been engaged in the following pages, but his passion for theology and his meticulous scholarship has been a constant example. I would also like to thank Paul Molnar (St. John's University) and Torrance Kirby (McGill University) who were examiners on my committee, as well as John Vissers and William Klempa (both of Montreal Presbyterian College) who were readers. Their perceptive, detailed, and probing questions and comments were challenging and encouraging. It was truly a gift to have my work read and evaluated by them all.

I would also like to thank Wipf & Stock for publishing the book, and especially Christian Amondson, who graciously guided me through the publishing process. Others have been involved in the process as well. Chad Hillier read early drafts of Chapters 2, 3, and 4 and offered valuable comments and suggestions. His friendship has also been extremely important in the last number of years. I would also like to thank staff and students from the Department of Religion and Culture at Wilfrid Laurier University and the Department of Religion at St. Jerome's University at the University of Waterloo. I received warm and generous support from many people while juggling (and cradling) adjunct teaching, dissertation writing, and newborns. Since 2009 I have been teaching, both full and part-time, at the Department of Religions and Cultures at Nipissing University. Nathan Colborne, Gillian McCann, and Susan Srigley have all been supportive of my teaching and scholarship in various ways. Thanks go to Nathan especially for numerous coffees and conversations.

The book of course would not have been possible without support from immediate and extended family. I would like to thank my parents, Victor and Linda Langdon, for their support and prayers. Brooke's parents have all been encouraging me along the way as well. And to answer Marty's question on time posed a few years back: I couldn't really think of anything better to do with the last seven and a half years. Thanks also to Paul and Emma Leonard for use of their cottage periodically for writing. I should also thank my church family in North Bay—too numerous to mention. Your friendship and communion as we worship and pray together have been a major source of God's grace in the last three years.

But the one individual who deserves the biggest thanks is my wife Brooke Langdon. She has been a constant source of support, encouragement, strength, and purpose. I really could not have completed the book without her companionship. Of course, things have been much more interesting since the arrival of Elam and Autumn. Elam's energy and joy is contagious, while Autumn's playfulness and reasoning is pure entertainment.

INTRODUCTION

Eternity, Narrative Time, and Analogy

> "The theological concept of eternity must be set free from the Babylonian captivity of an abstract opposite to the concept of time" (*CD* II.1, 611).

CHRISTIANS CONFESS THAT THE God of Israel became incarnate in Jesus Christ and works by the Holy Spirit in the Church for the salvation of humanity. What is more, Christianity has sought to hold together the living God of scripture with the best in philosophical reflection of what God may be like. The perennial attempt to define eternity and describe its relation to time has been one of the most difficult topics in the Christian quest to name and describe this God. How can Christians intelligibly hold together belief in a God who is not conditioned or limited by time and space, but who nevertheless acts within it?

To briefly take one important answer, in his *Summa Theologica* Thomas Aquinas, following Aristotle, argues that time is the measurement of created and human life in its movement, while eternity is the measurement of God's being: "for eternity is the measure of a permanent being, while time is the measure of movement" (Part I, Q. 10.4, answer).[1] Yet the measurement of divine life does not include movement. For Aquinas, and the theologians who preceded him, eternity is generally defined in its negative relation to time. While time is mutable eternity is immutable, while time is flowing eternity is static. To a large extent, then, Christian theologians did not allow the biblical view of the liv-

---

1. Although Aristotle only refers to the measurement of time; in his *Physics* he concludes that time is "movement in so far as it admits of enumeration" (IV, 11; 219b).

ing God or the doctrines of the Trinity and incarnation to inform their definitions of eternity, since these imply the activity and movement of God in time and history. This is not to say Christian theologians viewed God as absent from time and space, or that they denied the reality of the Trinity and incarnation, but that these positive doctrines did not supersede the negative relation found in the Greek tradition.[2]

Barth's attempt to positively relate God and time is one of the most significant attempts in modern theology. I will argue that he does not fall into this captivity of an opposition between eternity and time since he allowed the doctrines of the Trinity and incarnation to direct his struggles with this topic. Otherwise, Barth's view is quite similar to the traditional one. For example, he holds to the ontological distinction between eternity and time. Eternity is not time and time is not eternity. Or, there is an asymmetrical relation between eternity and time. Eternity is the prototype and time the type, time derives its existence from eternity. For Barth, however, eternity must be described with temporal and historical predicates. Not because eternity is controlled, trapped or limited by time, but because in the Christian revelation the triune God moves and is active in time.

Divine temporality may be expressed in two basic ways. First, God's inner triune life is described as the perichoretic relation between Father, Son, and Holy Spirit. And antecedent to the creation of the world, this God elected Jesus Christ to be the savior of humankind. God's eternal life, then, can be described using temporal categories such as movement, decision, event, act and life—even before the creation of time. Second, the eternal living God works and acts within created time and space. This occurs in the creation and preservation of the world and then in the covenantal relation between God and humanity—focused for Barth on the incarnation of the Son and the outpouring of the Holy Spirit. In this

---

2. Any acquaintance with Augustine or Aquinas, for example, will reveal their faithfulness to the doctrines of the Trinity and incarnation and God's activity in time. But they do not redefine eternity with the use of these beliefs. In *Summa Contra Gentiles* Aquinas, for example, states his procedure of remotion and then defines eternity. In Chapter 14 of Book 1 he states: "As a principle of procedure in knowing God by way of remotion, therefore, let us adopt the proposition which, from what we have said, is now manifest, namely, that God is absolutely unmoved." Following this in Chapter 15, eternity is defined: "But God, as has been proved, is absolutely without motion, and is consequently not measured by time. There is, therefore, no before and after in Him." Aquinas' point is that temporality and motion implies change, but God is not subject to change, therefore he is without time and motion.

second way, the eternal God must be described again using temporal categories and terms. Barth, then, can justify talk of divine temporality based on the triune being and activity of God.

Nevertheless, many interpreters have suggested Barth further entrenched an abstract and static view of eternity. This study claims the opposite, that Barth leads an exile from the philosophical captivity of eternity by a sustained reflection on the triune being of God. I will argue that far from defining eternity in atemporal terms the *Church Dogmatics* reveals a complex *analogia trinitaria temporis*. This will be demonstrated, first, by tracing the development of Barth's understanding of eternity and time from the *Romans* commentary into the *Church Dogmatics*. The strong diastasis found in *Romans* II gives way to a more creative and positive relation as evidenced in his discussion of the perfection of eternity in *CD* II/1. It will be argued, second, that the overcoming of an abstract view of eternity leads to a creative and complex relation of eternity and time that develops in all volumes of the *CD*. Throughout the various discussions of time in the *Dogmatics* a trinitarian pattern of times emerges that correspond the eternal being of God. I will argue that focusing on the doctrine of the Trinity reveals the conceptual coherence of Barth's view. The movement and life of the triune persons *is* God's eternity. Since God's immanent life is the differentiation and perichoretic relation of Father, Son, and Spirit—containing its own movement, order and succession—then eternity is its own particular time. This is not only true *in se*, when the immanent life of God is described, but also *ad extra*, in God's relation to created temporality. In fact, Barth's view of the relation between eternity and time can be described as analogous. Not only is God's dynamic eternity the source of time, but also that a trinitarian pattern of the eternity-time relationship emerges in the *CD*. The creation of time may be appropriated to the Father, the fulfillment of time to the Son, and the communion of time to the Spirit. These trinitarian dimensions of temporality correspond or are analogous to the eternal triune life.

Before outlining in more detail the book's argument, time itself must be discussed, after which, a brief review of Barth's understanding and use of analogy will be given. These discussions will help discern the complex contribution that a trinitarian construction of the eternity-time relation makes.

WHAT, THEN, IS TIME?

Time is generally discussed quantitatively as a formal feature of created and human existence. It is either described as the flow of past, present and future, or as the measurement of movement. Less discussed, however, is the qualitative character of time; that is, how time is filled—the content of time. The relation between form and content, quantity and quality, needs to be analyzed in order to understand Barth's contribution. To delineate the quantitative dimensions, the experiences and observations of time will be divided into subjective and objective forms, and then two basic definitions of time arising from these experiences will be noted. To suggest the qualitative dimension—how time is filled with content—Paul Ricoeur's concept of narrative time will be employed. This will demonstrate that the manifold nature of time may still be coherently understood, not merely as a formal feature of human and created existence but as something that has a narrative structure.

Experiences and observations of time may be roughly divided into endogenous (subjective) and exogenous (objective) approaches. The most basic form of endogenous time is the human experience of being awake and sleeping, resulting from natural light and darkness. These experiences are accompanied by various biological processes and a basic consciousness of time's process and duration.[3] Exogenous times are concerned with the rhythms and processes of the natural world, as well as cultural and social times.[4] Discussions of time in modern science add to this with the deep time of evolution and cosmology, and the technical discussions found in physics and relativity theory. The discovery of the space-time continuum, for example, has expanded understandings of the exogenous time of the natural world.[5]

Philosophical reflection on subjective and objective times has produced two main definitions of time in the western tradition. The first and most common is the rational-linear view; time is the movement from the past, through the present, and into the future. Concerning the human experience of time, Augustine's famous version of linear time as memory of the past, perception of the present, and anticipation of the future has held sway (*Confessions*, BK 11.XXI.20). Yet the linear passage

---

3. Achtner et al., *Dimensions of Time*, 8–9, and 12–26.
4. Ibid., 9–10 and 110–137.
5. On time in modern science see Davies, *About Time*.

of time is also found in objective times as well. Stemming from the experience of monotheism, first in Egypt and then in Israelite experience, history itself is viewed as a constant forward movement.[6] The linearity and unidirectionality of time are also assumed in scientific understandings of time. Barth assumes this basic division of time into past, present and future in most of his discussions. He assumes that the linear flow of time is the way in which God created the universe with time.

A second definition of time was put forward by Aristotle: time is the measurement of movement in regard to before and after (*Physics* IV, 11).[7] With this view a particular time has a beginning, duration and end. Originally, the basic units in this measurement were periods of the day, days, months, and years. With the invention of the clock in the middles ages however, social and economic time were measured and quantified by standards apart from the natural processes. The clock was originally invented to aid secluded cloister life and then applied to social and economic life.[8] This measurement approach was also significant for the discovery of relativity; times are measured differently (in reference to the speed of light) depending on one's perspective in relation to an object in motion.[9]

Thus, time may be approached as a subjective experience or a feature of the external world in general, whether defined as the flow of past, present, and future, or as a measured duration. Even so, these basic delineations do not necessarily lead to an integrated understanding of temporality.[10] In fact, one may be left with a scattered excess of measured times that have no coherence, quality, or character.

Paul Ricoeur, however, makes a strong case for integrating various approaches under the concept of narrative time. Rather than viewing time merely as the unidirectional and neutral succession of instants, he argues that temporality and narrativity be reciprocally understood.[11]

6. Achtner et al., *Dimensions of Time*, 27–64.

7. For a discussion of Aristotle's view, especially in relation to other ancient views, see Sorabji, *Time, Creation and the Continuum*.

8. Achtner et al., *Dimensions of Time*, 84–96.

9. On time in the theory of relativity see Davies, *About Time*, 44–77.

10. Paul Ricoeur, for example, perceptively argues that Aristotle's cosmological and Augustine's psychological approaches remain in fundamental tension. See Ricoeur "The Time of the Soul and the Time of the World," 12–22.

11. Paul Ricoeur, "Narrative Time," 169–190. In this article Ricoeur uses and expands Heidegger's phenomenology of time, while his argument is directed against the

6 God the Eternal Contemporary

Ricoeur specifically focuses on the role of plot in narrative, which suggests two major features of narrative time.[12] The first, a chronological feature, is the episodic dimension. The narrative is made up of episodes. The second, a nonchronological dimension, is configuration, in which "the plot construes significant wholes out of scattered events."[13] The plot structures a number of episodes into a narrative. Other features of narrative time include development and directedness; the end of the story pulls the narrative along.[14] The plot superimposes a sense of ending, so that time does not merely move from the past to the future, but toward a particular end that is contained even in the beginning.[15] Like objective approaches, moreover, narrative time is public. It is "a time common to the actors, as time woven in common by their interaction."[16] There is also the element of what Ricoeur calls intervention. Even though actors move with a certain amount of freedom, their time has been created and they do not control the consequences of their action. The actor is bound up in a world order.

Narrative time, then, includes both the measurement of objective time, as episodes have a specific measurable duration, and the subjective experience of linear time, as actors within the narrative experience the flow of time. Yet temporality takes on a particular quality as times are "for" this or that activity, which are included and directed by the overall narrative. As Ecclesiastes puts it, there is a season for everything: time to be born and die, plant and uproot, mourn and dance, etc. (3:1–8). *Time is not only quantified as the measurement of duration or existence*

---

dechronologizing of narrative in certain strains of literary criticism and historiography. While he agrees with much in Heidegger, Ricoeur criticizes him since the German philosopher focuses his view on individual temporal experience to the neglect of the communal and collective (ibid., 188–190).

12. As Ricoeur explains: "By plot I mean the intelligible whole that governs a succession of events in a story.... A story is *made out of* events to the extent that plot *makes* events into a story. The plot, therefore, places us at the crossing point of temporality and narrativity: to be historical, an event must be more than a singular occurrence, a unique happening. It receives its definition from its contribution to the development of the plot" (ibid., 171).

13. Ibid., 178. Ricoeur sees a similarity between configuration and other categories: Aristotle's "theme" in *Poetics*, the "point" of biblical parables, Kant's "thought" in *Critique of Judgment*, and "colligatory" terms in historiography (ibid., 179).

14. Ibid., 174.

15. Ibid., 179–80.

16. Ibid., 175.

in the flow of past, present and future, but takes on qualitative differences depending on the activity and relations taking place within it. The overall narrative directs the times within it, giving various times particular qualities as they are directed to an end.[17] What is important in Ricoeur's analysis for the present interpretation is the insistence on thinking about time within a larger overall narrative or framework, which in Barth has a trinitarian and christological focus.

As Ingolf Dalferth has pointed out, Barth readily incorporates non-theological perspectives on human experience of the natural world into his dogmatic project. In fact, Barth seeks to subsume these external perspectives with reference to the internal content of the Christian faith. This results in two basic components in Barth's theology: "[A] constructive or dogmatic component which generates the basic theological categories, and an interpretative component which applies those categories to elucidate our experience of natural reality in the light of faith. The first component is the backbone of his dogmatics and unfolds the universal perspective of Faith in terms of a complete reconstruction of reality on christological foundations. The second component reproduces the reality normally external to theology within theology by interpreting it in light of the perspective of Faith."[18] The first component moreover is focused on the eschatological reality of the resurrected Christ, which "has ontological and criteriological priority over the experiential reality which we all share."[19] There is then no understanding of humanity, the world, or cosmos that lies outside the dogmatic enterprise, including temporality.[20] There is no secular time as such; all time is understood with reference to the content of the Christian faith.

For Barth, moreover, the discussion of time must begin with the eschatological being of Jesus Christ. Specifically, "theology refers not to a reality past but a present reality—present neither in the sense of a historical past remembered by us nor in the sense of a permanent presence of timeless eternity. Rather it is the personal presence of the risen

---

17. There is generally little discussion of the qualitative dimension of temporality in theological contexts. Moltmann and Polkinghorne however come close to the qualitative dimension when speaking of time in an eschatological context. See Moltmann, *Science and Wisdom*, 109–10, and John Polkinghorne, *Science and the Trinity*, 156–57.

18. Ingolf Dalferth, *Theology and Philosophy*, 122–23.

19. Ibid., 115.

20. Ibid., 120–124.

Christ, the revelation of God's love towards us; Christ freely makes himself present to us through the Spirit by interrupting the continuities of our life and calling us into community with the living God."[21] This is the theological core of Barth's discussion of eternity and time. The eternal God meets temporal humanity in Jesus Christ; the risen and ascended Lord becomes present to believers through the awakening power of the Holy Spirit. But this christological focus does not exclude the work of the Father and Spirit in relation to time, rather it presumes it. There is, then, a distinct trinitarian content that fills the forms of time, the narrative qualification of time.

In addition to the trinitarian and christological filling of time, there are four basic forms of time that Barth includes. The first form is the rational-linear, time as the flow of past, present, and future. This follows closely Augustine's discussion and is the most common definition in western thought. A second form used by Barth is allotted time. This refers to the lifetime of each individual and focuses on one's movement from birth to death, a concern of modern phenomenology. This follows the definition of time as the measurement of movement, that is, the duration of time. The third form Barth includes is the objective time of the cosmos. This occurs in the rhythms and cycles of natural processes, though Barth understands this in relation to human existence. Finally, Barth speaks about general world history or the general world occurrence. It should be clear that Barth makes a limited choice in these forms. He focuses more on the discussion of human experience, only briefly mentioning exogenous or objective time, explaining it as the objective context for human temporality, never taking up the discussion of time in modern science. Moreover, Barth assumes that these forms are the common understandings of time; this is how God created the world with time. He rarely takes up the history of these concepts but merely assumes they are the common experience. Thus, it can be safely said that Barth makes no new contribution to the formal discussion of time; he assumes accepted definitions.

21. Ibid., 114. Douglas Harink also notes how all histories are taken into the time of the gospel. He contrasts Barth's view in his Romans commentary (along with the work of Giorgio Agamben) with views that fit gospel time into secular history or salvation history. These later views attempt to "inscribe the gospel into other supposedly 'larger' histories or narratives [and] end up losing that which Christ came to save by taking all things into the time of the gospel, which is to say, by gracing all things with eternal life" ("The Time of the Gospel," 30).

Distinguishing these forms of time is only the beginning. Since time is "for" or "of" this or that particular activity, these forms are empty of content and quality. Barth's contribution comes in interpreting these forms with reference to the content of the Christian faith, the internal dogmatic component of his view. What occurs in the *CD* is that time is "filled" with reference to the being and activity of the triune God, especially in reference to the eschatological reality of Jesus Christ. Moreover, the quantitative or formal nature of time does not change for the creature—it is still the flow of past, present, and future, or allotted time. What changes, however, is the *quality* of time according to the divine and human activity within it. For example, a Christian believer still lives in the flow of time and in the movement towards death, but she knows that her time is relativized in the presence of Jesus Christ by his Holy Spirit. Her own death is not a final end and she finds herself in the time of the community, which has a particular *telos* on its way to the final eschaton. Thus, while she finds herself in the ebb and flow of history and time, like anyone else (fallen time), her experience of time is lived within the time of the community; her temporal existence is actually filled with hope, even in the face of death and the end of her time. It is the movement of the triune God toward humanity that conditions, fills, and qualifies the experiences of time.

BARTH'S REJECTION AND USE OF ANALOGY

There is no proper Christian theology without analogy. One may not speak of God or think properly of the God-world relation without recourse to analogy, especially if the twin dangers of pantheism and deism are to be avoided.[22] Thomas Aquinas, for example, established the necessity of analogy when speaking of God.[23] Both univocal and equivocal forms of predication are inappropriate; the former views language in

---

22. Analogy has a long and complex history in western philosophy and theology. For an exhaustive treatment of the history of analogy see Hampus Lyttkens, *The Analogy between God and the World*; or Battista Mondin, SX, *The Principle of Analogy*, 1–6.

23. See *Summa Contra Gentiles* Book 1, chapters 28–36 and *Summa Theologica* Part 1 Chapter 12, "How God is known by us," and Chapter 13, "The Names of God." It should be noted that the line of interpretation that suggests Aquinas uses analogy as a linguistic category is being followed here (and that he does not have a developed analogy of being). See for example Ralph McInerny, *Aquinas and Analogy*. This does not mean no analogy of being can be developed in reference to and dialogue with Aquinas, but it seems that he reserves analogy for the problem of naming God.

reference to God and creation as identical, as if humans speak of God in the same way as created reality, while the latter sees human language as inadequate when speaking of a transcendence and mysterious God. Analogy, then, is the middle way between the univocal and the equivocal; it allows a true description of God (the point of univocity), while maintaining the ontological distinction and uniqueness of God (the concern of equivocity). Yet analogy is not only used in reference to naming God, but has also been employed to describe the God-world relation and as a theological epistemology.

While most would agree that analogous language is appropriate when describing God, which even Barth admits (*CD* II/1, 224–27), the use of analogy beyond predication is more controversial. The controversy, which continues from the last century, surrounds the issue of the *analogia entis*. Erich Przywara (1889–1973) introduced the concept into modern German theological discourse as a summary of Catholic theology. He argued that the *analogia entis* could be a middle way between the domestication of God in Protestant liberalism and the excessively transcendent God found in the Barth-Gogarten-Thurneysen school of the 1920s.[24] For Przywara *analogia entis* was a dynamic theory that attempted to synthesize the history of western thought. As James Zeitz notes, with this concept Przywara "develops into a symbol and banner for Catholic theology in general—in the debate with Barth. It becomes synonymous with his broader vision of integrating cultural movements, religious intuition and metaphysics."[25] But at the root of this synthesis lies the problem of humanity's existence and essence, argues Przywara. As Johnson summarizes, for "like God, the creature has a unity of essence and existence, but unlike God, the creature's unity is one of 'tension' rather than identity. …, the creature's essence appears within the context of existence only as becomingness, because its essence is realized

---

24. See Keith Johnson, *Karl Barth and the* Analogia Entis; and Joseph Palakeel, *The Use of Analogy*, 126–129. The term *analogia entis* is not found in Thomas Aquinas, as is often assumed, but is a product of commentary by Cajetan and Suarez, which was then found in Jesuit texts from the end of the 17th century. Przywara's construction of the *analogia entis* follows from this line, as he learned it from study at a Jesuit college in Holland and subsequently passed it into German theological discourse, while combining it with ideas from the fourth Lateran council (ibid., 155–158).

25. James Zeitz, *Spirituality and Analogia*, 117. This work looks at the complex development of Przywara's thought as it relates to and culminates in the concept of *analogia entis*. See esp. 117–165.

only 'over or above existence' – meaning it cannot be considered apart from its relationship with God, in whom the creature has its being."[26] The similar-dissimilar logic of the *analogia entis* solves this problem because it suggests that "the creature's existence testifies to God as its source, ... [and] because the creature remains dependent upon God for its existence at every moment."[27] There is, then, a natural knowledge and experience of God which the analogy of being articulates.

Barth's response to the doctrine of *analogia entis* is at least twofold: first, a negative polemic against the doctrine, and, second, a constructive alternative. The negative reaction is summarized in the infamous claim that the Catholic doctrine of the *analogia entis* is the invention of the antichrist (*CD* I/1, xiii). Barth understood the doctrine "as proposing *being* as a common ground between God and man, that is, God and man as sharing in the same being, which then is common to both. The ground of analogy in this case is creation and human nature and not God's revelation."[28] While Barth, following the lead of Przywara, may have been incorrect to assume the *analogia entis* as the sum of Catholic theology, he does seem to have legitimate concerns. Given his understanding of the doctrine, Barth suggests that it presupposes a higher concept beyond God and humanity, so that God is defined by a general concept of being. Following this, and perhaps more importantly, such a procedure would imply a second source of knowledge of God apart from that attained by faith in the revelation of Jesus Christ.[29] Moreover, the *analogia entis* implies that knowledge of God is direct and immediate, whereas for Barth it is indirect and mediated by scripture and preaching. Finally, the *analogia entis* suggests that knowledge of God is a movement of humans to God, as opposed to the gracious movement of God to humanity.[30] So it seems, given the definition Barth assumed, he had legitimate concerns.[31]

26. Johnson, *Karl Barth and the* Analogia Entis, 72.

27. Ibid., 73.

28. Palakeel, *The Use of Analogy*, 49.

29. Johnson repeatedly makes the important point that at the root of Barth's rejection of the *analogia entis* are Reform concerns of justification by faith and Luther's idea that we are *simul iustus et peccator*.

30. Palakeel, *The Use of Analogy*, 49–50.

31. It must be stressed here that we are primarily concerned with Barth's understanding of the doctrine. Betz questions Barth's notion that God and humanity are fitted into a preconceived notion of being and points out the christological content

Barth's constructive and positive response to Przywara was the *analogia fidei*. Rather than constructing a theology by beginning with a preconceived notion of being, wherein an understanding of God and humanity are straight-jacketed, Barth seeks to begin theology with the revelation of God in the death and resurrection of Jesus Christ. This knowledge arises from faith, a result of the work of the Holy Spirit in the believer. The faith of the believer is analogous to the God's knowledge of himself and to the activity and revelation of God in Jesus Christ (*CD* I/1, 227–47 and *CD* II/1, §§ 25–26). The *analogia fidei*, then, is basically an epistemological category that distinguishes Barth's approach from Przywara's.[32] Yet Barth's use of *analogia fidei* is not the only case of analogy in Barth.

Further to the epistemological and linguistic analogy of faith, there are other uses of analogy that describe the ontological order of things as such—what Christoph Schwöbel terms "a multidimensional network of analogies."[33] Thus, following the epistemological are ontological uses. This ontological use of analogy is most evident in Barth's varied employment of the *analogia relationis*. Found especially in the doctrine of creation, the intra-divine relation between the Father and the Son finds analogies in the relation of God and the world (I/1, 397; III/1, 14 and 50), the relation between Jesus Christ and God, and Jesus Christ and

---

of Przywara's position. Yet he does not highlight Przywara's notion of revelation in creation ("Beyond the Sublime," 404, note 17), a concern of Barth, and misconstrues Barth's view of revelation as trinitarian self-*interpretation* and theopantheistic (see "Beyond the Sublime," 5–6), whereas for Barth revelation is a trinitarian self-*disclosure* that includes the integral participation of the creature. Moreover, Betz's claim that Barth denies "any openness whatsoever of the creature to God, and thus any natural desire (*desiderium naturale*) for God" is incorrect. For a response to this see the article by Kenneth Oakes, "The Question of Nature and Grace in Karl Barth," 595–616. Thus while Betz chides Barth for his misreading of Przywara, his own reading of Barth is problematic. Nevertheless, Betz's aim in employing the *analogia entis* is laudable: see especially "Part Two," 20.

32. Palakeel, *The Use of Analogy*, 31–46 and 51–54.

33. Christoph Schwöbel, in the foreword to Peter S. Oh, *Karl Barth's Trinitarian Theology*, xi. See as well Johnson, chapter 7, "Analogy in Covenant," in *Karl Barth and the* Analogia Entis. Similarly, Palakeel notes the distinction between analogies used in predication (the epistemological and linguistic) and those that describe the ontological order of things (*analogia relationis* and *analogia operationis*), though he does not exploit this distinction (*The Use of Analogy*, 47). Both Palakeel and Peter Oh, while following Barth to different degrees, attempt to develop an *analogia entis* that is within the *analogia fidei*.

Introduction: Eternity, Narrative Time, and Analogy   13

the rest of humanity (III/2, 55–71 and 203–22).[34] This analogy of relation is also reflected in the relation between a man and a woman, parent and child, and neighbors (III/4, 116–323).[35] Thus while Barth remains faithful to the epistemological foundations of the *analogia fidei*, he is not opposed to using analogy in describing the relation of God and creation[36]—though he does not subsume these analogies under the rubric of the *analogia entis*.

Following this, I will be argue that within Barth's ontology there also functions an *analogia temporis* along with such concepts as the *analogia relationis*.[37] As Falk Wagner states, analogy generally refers to a "correspondence or similarity between two or more entities that are neither completely the same nor completely different."[38] The basic concept refers to a similar-dissimilar relationship. In the case of God and creation, or God and humanity, the dissimilarity must include the creator/creation distinction in which the aseity of God is preserved, while the similarity may include various features of God's life or the life of creation. In the case of the analogy of faith, the knowledge of God by faith arising in the believer is analogous or corresponds to the acts of God in the life, death, and resurrection of Jesus Christ. In the analogy of relation, the general relation between the God and the world is analogous to the intra-trinitarian relation of the Father and the Son. In the first case, knowledge of

34. See the summary statement in III/2, 323–324.

35. For an exposition of the analogy of relation see Gary Deddo, *Karl Barth's Theology of Relations*, 94–107. See as well Palakeel, *The Use of Analogy*, 24–31. On the analogy between the being of Jesus Christ and Jesus Christ's relation to culture see Paul L. Metzger, *The Word of Christ and the World of Culture*. Or, more recently, Peter Oh has argued that the perichoresis of the divine persons is reflected in ecclesial existence, *Karl Barth's Trinitarian Theology*, esp. 81–104. Although his main thesis that there was a methodical shift from the dialectical to the *analogia fidei* has been replaced by the work of McCormack, von Balthasar does point out the diversity of analogies in Barth as well. See Balthasar, *The Theology of Karl Barth*, 161–167.

36. In Barth, then, analogy is a more flexible concept than once assumed. Palakeel notes that this is based on his dynamic view of God as pure act; see *The Use of Analogy*, 59. Moreover, if we keep Barth's criticisms of the *analogia entis* in mind but note that he allows for the use of analogy in his ontology, then would it not be the case that there is an incipient *analogia entis* in his theology? For an argument along these lines see Peter Oh, *Karl Barth's Trinitarian Theology*, 40–67.

37. On Barth's actualistic and covenantal ontology see Bruce McCormack, "Grace and being"; and "The Ontological Presuppositions of Barth's Doctrine of the Atonement," 346–366.

38. Falk Wagner, "Analogy," 48.

God by faith corresponds to God's act; in the second, the intra-divine relation corresponds to the relation between God and creation. One way in which analogy has been preserved in Christian theology is the *via triplex*. To use the eternity-time relation: the ontological difference between eternity and time illustrates the dissimilar features (*via negativa*). The work of God creating and acting within time illustrates the similarity between eternity and time (*via positiva* or *via causalitatis*). Yet this work of God in time is possible, at least for Barth, only because God's own triune life includes the movement, order and life of the Trinity, a divine temporality (a *via eminentiae*).[39]

THE ANALOGY BETWEEN ETERNITY AND TIME IN THE *CHURCH DOGMATICS*

The forms of time Barth incorporates and the activity of the triune God in time have been mentioned. Important to note is that within his overall trinitarian narrative the quality of time varies for the human subject depending on their relation to God in Jesus Christ. While the forms of time do not change for the human subject, the activity and reality of the living God in time qualifies the experience of time, giving it a new character. Following this, the analogical nature of the eternity-time relation can now be explained.

It must be noted that Barth does not explicitly describe his view as an *analogia temporis*, though his language is highly suggestive of this. Thus the analogical interpretation is being suggested (though it seems that analogical reasoning and relations are inevitable in a proper Christian theology). Following this, the trinitarian appropriations that will be made in this book are not always stated as such by Barth. For example, while he is explicit in describing the times of the Son and the Spirit he does not state that the creating and preserving of time are the work of the Father, though this appropriation is faithful to what Barth says elsewhere about trinitarian appropriation. Moreover, when it is suggested that the eternal relations within the Godhead correspond to temporal activity within history, this again is a suggestion that Barth does

---

[39]. The way in which the *via triplex* and analogy are used in relation to Barth's theology is distinguished from the way in which Kim does so (see Eunsoo Kim, "Time, Eternity, and the Trinity"). He notes well that there is an analogy between eternity and time, though he does not outline the fuller trinitarian pattern I am suggesting. He also seems to misuse the *via triplex* as well.

not always explicitly state but which seems to be a faithful extrapolation of his view.

There are two basic ways in which the analogy between eternity and time are evident in the *CD*, which correspond to different understandings of time. First, Barth uses a formal definition of time—usually the flow of past, present, and future—suggesting that eternity is the simultaneity of these three modes. Whereas for created time past, present, and future are separated and even opposed, they are united in eternity. Based on a dynamic view of eternity, since the Father, Son, and Spirit are in an eternal relation of differentiation and perichoresis, *simul* will be interpreted in the first two chapters to mean that all futures are anticipated, all presents synchronic, and all pasts recapitulated by God's eternity. Or to reverse the relation, the pasts, presents, and futures of created temporality are anticipated and remembered in God's eternity. The division of time into past, present, and future is no threat to God's eternity, as it is to human existence. There is a basic analogy between eternity and time as all times are contained or anticipated in the simultaneity of God's eternity; eternity creates and preserves the pasts, presents, and futures of time. Although Barth does not explicitly use analogy to describe this relation, it is evident in the language he employs in describing the eternity-time relation. This will be the focus of Part I "Overcoming the Babylonian Captivity." In chapter 2, especially, we will trace Barth's conception of eternity into *Church Dogmatics* II where the formal definition of eternity is explicated. Yet couching the analogy between eternity and time in these terms is merely formal. It does not suggest how the activity of God and humanity *fills* time, it only suggests that eternity creates and preserves the flow of time—which in itself is important.

To unpack the richness of Barth's scattered discussions—the activity and presence of God in time and the trinitarian content—fuller explication is needed. This is the second way in which the analogous relation between eternity and time is found in the *Church Dogmatics*: the eternal triune being of God finds an analogous pattern in created, fulfilled and ecclesial time. This will be focus of Part Two of the book "Barth's *Analogia Trinitaria Temporis*." The content and qualification of the forms of time begin with the Father creating and preserving time itself. Yet, while time is meant for covenantal fellowship between God and the creature, humanity refuses this and lives in fallen time. The Father's creating and preserving time will be discussed in Chapter Three. The

Son enters time, however, and restores the fellowship between God and humanity. His time fulfills the original intention of created time, rescues fallen time, and provides the direction to all humans in their allotted times. According to Barth, the risen and ascended Lord now exists in the flow of time, while his life ruptures allotted time (his duration does not end with death, but begins anew with the resurrection; he is the contemporary of all time). Jesus Christ and time will be the subject of Chapter Four. But humanity still lives in its sinful time and must be awakened to the contemporaneity and presence of the risen mediator. This awaking of the believer to the presence of the Son is the work of the Spirit in ecclesial time. The Spirit is the agency of the risen and ascended Lord in the duration between the Son's first *parousia* (resurrection) and the final *parousia* (the eschaton). The activity of the Spirit fills this "middle time" by awakening, building up, and sending the community and individual believers. The Spirit and ecclesial time will be the subject of the fifth chapter. Therefore the Christian believer still lives in the flow of time and their allotted time (time as its basic *Existenzform*), but now lives with hope instead of despair, since they live in ecclesial time on its way to the eschaton. Time has a new *character* and *quality* for the believer given the activity of the Son and Spirit toward the creature, even in face of death and time's fleetingness.

Again, Barth does not use the term analogy to describe this fuller relation between eternity and time; it is an appropriation of my interpretation. Nevertheless it should be evident that it correctly interprets Barth. In fact, both the Son's and the Spirit's entering time correspond to the eternal relations within the Godhead. As Bruce McCormack states, "the condition of the possibility of the incarnation in time is to be found in the eternal generation of the Son. The condition of the possibility of the outpouring of the Holy Spirit in time is to be found in the eternal procession of the Holy Spirit from the Father and the Son. To the movement (the lived history) of the Son in time, there corresponds a movement in eternity. And so also with the Spirit."[40] It may also be added that the Father's eternal role as origin within the Godhead finds its analogy in creating and preserving time.

While narrating Barth's position as an *analogia trinitaria temporis* is the main purpose of this book, we will also notice along the way

---

40. McCormack, "The Ontological Presuppositions of Barth's Doctrine of the Atonement," 358–359.

Introduction: Eternity, Narrative Time, and Analogy 17

how Barth responds to a whole set of related concerns. He questions Augustine's insistence that the initial creation of the world was a timeless act, for example. He also subjugates the question of divine foreknowledge and future contingents, so prominent in the history of the debate, providing an alternative which focuses on the concrete encounter between God and the creature in time. In his discussion of human time, moreover, he provides alternative answers to the problem of the fleetingness of time (Augustine) and the movement toward death (Heidegger) offered by ancient and contemporary interlocutors. When reflecting on the times of Christ and the Holy Spirit he also tackles the modern problem of "faith and history" (Lessing) and suggests how the human creature may participate in eternity (without resorting to the mystical experience of timelessness). Barth's contributions to these debates will be highlighted as the discussion unfolds. Nevertheless, there are some important interpretive questions to ask of Barth's position, as many question whether he has properly led the way out of the Babylonian captivity that he so desired. To these we turn first.

PART I
Overcoming the Babylonian Captivity

ONE

Eternity as the Dissolution of Time?

THE CLAIM I AM making suggests that for Barth the doctrine of the Trinity is the basis for his discussion of eternity and time. This allows Barth to move beyond a timeless or static view of eternity to one which suggests that not only does the eternal God create and sustain created temporality but redeems and reconciles the creature in the times of the incarnate Son and Holy Spirit. Nevertheless, my interpretation is in contrast to some who suggest that in Barth we still have the "grin of the timeless cat,"[1] or the persistence of a static "eternal present."[2] Richard Roberts states it most dramatically in describing Barth's view of eternity: "Like some cancerous *Doppelgänger*, theological reality appears to inflate itself, drawing life from the reality it condemns, perfecting in exquisite form what could be seen as the most profound and systematically consistent theological alieniation [sic] of the natural order ever achieved."[3]

Such criticisms need to be accounted for if the interpretation offered in this book is correct. Do others misinterpret Barth's development or misunderstand what he suggests? Are there major shifts between *Romans* II and the *Church Dogmatics* in understanding eternity or is there continuity? Are there elements in Barth's Christology or pneumatology which undermine his intentions to positively relate eternity and time? In this chapter we will clear the ground by beginning to answer some of these questions. Four basic sets of interpretations will be

---

1. Jenson, *God after God*, 154. Hereafter *GaG*.
2. Moltmann, *Theology of Hope*, 57–58.
3. "Karl Barth's Doctrine of Time," 124–225.

examined below. The first set of interpretations suggest that, in one way or another, despite Barth's best intentions he ultimately reintroduces an atemporal or negative view of eternity. A second set focus on problems surrounding the fulfilled time of the Son, while the third set examines issues surrounding Barth's pneumatology and ecclesiology. The fourth section highlights those who suggest turning to the Trinity for understanding Barth on eternity. While there are issues and questions to keep in mind from the first three categories, I will argue that those who turn to Barth's trinitarianism provide the way forward in understanding his view on this important and complex topic.

THE CHARGE OF ATEMPORALITY

Many suggest that Barth reintroduces the traditional atemporal view of eternity or constructs a view with such tendencies. Barth, in these views, somehow betrays his best dogmatic intentions in being guided by residual philosophical categories or concepts that carry with them an atemporal construction. Representatives from this first group include Robert Jenson, Jürgen Moltmann, Richard Roberts, Colin Gunton and Alan Padgett.

The work of Robert Jenson provides one of the most substantial attempts in contemporary theology to reconstruct eternity and time in a positive relation. This attempt is noteworthy for the present discussion because his initial impetus arose from an engagement with Barth—though subsequently he moved beyond Barth. Highlighting the differences between the two will explain Jenson's concerns with Barth, but also highlight how Barth's view may be preferred to that of Jenson's.

Jenson's 1969 work *God after God: The God of the Past and the God of the Future, Seen in the Work of Karl Barth* was the first major work to take up the discussion of eternity and time in the Barth. Jenson correctly sees in Barth an attempt to overcome an abstract atemporal view of God. He points out that Barth reconstructs his doctrine of God by turning to the Gospel for a redefinition of God's being. He appropriately notes the importance of both Christology and the Trinity for Barth's construction. Jenson states, for example: "Jesus' existence is the one great event to which all others, from the creation of the world to the blessedness of the saints, are subsidiary. The story is the story of Jesus Christ, and *we and all creatures* occur solely in that we have roles to play in that story."[4] Or again, reflecting on Barth's trinitarianism in relation to eternity, he summarizes: "God comes to be understood not as a transcendent thing but as a transcendent happening, and his transcendence therefore understood not as his timelessness but as his radical temporality."[5]

In the end, however, Jenson finds Barth's view unsatisfactory, claiming that despite his best intentions Barth did not escape the atemporal tradition. For Jenson, the problem lies in Barth's distinction between God's being in himself and his temporal activity. [6] What Barth provides, Jenson argues, is nothing more than the Platonic view of time as the image of eternity. He rhetorically concludes: "But if the whole of God's temporal story is to be analogous to something else, what can this something else be—if not a timeless deepest reality of God? The notion of analogy of the whole of time to something else is itself the grin of the timeless cat."[7] Jenson must conclude that Barth has not made good on his intentions to rescue eternity from its Babylonian captivity of an abstract atemporality.[8] Yet, it is not altogether clear why Jenson is suspicious of the distinction between God *in se* and *ad extra*, which he argues must lead to Platonic timelessness. Jenson's negative judgment of Barth can be explained by noting the following four differences between their two views.

---

4. *GaG*, 69. On the importance of Christology see, 68–72.

5. Ibid., 96.

6. He summarizes the charge in the following way: "He wants to say that God is in fact what happens with Christ, that we are in fact actors in his story, that God's Trinity is in fact his being Creator, Reconciler and Redeemer. But he also wants to proclaim the freedom and transcendence of God over against what he is for and with us. He thinks that to do this he must postulate a reality of God in himself distinct from God-for-us," *GaG*, 153.

7. *GaG*, 154. On Barth's use of analogy and its similarity and differences from the western tradition, see 75 –78 and 83–86. Jenson's basic insight that Barth substitutes Jesus Christ and the Trinity for Being in the similarity-dissimilarity structure of analogy is on the mark.

8. It should be noted that Jenson tempers his judgment of Barth in later works. In *The Triune Identity*, for example, Jenson states that Barth makes progress in western trinitarianism because, first, he rigorously uses the gospel to define God's being, and, second, because the Trinity is defined in terms of act and repetition. See *The Triune Identity*, 136–138. Hereafter *TI*. In *Systematic Theology*, Vol. 1, when defining eternity as infinite temporality, he appropriates Barth's definition of eternity as pure duration. See *Systematic Theology, Vol. 1*, 216. Hereafter *ST*.

First, methodologically, Jenson's definition of eternity arises from reflecting on the problem of time itself. He suggests that religions offer different versions of eternity that are in fact answers to the problem of time.[9] That is, versions of eternity bring unity and coherence to the fragmented human experience of time in which the past is lost, the future is feared, and the present is ever slipping away. The problem of time remains programmatic in Jenson's definition of eternity even when he takes up the discussion of the Trinity. While Barth does define eternity using temporal predicates reflection on the problem of time as such does not serve the methodological role that it does in Jenson. Rather, the Trinity lies behind Barth's definition of eternity, even when he defines it as the *simul* of past, present and future. Moreover, as to be examined below, time is only problematic when its proper use for fellowship with God is refused ("fallen time"). In this way, created time becomes fallen, but still remains the good creation of God as a universal form of human existence.

A second feature of Jenson's view is the appropriation of Father, Son, and Spirit to past, present, and future respectively.[10] Barth by contrast refuses to identify any one of the divine persons with the three modes of time. While he defines time as the succession of past, present, and future, he does not reduce the divine persons to these three modes. Nevertheless, Barth does eventually appropriate time to the three divine persons; the creation of time to the Father, fulfilled time to the Son, and ecclesial time to the Spirit.

A third feature of Jenson's view, which is more problematic, is that God's work in time constitutes his being.[11] Jenson is not satisfied to say

9. See, for example, *GaG*, 62–63, 96; *TI*, 1–5, 21–25, 57–61, and 164–175; and *ST*, Vol. 1, 55–57 and 67. Douglas Farrow questions the conflation of the problem of time with the problem of sin; See "Robert Jenson's Systematic Theology: Three Responses," 93. It must be admitted, however, that Barth is not clear on the relation of created and fallen time until the discussions in *CD* III, which we will take up in chapter 4.

10. "The Father is the 'whence' of God's life; the Spirit is the 'whither' of God's life; and we may even say that the Son is that life's special present. If, then, when and whither do not fall apart in God's life, so that his duration is without loss, it is because origin and goal, whence and whither, are indomitably reconciled in the action and suffering of the Son," *ST*, Vol. 1, 218–219. For Jenson's explication of this see 218–221. See earlier hints as well *GaG*, 157–75 and *TI*, 24–25, 168–76.

11. "Since the Lord's self-identity is constituted in dramatic coherence, it is established not from the beginning but from the end, not at birth but at death, not in *persistence* but in *anticipation*. The biblical God is not eternally himself in that he persistently

that the eternal God acts in time, but moves beyond to suggest his being is somehow completed by his actions within time and history. Given this, Jenson must give priority to the future. One also wonders here, if Jenson makes God's being dependent on creation. As will become evident, Barth's view is less radical than Jenson's. While for Barth God clearly works in time, he never suggests that God's being somehow needs this work to constitute his being. Barth's view does include anticipation and futurity, but this does not in any way constitute God's being. God creates and works within time because he freely chose to do so.

Fourth, Jenson rejects reflection on God's being antecedent to creation, what Barth terms pretemporality. Though Jenson theoretically affirms God's pretemporality, there is no positive role for it. In answer to the question of whether God could have been the God he is without other persons, Jenson answers: "The dialectics of deity, as I have described them, equally compel us to say that he could, that God is independently personal, *and that we cannot know how*. As it in fact is, his personhood is not posited apart from us, and we cannot cognitively transcend this fact."[12] So while God, hypothetically, could have been personal apart from his relation to creatures and creation, we cannot know if this is the case.[13] This is closely related to his reinterpretation of the immanent-economic Trinity. Instead of allowing for an immanent Trinity prior to creation and the works of the economy, Jenson argues that the identity of the economic with the immanent Trinity is an eschatological reality.[14] Along with this, Jenson is hesitant to acknowledge the preexistence of the eternal Son, reserving his preexistence for a narrative pattern in Israel.[15] Again, Barth's view is different in affirming positive roles for God's pretemporality and the *logos asarkos* (albeit a limited one).

---

instantiates a beginning in which he already is all he ever will be; he is eternally himself in that he unrestrictedly anticipates an end in which he will be all he ever could be" (*ST*, Vol.1., 66). Similarly, Jenson seems to conflate eternity and time as well; see *GaG*, 132–33.

12. *TI*, 179. Italics added. See as well *ST*, Vol. 1, 141.

13. Fred Sanders interprets Jenson's view of the immanent Trinity as "the Counterfactual Hypothetical," see *The Image of the Immanent Trinity*, 107–12.

14. *TI*, 138–140.

15. See *ST*, Vol. 1, 138–142; and *TI*, 140; for a brief analysis of this and a critique of Jenson see Simon Gathercole, "Pre-existence, and the Freedom of the Son in Creation and Redemption."

Jenson's negative interpretation, then, is centered on a criticism of Barth's use of the immanent Trinity. This is insufficient for Jenson because it suggests an eternal reality of God apart from his action within and with creation and creatures. Jenson prefers a view of eternity that is only thought of in relation to God's activity within creation. Barth, with Jenson, argues for the temporal activity of God in creation and bases this on the gospel and its revelation. Yet in contrast to Jenson, Barth has a positive place for the immanent Trinity apart from his temporal activity of the world. As will be demonstrated, moreover, this immanent divine life is not a static being, but has its own order and "time." Thus, Jenson's negative assessment of Barth, even while he sympathizes with Barth, stems from programmatic differences.

Like Jenson, Moltmann is one who has both learned much from Barth and made the God-time relation a focus of his theological project. Whereas Jenson eventually tempered his critique of Barth and admitted learning from him, Moltmann's reading of Barth on eternity does not move beyond his initial critique. In fact, Moltmann's engagement with Barth on this issue is rather brief—though Barth has been a constant dialogue partner in Moltmann's corpus. Moltmann takes the "eternal Now" of the second *Romans* commentary as paradigmatic and critiques it based on his own concern to develop an eschatological view of history. His interpretation does not acknowledge any positive development in the *CD*, suggesting that Barth remained trapped in the Platonic tradition.

In his 1965 work *Theology of Hope* Moltmann interprets Barth's "transcendental eschatology" as espousing an "eternal Now," which is present and judges each moment of time. Eternity is less concerned with the beginning or end of time but critically judges each present. Moltmann sees a similarity to the historian Leopold von Ranke and Kierkegaard. More directly, however, is the influence of Wilhelm Herrmann. As a teacher of both Barth and Bultmann, Herrmann bequeathed to his students the importance of subjectivity in the act of revelation. Yet the question remained, "Does the 'self' of the self-revelation refer essentially to God or to man?"[16] While Moltmann thinks Herrmann clearly refers

---

16. Jürgen Moltmann, *Theology of Hope*, 52. Thomas Freyer has a similar interpretation of Barth as well in *Zeit – Continuität und Unterbrechung*. While he examines most of the major discussions of eternity and time in the *CD* he fails to see the importance of the Trinity to the extent I am suggesting. In fact, he states Barth's view is insufficiently trinitarian and instead focuses on God as the absolute subject, something similar to Moltmann's criticism (148–53), and exhibits the tendency of an "eternal now" (143–47).

to human subjectivity in the act of revelation, as does Bultmann following him, Barth interprets subjectivity primarily in reference to God—which is eventually interpreted with reference to the Trinity and the lordship of God in *CD* I/1.[17] According to Moltmann, however, this does not exorcise the eternal Now from Barth's theology. He rhetorically asks: "Does the doctrine of the Trinity mean the eternal trinitarian reflection of God upon himself? Does 'self-revelation' mean the pure present of the eternal, without history or future?"[18]

Even after Barth admits problems associated with *Romans* (see *CD* II/1, 635), Moltmann still insists that the self-revelation of God is the eternal Now that makes a future eschatological coming of God problematic. The God of Parmenides remains. He explains this in relation to Jesus' resurrection and eschatology: "To understand the revelation in Christ as self-revelation of God, is to take the question as to the future and the goal indicated by revelation, and answer it with a reflection on the origin of revelation, on God himself. With this reflection, however, it becomes almost impossible to see the revelation of the risen Lord as the ground for still speaking of an outstanding future of Jesus Christ."[19] That is, the self-revelation of God in the resurrection inevitably means a lack of promise and futurity in thinking of the eschatological future. While one may agree that there are problems with fulfilled time in Barth, it will be argued that this is not the result of an eternal Now, without past and future, haunting Barth's view in the *CD*. Rather, it concerns Barth's view of the cross and his use of the veiling-unveiling dialectic in interpreting this.

A similar interpretation of Barth is given thirty years later in *The Coming of God*.[20] Again summarizing Barth and Bultmann on eschatology, he states their view as "the transcendent breaking-in of eternity that plunges all human history into its final crisis. It is not history that puts an end to eschatology; it is eschatology that puts an end to history."[21] Again, the focus is on the second edition of *Romans* and its view of eternity as the eternal Now. Moltmann again suggests that Barth's view makes further divine activity in history problematic. Ultimately, then,

17. Moltmann, *Theology of Hope*, 53–55.
18. Ibid., 55.
19. Ibid., 58.
20. Moltmann, *The Coming of God*.
21. Ibid., 14.

even Barth's attempted correction in 1948 (III/2) Moltmann views as insufficient.[22] According to Moltmann, Barth's view of eternity is merely a reaffirmation of the Platonic tradition. His later work merely added to the problem by suggesting that eternity is before, with and after every moment. This does not begin the necessary eschatological reading of history.

In response to Moltmann, the following may be proposed. First, as will be discussed, the eternal or static Now of *Romans* was a view that Barth essentially left behind. Even in the *Göttingen Dogmatics*, Barth is beginning to construct a positive view based on the living God of scriptures. It is unwarranted, then, to dismiss Barth's discussion throughout the *Dogmatics* and to suggest he has not broken from the Platonic tradition—especially if the *CD* has not been more fully taken into account. It might be added, second, however, that there is indeed some concern with the way Barth constructs fulfilled time. Moltmann notes that the resurrection as the self-revelation of God implies a fulfillment of eternity in time that takes leave of a future fulfillment. In the next section, the problem of fulfilled time is more closely related to his view of atonement, and perhaps even his use of the veiling-unveiling dialectic. Yet, third, Barth does take into account God's futurity; not only in discussing fulfilled time in *CD* III and IV but even in the discussion of II/1. This includes Barth's exposition of the incarnation of the Son and outpouring of the Holy Spirit in time and history. Within this, he does have an eschatological view of history as moving toward its end in the final eschaton. Moltmann simply does not take into account Barth's trinitarian formulations, especially the discussions in volume's III and IV.[23]

A third atemporal interpretation is that of Richard Roberts. In his often insightful essay "Karl Barth's Doctrine of Time: Its Nature and Implications,"[24] Roberts attempts to unravel something of the "inner logic" of Barth's theology by focusing on the eternity-time relation. While the work has a number of positive contributions, it will be suggested that the essay's conclusions are unwarranted.

22. Ibid., 15–18.

23. It cannot go unmentioned that Moltmann's own theology takes up the critical task of rethinking the God and time relation. For an analysis of this see John J. O'Donnell, *Trinity and Temporality*, 108–58. Besides the earlier works which O'Donnell examines, Moltmann takes up the discussion of time in the following: *God in Creation*, 104–39; *The Coming of God*, 279–95; and *Science and Wisdom*, 85–110.

24. Richard H. Roberts, "Karl Barth's Doctrine of Time," 88–146.

First, however, Roberts is insightful on a number of fronts. He is sensitive to Barth's development in light of the philosophical background of Kant, Hegel and Kierkegaard.[25] He also notes the importance of the Trinity for Barth's definition of eternity in *CD* II/1: "Barth develops his exposition of 'pure duration' upon an explicitly Trinitarian basis of prototypical interaction and reciprocity without division. The relationship between the Trinitarian and the temporal doctrines is enhanced by similar terminology used by Barth in both contexts, thereby implying a continuity of argument."[26] Yet Roberts does not exploit this insight and turns elsewhere for interpretive tools.[27] This leads to a number of problems in his interpretation.

The first problem, like Moltmann, is the suggestion that the eternal and timeless Now of *Romans* continues into the *CD*. He concludes that in the "ensuing sections Barth's doctrines of God, Christ, and creation have been analysed from the standpoint of their dependence upon a set of temporal conceptions bound up with the doctrine of the divine act in the eternal 'Now.'"[28] The persistence of the eternal Now into the *CD* is presumed throughout Roberts's essay.[29] The place of the timeless Now in *Romans* cannot be denied, but as will be suggested in the next chapter the eternity-time dialectic of *Romans* was dropped nearly as soon as it was employed. Moreover, in Roberts's analysis of the period between *Romans* and the *CD* there is no mention of the Göttingen lectures which evinced a turning toward the Trinity and incarnation for the basis of dogmatics, and the first sustained reflection on the divine perfections in Barth's thought. As discussed below, in the *Göttingen Dogmatics* Barth makes an effort to move beyond the negative relation of eternity and time and begins to relate them positively.

While Roberts does well to note Barth's actualistic doctrine of God, a second problem arises with the failure to notice the relation of

---

25. Ibid., 91–96.

26. Ibid., 115–16. As will be shown below, the similar terminology and pattern of thinking between the doctrines of the Trinity and eternity is expounded by Hunsinger.

27. Ibid., 115–16. In fact, earlier Roberts states that the "relative worth of Barth's doctrine of the Trinity developed in the latter parts of volume I/1 of the *Church Dogmatics* is not of prime importance here" (ibid., 106). The exact opposite is the case.

28. Ibid., 144.

29. See as well 88, 98, 99, 103, 104, 105, 108, 109 and 140.

anticipation and actualization in Barth's view of the eternity.[30] As will be examined shortly in the interpretation of Padgett, for Barth God's eternity includes both an *anticipation* of his acts and their *actualization* in time and space. The eternal decisions of God in pretemporal eternity do not contradict their supratemporal realization. In contrast, when discussing the doctrine of election Roberts states that there is "an invidious contrast between on the one hand the eternal basis of election in the 'perfect presence' of God in the pre-, supra-, and post-temporality of 'primal history'. . . and on the other the realization of revelation in time in the life and death of Jesus Christ."[31] There is only a tension and contradiction, however, if there is no movement from decision and anticipation to realization and actualization. Yet this is not the case for Barth.

The third issue, and perhaps most problematic, is that Roberts assumes Barth's rejection of natural theology is a rejection of the natural order. This categorical error is constantly repeated in his essay and leads to his dismissive conclusions. Roberts argues that Barth alienates the natural order when he excludes non-theological views in his constructions.[32] Barth's theological method, focusing on Jesus Christ as the Word of God, does not exclude the importance of non-theological views or the reality of the created cosmos. As will be discussed in chapter 4, Barth does indeed have a theology of created time. Yet because of Roberts's reasoning, he makes the conclusion that in Barth we have "the most profound and systematically consistent theological alieniation [sic] of the natural order ever achieved."[33] By contrast, this project will demonstrate that Barth's doctrines of God, Trinity and incarnation do not alienate the created order but sustain a profound theology of eternity and time, which includes the grounding and fulfillment of human temporality.

In a study comparing Hartshorne and Barth, Colin Gunton provides a more nuanced interpretation of Barth. He notes well the place of time and movement within Barth's doctrine of God. Commenting on the use of "event" to describe God's being, he states:

---

30. Roberts does note the turn to God's being-in-act and its importance in the *CD*: 103, 105–8, 110–12, 121, 132 and 134.

31. Ibid., 118. See 119 as well.

32. "Barth is effectually calling into question not merely anthropocentric sources of revealed knowledge of God but natural knowledge of the natural world" (ibid., 123). For similar reasoning see 110, 114, 120, 124, 126, 130, 132, 136, 141, 142, 144, and 145.

33. Ibid., 124–25.

> One way of conceiving this is with the aid of the metaphor of movement. The incarnation is the movement of God into relation with the world he has created. Because this movement *is* God, there is no unmoved God behind or underlying it; rather it entails that God's being consists in a movement 'outwards' to what is not God. But because this movement is triune, and so not necessitated, it is a movement with a double aspect. God *is* movement towards the other, and this movement is expressed conceptually by the eternal relation of the Son to the Father in the Spirit. In its turn, this inner movement provides the ontological grounding for the outward movement we see to have happened in the life of Jesus.[34]

Thus God's being *in se* and his work *ad extra* is interpreted with kinetic terms. Gunton defends the metaphor of movement against critics who would suggest Barth compromises the ontological distinction between God and creation or inserts arbitrariness in God's activity. This cannot be the case because Barth always maintains the aseity of God and views God's becoming and movement as "triune and eternal."[35]

Yet Gunton's interpretation does express concern. Gunton is cognizant of Barth's attempt to overcome classical theism and its reliance on substantialist metaphysics, but he argues that Barth may not in fact escape this. This is seen in the ambiguity surrounding his discussion of eternity, which Gunton describes as "eminent temporality." He suggests that Barth's use of pure duration and simultaneity seem contrary and that his use of Boethius' definition is not clear. He concludes: "The truth appears to be that at times Barth defines eternity in light of (temporal) revelation while at other times he opposes it to time."[36] The result is that despite his insistence on the historical character of revelation, "Barth has failed to maintain the full temporal reality of the revelation event"; in fact, there is a persistent tendency "to contaminate the temporality of revelation with a conception of revelation as a timeless theophany."[37]

Granted, one must agree with Gunton that Barth is not always clear in his exposition and this could easily lead to ambiguity. Yet the difference between God's temporality and its "opposition" to time is not one of a negative correlation but rather of ontological distinction. The

34. Gunton, *Becoming and Being*, 167.
35. Ibid., 169, see 168–71.
36. Ibid., 180.
37. Ibid., 181.

distinction between eternity and time can be seen in two ways. First, as pointed out, God's immanent triune being has its own succession and order; eternal life, even antecedent to the creation of the world, is temporal in a particular way. This is one form of God's temporality. A second form used by Barth is that the eternal God acts within time and history; God is not timeless in the sense of being "above and beyond" time. Rather, God creates, preserves, and acts within creation—especially for Barth in the incarnation and the outpouring of the Spirit. Thus, the distinction between eternity and time in Barth is not recourse to timelessness, as Gunton suggests may be the case.[38] Gunton's interpretation is tempered, however, as he notes "that these criticisms are not of the whole of Barth's theology, but are made possible by the ambiguity in his understanding of time."[39]

One of Gunton's suggestions may be followed up, however. He notes in passing that "one is even tempted to wonder whether the very word *revelation* is not one of the chief culprits, in that it carries too heavy a load of inherited connotations to be able to bear the radical changes of meaning that Barth wishes to impose upon it."[40] In chapter 4 it will be argued that the veiling-unveiling schema used by Barth in his doctrine of revelation contributes to the problem of finality during the time of the forty days. This is not central to Gunton's critique as he proposes instead, following Jenson, that a subtle Platonism underlies Barth's theology.

A fifth interpretation in this category, focusing on Barth's discussion of eternity in *CD* II/1, is found in Alan Padgett's *God, Eternity and the Nature of Time*.[41] Padgett examines Barth's use of traditional language when constructing his notion of God's eternity; in particular, Boethius's definition of eternity as the total, simultaneous and perfect possession of unending life (*interminabilis vitae tota simul et perfecta possessio*).[42]

---

38. He makes five suggestions in his case; see ibid., 181–85.

39. Ibid., 185. Gunton then interprets Barth's doctrine of God in *CD* II/1 as evidence of Barth's positive relating of God and creation. See ibid., 186–212.

40. Ibid., 181.

41. Alan Padgett, *God, Eternity and the Nature of Time*. Others working in the field of analytic philosophy of religion simply dismiss Barth outright. William Craig, for example, accepts the judgment of Grace Jantzen that Barth's discussion is nothing more than "edifying nonsense," *God, Time and Eternity*, x.

42. 'Philosophiae Consolationis' V.VI.10, in *Boethius: The Theological Tractates and the Consolation of Philosophy*. The translation "total, simultaneous and perfect possession of unending life" is mine, though it is close to Steward's ("perfect possession

Padgett suggests that Barth's position is incoherent. While Padgett notes Barth's intent to positively relate eternity and time, he suggests that Barth's definition of eternity excludes the reality of time as the process or succession of past, present, and future.[43] As with other analytical philosophers of religion defending a positive relation of eternity and time, Padgett spends much effort defending the successive or process view of time (time flows as past, present, and future). This defence counters the arguments of some atemporal defenders who often reject a process view of time. Padgett explains: "Given the process view of time, it is simply contradictory to assert that all of the past, present and future can be one simultaneous Now to God. Those events that existed in the past, or will exist in the future, are not real and cannot be in 'eternity' any more than they exist (tenselessly) here on earth. It is incoherent, therefore, to assert that the time of Jesus Christ can be simultaneous with all other times."[44] Padgett suggests, then, that Barth's reference to the simultaneity of past, present and future implies the unreality of created time. That is, if for eternity past, present and future are simultaneous then this would exclude the *succession* of past, present, and future of created temporality; which in Padgett's view is essential. This critique, however, does not take into account how Barth interprets the concept of *simul*.

Padgett's interpretation assumes that Barth arrives at the notion of simultaneity in the same way in which Boethius did. For Boethius, eternity is defined with the use of the *via negativa*. Whereas time is limited and fleeting, losing the past and ignorant of the future, eternity is all encompassing, it views all of time at once. For Boethius, God sees all of time—past, present, and future—"as from a peak" (*Consolations*, 5.IV). This procedure would leave one with the impression that human time with its succession of past, present, and future is a non-reality for eternity. Padgett assumes this to be the same procedure as Barth, defining eternity in its negative distinction from time.

Barth, however, uses the *simul* of God's eternity in both a negative and a positive manner. First, negatively, he uses the concept of simultaneity to *distinguish* eternity from time. Barth states that "Eternity is the simultaneity of beginning, middle and end, and to that extent it is pure duration. Eternity is God in the sense in which in Himself and in all

altogether of an endless life").
  43. Padgett, *God, Eternity and the Nature of Time*, 143.
  44. Padgett, *God, Eternity and the Nature of Time*, 144.

things God is simultaneous, i.e., beginning and middle as well as end, without separation, distance or contradiction" (II.1, 608). This functions negatively in relation to time since "Eternity is just the duration which is lacking to time, as can be seen clearly . . . in the temporal present and in its relationship to the past and the future" (ibid.). The simultaneity or unity of eternity indicates the divine duration that is lacking in time.

More important, however, is Barth's positive use of *simul*. As he argues, to understand "duration without separation between beginning, succession and end is true only against a background of the decisive and positive characteristic that as true duration, the duration of God Himself is *the* beginning, succession and end" (II/1, 610). In fact, God's eternity "is itself that which begins in all beginnings, continues in all successions and ends in all endings" (ibid.). Barth, therefore, uses the notion of simultaneity, in distinction from Boethius, to argue that *in* God's eternal being all temporal modes of existence are anticipated before they are actualized in creating, sustaining, and redeeming creation.[45]

Moreover, the simultaneity of past, present, and future is actually a reference to God's will and determination for creation. For God, according to Barth, past, present, and future are not in contradiction since what God anticipates, he will actualize, and what he actualizes he has anticipated in his eternity.[46] Or, as Barth explains: "What distinguishes eternity from time is the fact that there is in Him no opposition or competition or conflict, but peace between origin, movement and goal, between present, past and future, between "not yet," "now" and "no more," between rest and movement, potentiality and actuality . . . In him all these things are *simul*, held together by the omnipotence of his knowing and willing, a totality without gap or rift, free from the threat of death under which time, our time, stands" (II/1, 612). This does not mean that created time—with all of its beginnings, middles, and ends—occurs all at once. It does mean, however, that all beginnings, middles, and ends are controlled by God's eternity.

To put Barth's view in other words, eternity contains the *anticipation*, *recapitulation*, and *synchronicity* of the different modes of time.[47]

---

45. For example, in discussing God's Sabbath rest in Gen 1, Barth makes the distinction between God's eternal anticipation and his acts in time; see *CD* III/1, 216.

46. The language of anticipation is Bruce McCormack's. See "Grace and being," 100; and "Barth, Karl" in *The Oxford Companion to Christian Thought*, 65–66.

47. George Hunsinger uses these terms to explain Barth's view of simultaneity when

Eternity as the Dissolution of Time? 35

In God's eternity all futures are *anticipated*, all presents are *synchronic*, and all pasts are or will be *recapitulated*. But all the anticipations, synchronisms, and recapitulations in God's eternity are the act of God himself and thus cannot be divided from his will and knowledge. While there is truly a distinction or succession of the past, present, and future in created time, these are held together in God's eternity, whether anticipated, synchronic or recapitulated. For Barth, the triune God is truly Lord of time.

Padgett's criticism of Barth's use of *simul*, therefore, appears unwarranted. His criticism would be correct if Barth was following the same procedure as that of Boethius.[48] For Barth, God as the triune being, with his own space and time, creates space and time as the form of the creature, out of his omnipresence and eternity.[49]

The assessment of these interpretations is based on the view that close attention must be paid to Barth's trinitarian theology when interpreting his view. The assessment can be summarized with the following points. First, Barth's theology of eternity and time developed significantly in the *CD* from the view of *Romans*. It is unwarranted to assume the negative view of *Romans* continues into Barth's dogmatic work. Second, and closely related, reading Barth on this issue must take into consideration, as much as possible, the full scope of the *CD*. As Barth was continuously developing his thought throughout his career the full breadth of his work must be kept in view. While this study is not exhaustive, it will be argued that examination of *CD* III and IV allows one to see the full trinitarian shape of Barth's view on this topic. Most of the interpreters above focused their attention on *Romans* and *CD* II/1. A third issue, as just illustrated with the discussion of *simul*, is Barth's tendency to reinterpret traditional categories in a unique manner. A sensitive reading of Barth must be contextually aware of Barth's particular use of theological and philosophical categories. A fourth concern, which most

reflecting on the life of Jesus Christ as eternal life; see *How to Read Karl Barth*, 241.

48. As Leftow notes, Boethius' definition of eternity appeals to Barth because of "the definition's talk of God's life" though Barth fills the definition with trinitarian content, "Response to 'Mysterium Trinitatis,'" 196.

49. While Barth agrees with Boethius that God's eternity is the fullness of unending life, Barth is referring to the fullness of the triune life, while Boethius is making a reference to all of created life. It seems that because Boethius is relying on the *via negativa* he ends up confusing the full life of God with the full life of creation; or in the least, he does not make the distinction clear enough.

interpreters mention or allude to, is the question of whether or not Barth pays sufficient attention to the temporality of the human creature. It will be demonstrated throughout this book that while Barth is theocentric and christocentric (the two are compatible) this does not necessitate the rejection of the human creature nor their temporal existence. Defending these claims will be demonstrated in the chapters that follow.

THE PROBLEM OF FULFILLED TIME

A second group of interpretations is centered on Barth's christocentrism. Rather than claim that he imports atemporality, these criticisms suggest that the explication of Christology and time somehow inhibits a proper view of human time in general or the time of the church. The most persuasive of these interpretations note that the forty days of resurrection time are described as the fulfillment of eternity in time. This tendency of Barth is problematic because it leaves the impression that the time of the church, the ascension, and future *parousia* receive unbalanced or inadequate attention. Representatives of this category include Albert Brandenburg, David Ford, and Douglas Farrow.

Albert Brandenburg's essay on time and history in the *CD* surveys well Barth's various discussions, highlighting especially Barth's christocentric interpretation of time.[50] He concludes, for example, that fulfilled time for Barth is the "pure unveiling presence with the resurrection and the 40 days."[51] He also notes the importance of the time of community in *CD* IV, which corresponds to the second form of the *parousia*, too often overlooked in secondary literature.[52] Yet he argues that Barth neglects time and history apart from that of Jesus Christ. As he states: "The unmistakable idealist development of Barth is so strong that he can find no access to this historically grounded reality, the 'flesh has been assumed.'"[53] While he is sympathetic to Barth's use of Chalcedonian Christology, he argues that Barth does not give sufficient attention to time and history apart from the history of Christ. For example, Barth's

---

50. Albert Brandenburg, "Der Zeit – und Geschichtsbegriff bei Karl Barth," 357–78. He includes the times of expectation and remembrance in I/2; eternity and time in II/1; election in II/2; the times of creation in III/1; human temporality in III/2; and the problem of faith and history found in IV.

51. Ibid., 362.

52. Ibid., 375.

53. Ibid., 358. Translation mine.

division of fulfilled and fallen time rejects the time of creation apart from Jesus' history, whether understood as history in general or the reality of creation. So whereas Bultmann "de-historises" the acts of God in history, Barth simply neglects time and history apart from the biblical picture of reality.[54]

Granted, Barth's doctrine of creation is understood in light of the covenant and his view of human time is read christologically, but he does not neglect time and history in general. First, to be discussed in chapter 3, he does include the reality of objective cosmic time in his exegesis of Genesis 1. Second, in his explication of human temporality Barth states that time is a part of the universal form of existence (*Existenzform*) of the creature. Brandenburg's focus on fulfilled and fallen time does not give sufficient weight to time as a permanent and universal concept in Barth's anthropology—just as the concepts of the *imago dei* and the unity of soul and body are. Third, it must also be pointed out that the driving force of Barth's discussions is his trinitarian theology. While Brandenburg mentions time in creation, fulfilled time, and even the time of the community briefly, he does not note how these are held together with the doctrine of the Trinity. So while Barth is definitely christocentric this is not at the expense of theocentrism. Brandenburg's criticism, in the end, remains general, though he does point to neglected sections in the *Dogmatics*.

David Ford in *Barth and God's Story*, using literary analysis and a focus on narrative, asks whether or not the forty days of Jesus' post-resurrection history bears the weight Barth gives them. Barth's emphasis, he argues, leads to a distortion in which "the content of the Gospel accounts of the resurrection appearances does not bear out Barth's claim that they represent a unique fulfillment and completeness, a manifestation of eternity in time. They have much more the character of 'sending' into the future, and there is at least as much promise as fulfillment."[55] That is, while Barth speaks of resurrection time in terms of final fulfillment, the gospel narratives do not. The problem behind this, Ford argues, lies in Barth's conflation of resurrection and *parousia*. "His absolutising of the Forty Days goes well beyond the perception of their literary function. It is related to his modification of the traditional paradigm, for in that paradigm the resurrection and Parousia were not at all one event for

54. Ibid., 376–78.
55. David Ford, *Barth and God's Story*, 145.

Jesus, and there was little temptation to transfer "the sense of an ending" to the resurrection. The resurrection and the appearances are immensely important in the story even when they are recognized as in one sense interim events. Barth's virtual 'closure' at this point overburdens them . . . and violates the 'realistic' element as one link in a chain of events."[56] The NT narrative, according to Ford, presents the resurrection appearances and final *parousia* as links in a "chain of events." Thus Barth's emphasis on the forty days as the fulfillment of eternity in time does not respect the difference and unity of the full history of Jesus Christ.

Ford's critique is important for at least three reasons. First, that the fulfilled time of Jesus Christ must take into account the successive nature of Jesus-history is correct. This must include not only the life and ministry of Jesus, the cross and resurrection, but also the ascension, heavenly session and final return; all of this while providing the basis for the outpouring of the Spirit and the time of the church. Any distortions in this succession must be critiqued. Second, however, Ford needs to take account of the further development of Barth's thought. Though Barth tends to focus on the forty days, the problem of fulfilled time becomes more complex when it is asked how Barth develops his position in *CD* IV. Ford's analysis focuses upon I/2 and III/2. In *CD* IV Barth makes the interval between the first and final *parousia* more explicit. The time of the church there becomes the second form in Christ's threefold presence. This will be taken up in chapters 4 and 5. It will be suggested that the apparent conflation of resurrection and *parousia* does not prevent Barth from developing Jesus-history further. Yet it may be asked, third, if the problem with fulfilled time is simply a matter of poor narrative arrangement or is there something else within Barth's theology that causes this problem? Here the interpretation of Douglas Farrow is the most thorough.

Farrow's questioning of the finality given to the forty days is with the purpose to pursue a fuller doctrine of the ascension and heavenly session. While Ford points out that Barth put too strong an emphasis on the forty days, Farrow seeks to discern the underlying reasons for this problem. The basis of his critique is the finality given to the cross for the history and activity of reconciliation. That is, the work of salvation is completed at Golgotha to such an extent that the resurrection and ascension are merely the noetic realization of this, first to the apostles

---

56. Ibid., 145–46.

and then to the church. This is problematic because it cuts off the continuing soteriological work of Jesus Christ in the time of the church and the eschaton. While the crucified Jesus rose, ascended, and will return, the implications of this for humanity and cosmos are truncated, being reduced to a noetic participation.

Farrow does however begin with a basic appreciation of Barth. He states that Barth's *CD* IV is "one of *the* major works of ascension theology."[57] And more germane for the present discussion, he affirms Barth's attempt at grounding the time of the church, the time between the times, in the contemporaneity of Jesus Christ.[58] This contemporaneity of Jesus Christ, moreover, is disclosed in the resurrection and ascension.[59] Yet Barth's view, Farrow argues, is not without its problems. The problem centers on Barth's view of reconciliation. It implies "that Jesus-history is entirely complete at Calvary, for the nadir of the divine descent necessarily coincides with the pinnacle of human ascent. All that remains, says Barth, is that we should see and hear and share in what has already been done. Jesus-history from the standpoint of the Emmaus Road is pure revelation, pure unveiling, pure contemporaneity. Nothing is added except our histories."[60] As interpreted by Farrow, Barth's view of the cross brings a certain closure to the work of reconciliation that is not born out by the NT narrative. This focus of Barth has numerous effects. There is the conflation of resurrection and ascension, which Farrow argues even the idea of threefold *parousia* does not solve.[61] The difference between church and world, moreover, is basically a noetic distinction, since all humanity is in reality contemporaneous with Christ. That is, the resurrection, ascension, intercession, and *parousia* have little effect in the reconciling of God and humanity, they merely function in the ap-

---

57. "Karl Barth on the Ascension," 127.

58. *Ascension and Ecclesia*, 232-241; Cf. "Karl Barth on the Ascension," 136-38.

59. "That contemporaneity is what the resurrection and ascension disclose, and in disclosing render effective. They make it clear to us that Jesus himself is seated at the right hand of God; that he alone has secure and concrete reality; that his present is in fact more real than ours. For the time being this presence is a mysterious one, for the ascension is not the parousia. But through the resurrection and the ascension God has laid claim to Jesus-history as his very own act and declared it to be his one definitive Word; with Barth that is always the crux of the matter" ("Karl Barth on the Ascension," 136-37; see as well 138).

60. Ibid., 245. See 245-248 as well, or "Karl Barth on the Ascension," 139-142.

61. *Ascension and Ecclesia*, 248.

prehension by believers of a work already completed on Calvary. What is more, he argues that the appropriation of the *triplex munus* to the Chalcedonian pattern leads to a neglect of the priestly office.[62]

Farrow gives two reasons for this problem in Barth. First, in regard to the discussion of *CD* IV especially, the two natures of Jesus Christ are correlated with the two states of humiliation and exaltation, so that the descent of God and the ascent of humanity correspond on the cross.[63] Thus the Chalcedonian pattern is imposed on the biblical narrative, affecting an unnecessary closure. Second, Farrow suggests there is an underlying negative correlativity between God and creation. The appropriation of deity to descending and humanity to ascending means that divinity and humanity are "logically correlative" or "polar opposites."[64] Farrow attempts to trace the problem of correlativity into different levels of the *CD*, claiming that there is "a contrariety which requires an atoning act from the very outset."[65] These issues come to a head with Barth's view of the cross as a divine self-humiliation and a self-alienation.

> 'The secret of the cross is simply the secret of the incarnation in all its fullness' [*CD* IV/2, 293], says Barth. And with this statement it is obvious enough that God's 'non-contradictory' relation to the world, just at the point where God truly is related to the world, is something that can only be achieved by the death of God. It is obvious too that resurrection cannot be allowed to be anything more than a revelation of the secret, or ascension anything more that the establishment of its eternal vitality. For if the

---

62. "Karl Barth on the Ascension," 143.

63. But Farrow asks concerning this: "Can we afford, even occasionally and as a purely formal device, to use one element in the story of Jesus to speak primarily of divinity and another primarily of humanity? Does that not endanger the story itself, not to mention a sound theology of the incarnation?" (ibid., 243, cf. 243–250). See as well "Karl Barth on the Ascension," 134–135; and "Ascension and Atonement," 78–82. Similarly, G.C. Berkouwer noted the problems created for time and the successive nature of the NT narrative by reconfiguring the two states of humiliation and exaltation. See *The Triumph of Grace*, 314– 319.

64. "Karl Barth on the Ascension," 141. Dale Dawson sees something similar when he notes in Barth an antithesis between God and humanity, Jesus Christ and humanity, and even within the Godhead—between Father and Son. See Dale Dawson, *Resurrection in Karl Barth*, 158–161 and 218–219.

65. Ibid., 146. He examines election, the close connection of creatureliness and sin, sin as Nothingness, the naturalness of death, and the rejection of inherited sin from Adam, ibid., 143–146.

humanity of God *means* God's self-alienation, a new life beyond the cross is—apart from its revelatory power—meaningless.⁶⁶

The reconciliation between God and humanity, therefore, must first occur within God before humans can participate in it, and this is what the death of Jesus accomplishes.⁶⁷

Now the way out of this problem for Farrow is by rejecting the identification of states with natures and seeing the descent and ascent as movements of *the God-man* and not of his divine and human natures separately.⁶⁸ This, he argues, would resist the fulfillment of eternity during the forty days, and also open up a fuller appreciation for the ascension and final *parousia* as new events in Jesus-history, and thereby space for the ecclesial time of the Spirit.⁶⁹ The fruit of Farrow's examination, however, comes when he suggests how one may move beyond Barth. Rather than the resurrection and ascension being merely the unveiling of the cross, they are "a fresh beginning for Jesus. Seen thus, as the beginning of the liberty of the sons and daughters of God, and hence of the whole of creation, for genuinely new events—for the parousia and for what lies *beyond* the parousia."⁷⁰ Farrow's critique, then, stems from a call for a fuller view of salvation. Salvation is not just the reconciliation between God and humanity on the cross and the noetic participation of believers after the fact, while it includes such participation, but must include the ongoing work of Jesus Christ in the heavenly session, *parousia*, and beyond.⁷¹

---

66. Ibid., 147. It might also be asked here if this problem of correlativity is behind Barth's view of the cross as the second or eternal death, which seems at times to imply a decision and event between the Father and the Son quite apart from his humanity.

67. Farrow also suggests, though he does not fully develop the idea, that Barth's actualism only compounds the problem, ibid., 147–148.

68. *Ascension and Ecclesia*, 249–250; "Karl Barth on the Ascension," 141; and "Ascension and Atonement," 79.

69. Ibid. On the negative effects of this for ecclesiology see 250–54. Similarly, Thomas Freyer notes that the work of the Holy Spirit is reduced to the subjective and noetic realization of the work completed by Jesus Christ, *Zeit – Continuität und Unterbrechung*, 176–179. Though he views the problem as symptomatic of Barth taking over idealist notions of time (ibid., 147–153 and 180–181) and not symptomatic of Barth's doctrine of reconciliation and the cross.

70. "Karl Barth on the Ascension," 149.

71. A fuller examination of Barth's soteriology lies beyond this work. For a fuller discussion see David Lauber, *Barth on the Descent into Hell*.

In response to Farrow the following points can be made. First, there is a basic agreement. Much like Ford, it will be pointed out in chapters 4 and 5 that there is indeed a tendency in Barth to finalize the forty days as fulfilled time and thereby reduce the ascension and *parousia* to noetic realization of the reconciliation completed on the cross.[72] This will be complemented by suggesting a larger role for the veiling-unveiling dialectic that Barth uses in connection to this. Yet, second, it must also be pointed out that Barth does make room for an ascension time with a corresponding pneumatology and ecclesiology. Of course, this may not be as full as deemed necessary, but the being and activity of the church are not altogether neglected. It is not as if there is no history after the cross, then, but that its quality and character tends to be reduced to noetic participation. This history after the forty days that accounts for the novelty of ascension, church, and *parousia* will be pointed out.

Third, while the individual points at which Barth may exhibit negative correlativity between God and creation will not be taken up, it will be argued that Barth's theology of eternity and time does not succumb to this tendency. In *CD* III/1 and III/2, for example, Barth makes a distinction between created and fallen time (though admittedly this is not clear in II/1) and so time's fallenness is not inherent in its being created. Fallen time, rather, is a result of human sin filling the created time humans are given. On this account, Barth does not fall into the situation of a negative correlativity. Fourth, Farrow, though only hinting at the issue, suggests Barth's actualistic doctrine of God contributes to the problem of fulfilled time.[73] It will be argued, however, that Barth's version of God's being as act or event serves the positive relation of eternity and time. In connection with God's eternity, God's action in history includes differentiation and unity between past, present, and future acts. That the eternal God acts in time does not imply the dissolution of human time

---

72. Farrow's point does not seem to be that Jesus-history actually ends or that the cross is insufficient for salvation but that this further Jesus-history could be given more soteriological substance by Barth (*contra* Dale Dawson, *Resurrection in Karl Barth*, 132 and 185–188).

73. See, for example, *Ascension and Ecclesia*, 291–292, where Farrow argues the *simul* doctrine is a view of eternity had by the negative judgement of time, which ends up, by way of fulfilled time, choking creaturely time (ibid., 291). Here he refers to a brief discussion of the eschatological preservation of time (III/3, 84–90) which seems to suggest the dissolution of human time in the eschaton. This issue will be taken up in chapter 5.

but its true grounding. Even the *simul* concept does not imply the necessity of completeness.

Nevertheless, the criticisms of Ford and Farrow do point to Barth's emphasis on the forty days as the fulfillment of eternity in time. While Ford basically points out the problem, Farrow's account, based on the call for a fuller soteriology, notes that the basic problem is associated with the completion of salvation on the cross.

CRITICAL ISSUES IN PNEUMATOLOGY AND ECCLESIOLOGY

One of the original contributions of my interpretation is suggesting that Barth's view of the eternity-time relation includes the ecclesial time of the Holy Spirit which compliments the times of the Father and Son. Yet there are some serious questions asked of both Barth's pneumatology and ecclesiology that are relevance for his discussion of ecclesial time, especially as to the quality of this "time between the times." These issues include the claim that there is a basic orientation to the past in Barth's theology, that his christocentrism negatively effects pneumatology, and the tendency toward a disembodied ecclesiology.

First, it has been suggested that Barth's discussion of the eternity-time axiom is heavily weighted toward God's being and activity in the past, with either the focus on pretemporal election or the work of the cross. While the doctrines of election and reconciliation point us toward God's pretemporality and work on the cross, the work of the Spirit drawing the church toward the eschaton is reduced if not absent altogether.[74] Wolfgang Vondey, for example, suggests that in Barth "the Spirit directs humankind back in time to Christ but does not point forward to the completion of God's work of salvation in the future."[75] While it is true that the Spirit for Barth points humanity toward the new possibilities that are found in the fulfilled time of Jesus Christ, this is not merely a looking back but also a looking forward. As will be demonstrated in chapters 4 and 5, it can be argued that even if pneumatology is "subsumed" under Christology, the activity of the Spirit in the eschatological future is ingredient to Barth's view.

---

74. See, for example, Jenson, *God After God*, 172–175; and Colin Gunton, *Becoming and Being*, 182.

75. Wolfgang Vondey, "The Holy Spirit and time," 398.

A second issue, or perhaps a cluster of issues, concerns the relation of Christology and pneumatology. The criticisms here suggest that Barth's christocentrism restricts the person and work of the Spirit. This problem is tied to Barth's complex trinitarian theology, including his use of the *filioque*, and issues surrounding the agency of the Spirit.

As will be noted in the next chapter, the linear triune movement of Revealer, Revelation, and Revealedness is key for Barth's doctrine of the Trinity. In Barth's view, the Holy Spirit completes the movement of God's self-revelation by imparting this knowledge unto humanity; the Spirit is the third moment in the veiling-unveiling-impartation schema.[76] In *CD* IV, this pattern is again found when the Spirit imparts to believers knowledge of the atonement completed on the cross. Yet this linear-revelation model of the Trinity is combined with other elements as well. Gary Badcock suggests that Barth unsuccessfully combines the linear concept of divine self-communication with a *filioque* doctrine, wherein the Spirit is the bond between Father and Son:

> The problem here is that the Holy Spirit is presented as a middle term between the Father and the Son, rather than as the third term in a divine self-communication, bringing the process to fulfillment. The earlier Revealedness paradigm, therefore, is in conflict with the pneumatology enshrined in the *filioque*. The Revealedness idea, in short, ought to issue in an inner-trinitarian version of the pre-Nicene trinitarian taxis 'from the Father, through the Son, in the Holy Spirit,' which from the beginning connoted more than the order of transmission in the saving approach of God to the world. Here, too, the Spirit appears truly as the Spirit of the Son, but as the final moment of the divine outreach in the economic sense, and as the third moment of the divine overflow from the Father in the inner-trinitarian sense.[77]

Thus Badcock sees a tension between the *filioque* doctrine, especially as the Spirit is understood as the bond between Father and Son, and the idea of the Spirit imparting salvation unto believers. Barth's exposition

---

76. The criticism that Barth's focus on epistemology and revelation limits his view of the Trinity and salvation is being left out here. For such criticism see Alan Torrance, *Persons in Communion*. Contra this, Hunsinger suggests that Barth's notion of knowledge includes communion; see "The Mediator of Communion," 170, n. 25.

77. *Light of Truth and Fire of Love*, 183. See as well the important discussions by Rowan Williams ("Barth on the Triune God") and Robert Jenson ("You Wonder Where the Spirit Went") who similarly note the de-personalising of the Spirit that the *filioque* implies.

in *CD* IV however views the linear-revelation and *filioque* models in conjunction. As will be argued below, it is precisely because the Spirit is the eternal bond between Father and Son that the Spirit is the mediation between Jesus Christ and believers, the third moment in the triune movement toward humanity. The Spirit's temporal role *ad extra* is analogous to his eternal role *in se*.

Another issue closely related to Barth's use of the *filioque* is the charge of pneumatological subordination. It is suggested that Barth reduces or collapses the work and person of the Spirit into that of the Son; practically resulting in a binitarianism rather than a trinitarianism.[78] Recently, David Guretzki has thoroughly examined Barth's use of the *filioque* and rightly concludes that Barth is no subordinationist if this means denying the divinity of the Spirit, which the *filioque* protects, or even the ontic work of the Spirit. But he does point out that Barth generally reads NT passages on the relation of the Spirit and Jesus Christ "through the lens of the post-resurrection, post-ascension giving of the Spirit."[79] Thus it may be the case that this restricts the relation of the Spirit to the humanity of Jesus Christ throughout the *CD*—though this is not a focus of his study.[80] He does suggest however that Barth's use of the *filioque* to describe the eternal relation of the Father and Son implies a non-agential view of the Spirit: "the Spirit is technically not an external 'agent' to the Father and Son, but is internally related to Father and Son as the one who proceeds eternally from their shared being as

---

78. Robert Jenson makes the strongest case for this, see "You Wonder Where the Spirit Went"; while Williams has some similar criticisms, "Barth on the Triune God." Hunsinger notes both agential and non-agential description of the Spirit, but does not suggest this as problematic, "The Mediator of Communion," 153.

79. David Guretzki, "*Filioque* in Karl Barth's *Church Dogmatics*," 262.

80 In other words, that the Son is the giver of the Spirit ought not to displace the fact that he was conceived and anointed by the Spirit (Matt 3:16; Mark 1:20; Luke 3: 21–22; and Luke 4:16–19). Or, as James Buckley rhetorically asks, what "about the story of the Spirit in creation, speaking through the prophets, the One of whom Jesus was conceived and who descended upon (Mk 1:10) and abided with (John 1:32) Jesus and who raised Jesus from the dead (Romans 4:1)?" ("A Field of Living Fire," 88). Perhaps the best way of describing this tendency in Barth is to say that his pneumatology is "Pentecostally-centered" (Guretzki, "*Filioque* in Karl Barth's *Church Dogmatics*," 262). There is evidence in Barth, however, that the Spirit is central for the birth and incarnation; see Hunsinger, "The Mediator of Communion," 160; and Rosato, *The Spirit as Lord*, 68–69. For a study focused on re-conceiving inner trinitarian relations with attention to a fuller view of the Spirit, though not in specific dialogue with Barth, see Thomas Weinandy, *The Father's Spirit of Sonship*.

the Father of the Son, and the Son of the Father."[81] This will be apparent in examining ecclesial time, when it is pointed out that the Spirit is the self-attestation of Jesus Christ and his work is confirmatory. It will be suggested that Barth oscillates between agential and non-agential description of the Spirit, at times seeming to collapse the work of the Spirit into the agency of the Son.

A third issue concerns the tendency of Barth toward a disembodied ecclesiology. The focus of Barth's ecclesiology is on its invisible Lord who acts in and upon believers by the Spirit. In this account the church is the event of his presence by the Spirit, but not essentially embodied or continuous in concrete ecclesial practices or institutions. The church for Barth, it seems, is occasionalistic.[82]

Nicholas Healy diagnoses well this problem in Barth. To begin with, Barth has three main ecclesiological principles. The creedal rule, first, states that "the church is an object of belief . . . insofar as it is the 'event' (CD IV/1 651) of the calling and upbuilding of people by the Holy Spirit."[83] Second, the human agency rule suggests "that the reality of the church is made concrete and visible in the form of human activity."[84] The third and more fundamental rule, christological primacy, "requires that we understand ecclesiology to be a function of Christology."[85] The problem, as Healy sees it, is the reduction of human agency. This is evident when Barth chooses *concepts* over *narrative* to describe the church,

---

81. Guretzki, "*Filioque* in Karl Barth's *Church Dogmatics*," 254. Note here that this is not a double procession; the Spirit does not proceed from *both* the Father and the Son. This is one of the corrections Guretzki makes to interpreters of Barth: "the Spirit proceeds from the-common-being-of-the-Father-and-the-Son" (ibid., 177–178, italics removed).

82. Occasionalism is the theory that denies efficient causality between physical objects, implying that God is the immediate cause of every physical event. This view is not being attributed to Barth. Rather the term is used to describe Barth's tendency to abstract ecclesiology from continuous concrete practices and institutions, focusing instead on the community as an event of the Spirit. Barth's ecclesiology is occasionalist in that God is the immediate cause of the church as event while ecclesial embodiment, the concrete cause and effect of ecclesial life and practice, seems optional.

83. Nicholas Healy, "The Logic of Karl Barth's Ecclesiology," 254–55. Healy, it should be noted, provides a more positive reading of Barth's ecclesiology in "Karl Barth's ecclesiology reconsidered," 287–299. In this later article he appreciates more Barth's primary focus on the church as the work of Jesus Christ by his Spirit. Nevertheless, on my view, his 1994 critique still highlights a weakness in Barth's ecclesiology.

84. Ibid., 255.

85. Ibid.

leading to an unnecessary bifurcation. Barth makes "a strong logical distinction between the true and concrete church, on the one hand, and the church of merely human and therefore sinful agency on the other."[86] There is a sharp distinction between the true, real, *wirkliche Kirche* and the apparent, make-believe, *Scheinkirche*. This logical distinction however threatens to turn into a real distinction. For example, Barth cannot discuss the "sinfulness of the church *qua* church," but resorts to the *Scheinkirche*:

> But by doing so he seems to be saying that the church which is really (*wirklich*) the church is in essence a perfect reality. Indeed, such a view would seem to follow necessarily from the definition of the church as denotatively the Body of Christ, for Christ, of course, does not sin. So when the 'church' sins it cannot be the action of the Body of Christ. It must therefore be something else that sins, some other entity, namely the 'false' church. At such time, the true church must be understood either as non-existent or else perhaps existent in another place. According to Barth, then, sometimes at least the unfaithful Bride of Christ is a different entity than the true Body of Christ.[87]

In the end, Healy continues, Barth's ecclesiology leans toward abstract concepts. In scripture, by contrast, there is no "division between the empirical church and its essential reality. God is regarded as continually present and active within the one, all-too-human church, a church that remains such in spite of its faithlessness. Scripture speaks both theologically *and* concretely about Israel and the church."[88] In other words, Barth divides the true church from the ongoing history of the community. Healy's proposed modification is to recover narrative and not rely solely on concepts for ecclesiology. Narrative would allow for the concrete lived experience and particularity of ecclesial existence.[89] Yet the recovery of narrative may only be a result of what is really needed, a more robust and embodied pneumatology.

Reinhard Hütter insightfully examines Barth's 'dialectical catholicity' as a critique of both Roman Catholicism and liberal

---

86. Ibid., 258.
87. Healy, "The Logic of Karl Barth's Ecclesiology," 259. See, as well, 261 on human agency.
88. Ibid., 264.
89. Ibid., 266–68.

Neo-Protestantism. According to Barth, both ecclesiologies misconstrue theological identity and authority; the first locates these in the institutional church the second in the modern turn to the self.[90] Barth criticizes both these views by beginning with eternal election. Barth's view of election, Hütter points out, "secures the Gospel protologically . . . as the free eternal decision of God's will to determine all of the Triune God's activity in time through the election of Christ. The eternal reality of this election is mirrored by a community in which God's act in Christ becomes public for all of humanity and whose vocation is nothing less and else than witnessing to God's election in Christ by communicating it to all the world through word and witness."[91] Following this, the "one true Church can only exist as an event in which, due to the Holy Spirit's action, the human witness fully coincides with its referent, God's graceful election of Christ. . . . Only eschatologically in the full consummation of all will the Church coincide perpetually with its referent."[92] This "transcendental ecclesiology" allows Barth to critique both Roman Catholicism and Neo-Protestantism because the identity of the church is never fully embodied, whether in institutional structures or individualism. "In other words," and this is where catholicity is predicated of Barth's view, "ecclesial difference does not matter as long as the nature and location of the identity of Christ's Body is rightly understood."[93] The problem with focusing on the eschaton as the place of perfect correspondence between human response and divine election is that the practice and institution of the church in the middle time is downplayed. Hütter's modification of Barth's transcendental or disembodied ecclesiology is on the right track. He turns to pneumatological embodiment in concrete ecclesial practices, specifically Luther.[94]

This problem with Barth's ecclesiology has already been anticipated in examining questions of Christology and time. Ford and Farrow

---

90. Reinhard Hütter, "Karl Barth's 'Dialectical Catholicity,'" 142.

91. Ibid., 145.

92. Ibid., 146.

93. Ibid., 147.

94. Ibid., 149–52. These include: "(1) the proclamation of God's Word and its reception in faith, confession, and deed, (2) baptism, (3) Lord's Supper, (4) the office of the keys, (5) ordination and ordained office, (6) prayer, doxology, catechesis, and (7) the way of the cross" (ibid., 149-150). Given this strong focus on ecclesial practice it is not surprising that Hütter has subsequently been received into the Roman Catholic Communion.

suggest that Barth's view of completed salvation on the cross renders ecclesial existence merely a noetic participation. Hütter is correct that an embodied pneumatology with concrete ecclesial practices is needed, but it might also be added that this is necessary not only because Barth has a transcendental view of the church, but because salvation is completed on the cross. A fuller view of salvation is needed, one in which the regeneration of believers in the church through concrete pneumatological practices complements the judgment of sin on the cross.[95]

The critical issues surrounding Barth's view of the church arise then from christological and pneumatological issues, and not necessarily from his actualism or his conceptual use of the body of Christ.[96] As will be examined in chapter 5, the problems of pneumatological agency and ecclesial disembodiment manifest themselves in the discussions of ecclesial time.

TRINITARIAN READINGS

Other interpreters have found Barth's trinitarianism more central to the eternity-time relation. It is not as if the above interpretations miss Barth's trinitarianism. Jenson and Gunton receive much direction from Barth and most interpretations from the second and third group seem to assume it. But the central role of the Trinity in Barth's definition of eternity must be more explicitly acknowledged. In this regard, Eberhard Jüngel, Wolfhart Pannenberg, and George Hunsinger provide important interpretive clues.

---

95. Even Hunsinger admits Barth could have made more room for "gradual or cumulative regeneration within the spiritual life of the believer. Although such a place cannot be completely ruled out (e.g., IV/2, pp. 566, 794), it seems undeniable that in Barth's soteriology this aspect is underdeveloped and excessively diminished" ("The Mediator of Communion," 167–68). Jenson suggests that a non-*filioque*/non-*vinculum* view of the Spirit would lead to a fuller view of the Spirit's agency and greater appreciation for the church as a soteriological instrument; see "You Wonder Where the Spirit Went," 302–4. Of course, Jenson's own solution to this issue is not unproblematic; on Jenson see Burgess, *Ascension in Karl Barth*, chapter 8.

96. I have less suspicion of Barth's actualism than Farrow does (see his *Ascension and Ecclesia*, 244–246, 286–87, and 291–93, and "Ascension in Karl Barth," 147). Alternatively, it may be argued that the actualistic and covenantal ontology Barth develops could help articulate a greater emphasis on Jesus-history beyond the cross, resurrection, and Easter time. On Barth's ontology see Bruce McCormack, *Orthodox and Modern*, especially the essays in "Part 3: Karl Barth's Theological Ontology."

In his important paraphrase of Barth's doctrine of God, Eberhard Jüngel highlights well divine temporality and historicity in Barth's view.[97] Since for Barth the doctrine of the Trinity is central, God's being contains its own movement and order. Jüngel's work gives a commentary on fundamental sections of the *CD*. Jüngel begins in the prolegomena with the revelation of God (*CD* I/1). God's self-revelation is that of revealer, revelation, and revealedness, which is grounded in the triune self-differentiated being of God. Christian revelation is not based on an *a priori* concept of revelation but on God's revelation in the gospel.[98] Moreover, the doctrine of revelation corresponds to the self-relatedness of God's own being. The being of God is a "being which is differentiated in itself and so related in its differentiations, so that the relation constitutes the distinction."[99] Moreover, the inner unity of God's being is expressed in the doctrine of perichoresis, while the outer unity in his works is expressed with the concept of appropriation.[100] After a chapter on Barth's epistemology in *CD* II/1,[101] and a discussion of God's being-in-act, Jüngel seeks to show the concrete being of God in Barth's discussions of election and the cross.[102] While these fine discussions are important, it is Jüngel's conclusions that need to be highlighted for the present interpretation.

In contrast to Platonic metaphysics, which excludes event and movement from the divine essence, Barth's doctrine of God includes event, relatedness, and self-movement.[103] This can be explained with the concept of double relationality in Barth's doctrine of God: "This means that God can enter into relation (*ad extra*) with another being (and in this very relation his being can exist ontically, *without* thereby being ontologically dependent on this other being), because God's being (*ad intra*) is a being *related to itself*. The doctrine of the Trinity is an attempt to think through the self-relatedness of God's being."[104] This implies, moreover, that it is appropriate to apply historical predicates to

---

97. *God's Being is in Becoming*.
98. Ibid., 28–37.
99. Ibid., 39.
100. Ibid., 42–53.
101. This is chapter 2, "God's Being-As-Object," ibid., 55–74.
102. Ibid., respectively 75–82, 83–98, and 98–104.
103. Ibid., 108–12. For a succinct summary of Jüngel's argument see 120–21.
104. Ibid., 114.

the divine being; not only in his revelation but also in his inner triune being. This historicality, however, must not be understood in a generic sense, that God *is* history, but rather as a descriptive of God's revelation and triune being. For God is historical in a more fundamental way. The "Yes" of eternal election reflects this in Jüngel's view: "This *Yes* of God to himself constitutes his being as God the Father, God the Son and God the Holy Spirit. And at the same time, from the beginning, it constitutes the historicality of God's being, in which all history has its ground."[105] In fact, "the being of God takes place as the history of the divine life in the Spirit. And in the history which is constituted through this correspondence God makes space within himself for time. This making-space-for-time within God is a continuing event. The space of time conceived as a continuing event we call eternity."[106]

Jüngel's insight, then, is that for Barth God's eternity—which is the triune life—calls for historical and temporal description. Not only because God reveals himself in time, but also because the divine life has its own independent historicality as Father, Son, and Spirit. God's eternity is the prototype of history and time. That is, divine temporality in Barth can be spoken of in two ways. First, God is temporal in his eternal life *in se*. Second, God is temporal in the sense that he works in time and history *ad extra*. While Jüngel examines this in relation to election and the cross, the following chapters will examine it in the creation and preservation of time by the Father, the fulfillment of time by the Son, and in the ecclesial time of the Spirit.

Wolfhart Pannenberg has given the eternity-time relation a central place in his theological corpus. This is evidenced not only in his systematic work but also in his work in prolegomena and metaphysics.[107] Like Jenson and Moltmann, Pannenberg is highly appreciative of Barth's work but ends up critiquing Barth in light of his own constructive proposal. This reading of Pannenberg's interpretation of Barth will rely on his later work *Systematic Theology*.[108]

Pannenberg, like Barth, seeks to redefine the eternity of God in light of the revelation of the triune God and to appropriate critically the traditional discussion. In *ST* vol.1 Pannenberg seeks to relate positively

---

105. Ibid., 111.
106. Ibid.
107. On this see Mostert, *God and the Future*, 89–182.
108. Pannenberg, *Systematic Theology*, Vols. 1–3.

the eternal God to the created order, and credits Barth with connecting God's eternity with his triunity. Understanding the relation of eternity and time "is possible only if the reality of God is not understood as undifferentiated identity but as intrinsically differentiated unity. But this demands the doctrine of the Trinity. Barth finely stressed this and spoke of an "order and succession" in the trinitarian life of God which includes a 'before' and 'after'. The last point can be made only with reference to the manifestation of the Trinity in the economy of salvation."[109] Besides recognizing the importance of the Trinity for Barth's view of eternity, Pannenberg also notes the centrality of the incarnation for Barth—what Pannenberg describes as the "in-temporality" of eternity. He summarizes Barth's view of eternity by describing it as the "source, epitome, and basis of time."[110] Pannenberg's analysis, however, does not note in Barth the relation of eternity to the creation of time nor the time of the church; which will make up important parts of this project.

However, in seeking to read together NT eschatology along with Plotinus and Boethius, Pannenberg relates eternity to time with an emphasis on futurity: "Eternity as the complete totality of life is thus seen from the standpoint of time *only* in terms of a fullness that is sought in the future."[111] Here a basic difference between Barth and Pannenberg can be discerned. While Pannenberg sees the relation between eternity and time more or less exclusively in terms of futurity, Barth views the relation with reference to God's pretemporality, supratemporality, and posttemporality. Thus eternity is related to the past, present, and future in terms of recapitulation, synchronicity, and anticipation, and not exclusively as the power of the future. Eventually, then, Pannenberg critiques Barth's position in *ST* vol. 3.

In volume 3 Pannenberg repeats the basic contours of his view of eternity while relating it to the final *parousia*.[112] Here he criticizes Barth for not relating eternity positively to the final eschaton, stating that Barth "still did not do full justice to the distinctive priority given to the eschatological future in primitive Christian eschatology."[113] This

---

109. Pannenberg, *ST* 1, 405.

110. Ibid., 406.

111. Ibid., 408, emphasis added; see 405–09. On the focus of futurity see *ST* 2 as well, 84–102 where the Holy Spirit is viewed as a "force field" of the future.

112. See especially 595–607.

113. *ST* 3, 595.

charge seems unwarranted for two reasons. First, unlike Pannenberg, Barth never was able to complete his dogmatics with a full-fledged eschatology, thus one cannot finally adjudicate on what Barth was never able to complete. Second, there are places where Barth relates the eternal God to final things. This will be discussed below in chapter 4. After this we may judge whether or not Barth does justice to the eschatological futurity of God. Nevertheless, Pannenberg does note the importance of the Trinity and incarnation for Barth, pointing to their positive use for the eternity-time relation.

George Hunsinger in his article "*Mysterium Trinitatis*: Karl Barth's Conception of Eternity" also highlights the doctrine of the Trinity as the key to interpreting Barth's view of eternity and time. He argues that Barth's motive on this issue is "to think through the conception of eternity in thoroughly trinitarian terms. Eternity for Barth is not the container in which God lives. It is a predicate of God's triune being."[114] The result is that by "granting primacy to the divine freedom at the heart of God's trinitarian life, Barth can side with the traditional view on eternity's radical otherness and perfect transcendence while also incorporating themes of dynamism, teleology, and immanence that characterize the more modern view."[115]

First, Hunsinger notes the trinitarian background as found in *CD* I/1. He highlights the three main features of Barth's discussion. "God is self-identical in being (*ousia*), self-differentiated in the modes of being (*hypostases*), and self-unified in eternal life (*perichoresis*)."[116] Describing God's triune life as *ousia*, *hypostases*, and *perichoresis* cannot be fully understood but only adequately described. This description, Hunsinger suggests, takes up a dialectical strategy in which neither concept is allowed to isolate the other, but all must be held in tension—though Hunsinger suggests Barth gives a logical priority to the self-identify (*ousia*) of God.[117] Hunsinger then proposes that this dialectical strategy of holding different conceptions in tension in order to preserve the mystery of God is found in the description of eternal life: "God's life in and for himself, his one *ousia* in three hypostases in the process of perichoresis, is a perfect work (*opus perfectum*) that occurs in perpetual

114. Hunsinger, "*Mysterium Trinitatis*," 188–89.
115. Ibid., 189.
116. Ibid., 190. See as well a brilliant summary on 196.
117. Ibid., 191.

operation (*in operatione perpetuus*) (I/1, p. 427). In the dynamism of his one eternal life, God, who is his own basis, his own goal, and his own way from the one to the other, continually becomes who he is."[118] Hunsinger, second, moves into a discussion of eternity found in *CD* II/1. He suggests that the same "theological grammar that governs Barth's doctrine of the Trinity is being applied with suitable modifications to his concept of eternity."[119] This does not mean that Father, Son and Spirit are identified with past, present and future—as is the case with Jenson—[120] but that Barth's dialectical strategy of relating eternity as "pure duration," "beginning, middle, and end," and "simultaneity" corresponds to that of relating *ousia*, *hypostases*, and *perichoresis*.[121] Eternity is thereby understood as "the mutual coinherence of three concrete temporal forms, distinct but not separate, that exemplify an undivided duration, identical with the *ousia* of God."[122]

These distinctions are then used by Barth to distinguish and relate eternity and time. As pure duration, eternity does not share the dissolution and separation between past, present, and future. This is expressed with the idea that beginning, middle, and end are simultaneous in eternity. Yet eternity does contain distinctions between beginning, middle, and end, and thus creates and coexists with all beginnings, middles, and ends of creaturely time. Although eternity is ontologically distinct from time, eternity is understood by Barth as God's own time, since it has its own immanent order and succession and is contemporary with time.[123] Hunsinger then notes the importance of the incarnation in *CD* II/1 as both the entry of eternity into time and the elevation of time into eternity. As fully God, Jesus Christ participates in God's eternity and, as fully human, takes up and heals time. Hunsinger finishes his essay with a brief review of eternity's preceding, accompanying and fulfilling of time with as pre-, supra-, and posttemporality.[124]

---

118. Ibid., 193.

119. Ibid., 198.

120. Jüngel also hints at this identification. See "Theses on the Eternality of Eternal Life," 166–67.

121. Hunsinger, "*Mysterium Trinitatis*," 197–98.

122. Ibid., 198.

123. Ibid., 197–202.

124. Ibid., 203–5 and 206–9, respectively.

The value of Hunsinger's essay is at least threefold. First, he illustrates that the best way to understand Barth's position is by a close reading of the *CD* itself.[125] While Barth takes up traditional notions such as simultaneity, one must be attentive to the way in which Barth employs and develops these terms, lest one assume he is reintroducing ideas that imply timelessness. Second, Hunsinger notes Barth's trinitarian pattern of thinking. Without reducing the Father, Son, and Spirit to the temporal modes of past, present, and future, Barth's dialectical relating of *ousia*, *hypostases*, and *perichoresis* is applied to the definition of eternity and its distinction from and relation to time. Third, Hunsinger's discussion correctly assumes that Barth's view is founded on the doctrines of the Trinity and incarnation. While Hunsinger's analysis is focused on the discussion of eternity in *CD* II/1, this book will reach into important discussions found in volumes III and IV of the *CD*.

Reading Barth on the eternity and time, then, is a complicated endeavor. Not only because thinking about eternity and time is difficult in and of itself, but also because Barth's theology is vast, complicated, and develops over time. However, the charge that he exhibits an atemporal view of eternity is incorrect, though there are some issues concerning Christology and pneumatology that will have to be taken up in the chapters that follow. Another claim I have made in this chapter, however, is that Barth's view of eternity significantly develops from the second *Romans* commentary into the *Church Dogmatics*, and that this is a result of his reflection on the doctrines of the Trinity and incarnation. In the next chapter I will demonstrate Barth's overcoming of an atemporal or abstract view of eternity by tracing this development.

---

125. See as well the comments by Dawson, *Resurrection in Karl Barth*, 27 n. 88.

TWO

Rethinking Eternity and Time

That Barth leads a return from the Babylonian captivity of an abstract view of eternity will be obvious by the end of this chapter. I will demonstrate this, first, by tracing Barth's view on eternity and time from *Romans* II into the *Göttingen Dogmatics*. It will be noted that Barth very quickly abandons the negative view of eternity suggested in his 1921 commentary. That is, the "eternal Now" does not become Barth's primary view of eternity as his theology develops. Second, there will be an examination of the doctrine of the Trinity as found in *CD* I/1. This provides a basis for my argument that the Trinity is decisive in Barth's dynamic understand of eternity as evinced in later parts of the *Church Dogmatics*. In the third section the perfection of eternity in *CD* II/1 will be examined demonstrating how Barth was able to develop a dynamic view of eternity. This section will also briefly take up the relation of eternity and election as found in *CD* II/2. I will highlight the continuities and development between the two parts concerning Barth's understanding of eternity. The discussions of the Trinity, the perfection of eternity, and election will be foundational for the chapters that follow when Barth's *analogia trinitaria temporis* is explicated in detail.

ETERNITY AND TIME IN *ROMANS* II AND THE *GÖTTINGEN DOGMATICS*

Various commentators have correctly asserted that the relation of eternity and time in *Romans* II is predominately negative. In distancing himself from his liberal teachers, Barth needed to draw the sharpest possible line between God and history, eternity and time. The protest of *Romans* is that eternity is not time, the Spirit of God is not history, and knowledge of God is not religious experience. Barth seeks to point out this Krisis in human knowledge of God. While the relation of eternity and time is found throughout the commentary, it is not the major theme of the work however. In fact, the perfections of God do not receive sustained attention; it is after all a commentary.[1] Eternity and time are briefly examined in *Romans* only to mark out the different way in which this relation is worked out in Barth's dogmatics, especially as it begins in the *Göttingen Dogmatics*.

The clearest description of the relation is found in Barth's reflections on the work of love expounded in chapter 13. Here he reflects on the possibility of works of love toward one's neighbor, suggesting that the relation of eternity and time grounds the when and where of "the incomprehensible work of love" (*Romans*, 497). He defines the relation in the following manner: "Between the past and the future—between the times—there is a 'Moment' that is no moment in time. This 'Moment' is the eternal Moment—the Now—when the past and the future stand still, when the former ceases its going and the latter its coming" (ibid.). Eternity, then, is a constant timeless Moment, likened to the present but does not pass away. It is not time, but accompanies and transcends time as the "*Now* that lies invisibly in the midst, incommensurable with it and unable to approach it" (ibid, 499). In the face of this hidden eternal Moment, every "moment in time bears within it the unborn secret of revelation, and every moment can be thus qualified" (ibid., 497). As Barth put it earlier in the commentary, there is a line of intersection between eternity and time (ibid., 47). Eternity can either judge and critique each human present or empower it for loving action. In *Romans*, then, the relation of eternity and time is not necessarily negative, since eternity grounds "the opportunity for the occurrence of love" (ibid., 498). This intersection of eternity and time, nevertheless, does not present the creation, preservation, and fulfilling of time that Barth develops in the *CD*. In fact, eternity is here viewed as a static Now, similar to what is found in some of the traditional discussions.

---

1. On the significance of *Romans* as a commentary, with directions on the importance of this genre for Barth and his relation to modern exegesis, see John Webster, "Karl Barth" in *Reading Romans*, 205–23.

As one might expect, the diastasis of eternity and time in the commentary is most prominent. For example, in contrasting the relation of the flesh and the Holy Spirit Barth suggests the following dualism: "In time, it has already been decided that we are all *in the flesh*: in eternity, it has already been decided that we are all *in the Spirit*. We are rejected *in the flesh*, but elected *in the Spirit*. In the world of time and of men and of things we are condemned, but in the kingdom of God we are justified. Here we are in death, there we are in life" (ibid., 284). The relation of flesh and Spirit does not reflect an equilibrium but an "infinite preeminence which the one has over the other, whereby time is swallowed up in eternity" (ibid., 285).[2] There is also a focus on the future eschaton that is negatively related to the present. Time is not seen as moving toward or being fulfilled in the eschaton, rather the "*futurum aeternum* towers above our life, casting over it everywhere the shadow of doubt and shock, of uncertainty and impossibility. What in God we are, and know, and will, rises like an overhanging precipice over our past and present and future" (ibid., 200).[3]

Yet there are also passages on the positive relation of eternity and time. Again the eternal future, which we groan for (ibid., 312), gives us promise (ibid., 377) and the hope of resurrection (ibid., 223). Moreover, the work of the eternal Spirit in creating faith is God's eternal Yes (ibid., 152), so that in this temporal life one may come to know God (ibid., 310–11). And while "the knowledge of God is eternal and unobservable: it occurs altogether beyond time," God is still able to call humans to love and know him: "Since love beareth all things, believeth all things, hopeth all things, endureth all things (I Cor. xiii. 7), human past, present, and future, is, as such, already the eternal Future. Love is the existential recognition of God; for it is God's recognition of men" (ibid., 325).[4] So while the relation between eternity and time in *Romans* follows the diastasis between God and humanity, which the whole work supports, there is sill the possibility of temporally knowing God in faith and love. To reiterate, however, this is not the trinitarian view developed throughout the *Dogmatics*, but the static and hidden Now which either judges each human moment or creates faith and love.

2. See as well 91, 328–29, 360, 414, 417 and 482–84; on the equating of death with eternity and life with time see 120, 121, 238, 250 and 327.

3. See as well 191, 202 and 515.

4. See as well 331–32, 382 and 457.

But what significance does the *Romans* commentary have for Barth's further development on this issue? Bruce McCormack argues that in *Romans* II the eternity-time relation assumes a subordinate role to the veiling-unveiling dialectic; and that while the latter remains and develops with reference to the incarnation and Trinity (which is evident in the Göttingen lectures), the former is eventually replaced. McCormack argues that there is a more positive relation, and even nascent trinitarianism, between God and humanity found in the veiling-unveiling dialectic—which is the basis of human knowledge of God.[5] God is not known through a natural theology but indirectly reveals himself in the mediation of Jesus Christ.[6] Revelation, in the narrowest sense, occurs in the resurrection, and the cross as the gracious event of God abandonment is only known because of the light of the resurrection.[7] McCormack summarizes this in the following:

> In the dialectic of veiling and unveiling which occurs in the cross and resurrection, Barth sees the actualization of a relationship of correspondence between the hidden God and the death of this man in God-abandonment. God is revealed as the God who shows His faithfulness to the human race in the negation of every last temporal possibility up to and including death itself. . . . That the event of the cross can become *the* parable of the Kingdom means that in and through it is revealed the fact that the Kingdom of God is realized only through the negation of all human, historical, temporal possibilities. The Kingdom of God lies on the other side of the 'line of death' which separates eschatology from history, time from eternity.[8]

Thus, while the concentration here is on the negation of human possibilities in the death of Jesus, the cross, in light of the resurrection, reveals God's faithfulness to humanity. Yet Barth's eschatology here does not reveal any positive telos in the time of the community as the movement toward the eschaton, which he will develop later. Nevertheless, following this objective revelation of God *in* history, there is still the subjective

---

5. This reasoning follows McCormack's larger proposal that there is more continuity between *Romans* II and *CD* than once assumed; see *Barth's Dialectical Theology*, 244–45.
6. Ibid., 246–251.
7. Ibid., 251 ff.
8. Ibid., 255–256.

realization of this by the human subject in the work of the Holy Spirit.⁹ In *Romans* II, then, there is a nascent form of the epistemology found in the trinitarianism of *CD* II/1.¹⁰ What is missing in *Romans*, however, is "sufficient attention to its ground in God himself."¹¹

Nevertheless, in *Romans* Barth did describe eternity in predominately negative terms. Critics of Barth were quick to point this out and suggest its negative repercussions for the relation of God and history. The importance of this negative view, however, is not to be misunderstood. For as McCormack argues, "It is clear from the foregoing analysis of Barth's epistemology that God can do things which eternity (treated as an abstract principle) cannot. God can raise Jesus from the dead bodily; He can create the knowledge of God and faith in the sinner living in time. Unlike eternity, which can only limit or bound time, God can realize new possibilities in time. In a very real sense, the inadequacy of the time-eternity dialectic for witnessing to *all* that Barth wanted to say rendered it outdated from the very moment it was first articulated."¹² It is arguable, therefore, that the view of eternity and time in *Romans* is not traceable into the *CD* because it was not significant for Barth in the first place. The negative relation of eternity and time in *Romans* functioned primarily to critique any notion that knowledge of God could be had by way of abstraction from history. It is basically a rejection of natural theology, especially in the Protestant liberal form of Barth's teachers. Yet knowledge of God and his work in the cross and resurrection of Jesus Christ is an actual possibility.

According to McCormack, the final rejection of the eternity-time dialectic of *Romans* was secured when Barth discovered anhypostatic-enhypostatic Christology in his Göttingen lectures. This ancient Christology preserved the distinction of God and humanity, even while bringing them into connection when the second person of the Trinity took on human nature. A focus on Jesus Christ, as both fully God and fully human in one person, meant that "the time-eternity dialectic could now gradually be dispensed with with no loss of the critical distance between God and humankind which that dialectic had once secured."¹³

9. Ibid., 256–259.
10. Ibid., 262.
11. Ibid., 261.
12. Ibid., 265.
13. Ibid., 328. McCormack also notes that this Christology also served to preserve

Now that the eternity-time relation of *Romans* had ceased to serve its original function, Barth would eventually develop a more positive relation in the Göttingen lectures. Barth, for the first time, begins to reflect on his theology in the more systematic form of dogmatics.

While the shift to dogmatics may have surprised many, even those associated with *Zwischen den Zeiten*, Barth hesitantly took up the task of dogmatic lectures.[14] In 1924 and 1925 the importance of Trinity and Christology for Barth's theology begins to emerge—not even three years after the revision of *Romans* in 1921. For the present concerns, there is a definite shift in the discussion of eternity. With the Protestant scholastic collections of Heppe and Schmid in hand, Barth provides a sustained discussion of the attributes of God.[15] In a critical discussion of the *via triplex*, he suggests that his method is a "way of revelation" (*GD*, 398–401). Like the *CD* he divides the attributes into two basic categories and pairs them off. The positive or communicable attributes of God's personality are life and power, wisdom and will, love and blessedness (ibid., 401–26); While the negative or incommunicable attributes of God's aseity are uniqueness and simplicity, eternity and omnipresence, and immutability and glory (ibid., 426–39).

While there are further developments found in the *CD* (especially in taking up the medieval discussion and developing pre-, supra-, and posttemporality), Barth does begin to relate eternity and time in a more positive manner. First, he states, negatively, that God is not limited by time and space as humans are, nor can eternity and omnipresence be understood as infinite time or space.[16] Yet reflection must not end with the veiling-unveiling dialectic. The divinity of the Son is veiled in his humanity until the revelation of the resurrection and the imparting of faith by the Spirit: "Because of His unintuitability, God can only be known in Jesus where He condescends to grant faith to the would-be human knower; where He unveils Himself in and through the veil of human flesh" (ibid., 327).

14. *Göttingen Dogmatics, Vol 1*. Hereafter *GD*.

15. It might be noted that the order of things in these lectures resembles that of the *CD*: Trinity and incarnation are a part of the prolegomena, epistemology immediately proceeds the nature and attributes of God, and election is treated within the doctrine of God.

16. "We do not begin to conceive of God's eternity and omnipresence by infinitely extending time and space but by negating them. . . . God is he for whom the limit of time and space has no necessary meaning, not even as a necessary correlate, as one can hardly deny in the case of the concept of infinity" (*GD*, 434).

the negation;[17] rather "God's freedom has to be God's lordship over time and space. It is lordship backwards only if he created time and space, and forwards only if he rules them, only if he is present every moment in them as the Lord. God is the author and Lord of time. He is the fabricator of all times" (*GD*, 435). To support this positive relation, following 17th century reformed scholastic Franciscus Burmann, Barth defines eternity as "coexistence" (ibid., 436). Moreover, "Eternity is the quality of God in virtue of which he contains in himself the meaning of time. Eternity is simultaneous duration. We recall the biblical saying: 'My times are in thy hand' (Ps. 31:15)" (ibid.). So here Barth can be seen struggling to move beyond the predominately negative description of eternity in *Romans*. He explicitly combines a negative and positive relation: negatively, eternity is to be distinguished from time; positively, the eternal God is Lord of time, in his eternity he created and sustains time. His eternity coexists and contains the meaning of time.

Thus, interpretations that suggest Barth replicates the eternal Now of *Romans* in the *CD* appear incorrect. As McCormack suggests, the diastasis of eternity and time may have been surpassed as soon as Barth used it, and it was certainly replaced in the Göttingen lectures. Now Barth is free to reconstruct the eternity-time relation with specific emphasis on the doctrines of the Trinity and incarnation.

TRINITY IN *CD* I/1

Fundamental to both the structure and content of the *Church Dogmatics* is Barth's doctrine of the Trinity. Indicative of this is the fact that Barth places the doctrine in the first volume of the *CD*, where one might expect a traditional prolegomenon. As Barth put it: "In giving this doctrine a place of prominence our concern cannot be merely that it have this place externally but rather that its content be decisive and controlling for the whole of dogmatics" (303). Or, as John Webster states, "In one very important sense, the whole of the *Church Dogmatics* is a doctrine of the Trinity, both in its architectural conception and its specific content."[18]

Since his doctrine of the Trinity is found in the prolegomena, Barth couches the discussion in terms of God's self-revelation: the "basis or

---

17. In a shot at reviews of *Romans*, Barth states: "If I were the theologian of negation that I am rumoured to be, I could hold a perfect orgy here" (ibid., 435).

18. Webster, *Barth*, 72. On Barth's trinitarianism see as well William Stacy Johnson, *The Mystery of God* and Paul Molnar, *Divine Freedom and the Doctrine of the Trinity*.

root of the doctrine of Trinity . . . lies in revelation," but it is "also an interpretation of the God who reveals himself in revelation" (*CD* I/1, 311). This beginning with revelation gives Christian theology the ability to speak of God's difference. For, according to Barth, within this self-revelation of God there are implied three questions: Who is God in his revelation? What is he doing? And what does it effect? (I/1, 295–97). For Barth, these three questions show the identity of the self-revealing God to be revealer, revelation, and revealedness; or, Father, Son, and Holy Spirit. Within this revelation of God, however, there is both "unimpaired unity" and "unimpaired differentiation" as "this threefold mode of being" (I/1, 299).

For Barth, the material basis of revelation in scripture begins with a focus on self-unveiling, or the incarnation of the Son (I/1, 315–320). According to the biblical witness, this means that God "takes form, and this taking form is His self-unveiling" (I/1, 316). This taking form means "a being of God in a mode of being that is different though not subordinate to His first and hidden mode of being as God" (I/1, 316). This is expressed in the gospel story as Easter, for the resurrection of Jesus Christ demonstrates that he is a second mode of the divine being. Behind this occurrence, however, is also the God who cannot be unveiled. This mode of God is the Father, the creator who is by essence "inscrutability, hiddenness" (I/1, 320). For behind "the *Deus revelatus* . . . is the *Deus absconditus*" (I/1, 321). In this second mode of being, "God the Father is God who always, even in taking form in the Son, does not take form, God as the free ground and the free power of his being God in the Son" (I/1, 324). The fatherhood of God is expressed in the death of Jesus Christ on the cross, Good Friday. The cross points to the veiled Father, who is the source of revelation (I/1, 331). Yet the revelation of God in these two modes is still incomplete without the imparting of revelation to humans (I/1, 324–332). The revelation of God is not an abstract mythology, but is directed to "a specific man occupying a very specific place, a specific historical place" (I/1, 325). Barth explains this imparting in the following way: "in the Bible revelation is a matter of impartation, of God's being revealed, by which the existence of specific men in specific situations has been singled out in the sense that their experiences and concepts, even though they cannot grasp God in his unveiling and God in his veiling and God in the dialectic of unveiling and veiling, can at least follow Him and respond to Him" (I/1, 330). This is described as "an effective encounter between God and man" (I/1, 331), but it is at the same time "an act of God himself" (I/1, 330). This third mode of God's being, who brings about the impartation, is the Holy Spirit (I/1, 332). The material basis in the New Testament is the outpouring of the Spirit on the apostles after the ascension of Jesus.

These three economic moments of the biblical revelation correspond to the three immanent modes of the divine being. Barth explains: "The concept of the revealed unity in the revealed God, then, does not exclude but rather includes a distinction (*distinctio* or *discretio*) or order (*dispositio* or *oeconomia*) in the essence of God. This distinction or order is the distinction or order of the three 'persons', or, as we prefer to say, the three 'modes (or ways) of being in God'" (I/1, 355).[19] God in the three modes of being (*seinsweisen*) "is God three times in different ways," and "this difference is irremovable" (I/1, 360). So within the immanent divine life there is a true difference and distinction of the divine persons or modes of being, a *repetitio aeternitatis in aeternitate* (I/1, 366). There is no hidden fourth substance behind this differentiation and order within God.

In faithfulness to the classical discussion, the basis of this distinction within the immanent Trinity is found in the doctrine of "distinctive genetic relations," wherein the modes of being "stand in dissimilar relations of origin to one another" (I/1, 363): *paternitas, filiatio*, and *processio*.[20] First, Barth points out the relations of "begetting and being begotten," and a "bringing forth which originates in concert in both begetter and begotten" (ibid). Second, corresponding to these relations of origin, Barth attributes the works of God *ad extra* to particular persons. The Father is the basis of "authorship," "source," and "grounding" as the revealer; while the Son is the basis of "the event of making manifest" as the revelation; and the Spirit the basis of "goal" or "purpose" as revealed-

---

19. On the caution quotes around person, see Barth's discussion of person and his preference for mode of being (*Seinsweisen*), I/1, 355–360. Thomas Torrance also notes in the 1975 English edition of *CD* I/1 (with the apparent permission of Barth) that *Seinsweisen* may also be translated as "way of being" so as to avoid the modalist connotations suggested by "mode of being" (viii). Thus the terms may be used synonymously.

20. "The relations in God in virtue of which He is three in one essence are thus His fatherhood (*paternitas*) in virtue of which God the Father is the Father of the Son, His sonship (*filiatio*) in virtue of which God the Son is the Son of the Father, and His spirit-hood (*processio, spiratio passiva*) in virtue of which God the Spirit is the Spirit of the Father and the Son" (I/1, 365).

ness (ibid). A page later, in the fine print, these relations and distinctions within the Godhead are connected to God's work as creator, reconciler, and redeemer: "We might say further that the fact that God is the Creator is the presupposition of the fact that he can be the Reconciler and the fact that the Creator is the Reconciler is the ground of the fact that he can be the Redeemer" (I/1, 364). Therefore, the full shape of God's works *ad extra* corresponds to the order of his being *in se*.

Another important doctrine taken up in Barth's discussion of the immanent Trinity is the perichoresis of the divine modes of being. With the use of perichoresis, Barth avoids the idea of a mathematical unity of one and instead affirms that the unity of the one God is found in the perichoresis of the three divine persons. While the doctrine of genetic relations is the foundation of the difference in the divine life, the perichoresis of the persons is the foundation of divine unity. Barth explains this in the following way: "The triunity of God obviously implies, then, the unity of Father, Son and Spirit among themselves. God's essence is indeed one, and even the different relations of origin do not entail separations. They rather imply—for where there is difference there is also fellowship—a definite participation of each mode of being in the other modes of being, and indeed, since the modes of being are in fact identical with the relations of origin, a complete participation of each mode of being in the other modes of being" (I/1, 370). The life of the immanent Trinity, therefore, is not exhausted by the subsisting relations of the divine persons but also includes a participation of each person in the other.[21] Barth also argues that such a doctrine has its material basis in scripture. For in the testimony of scripture what "is always stated implicitly or explicitly . . . is not, of course, the identity of the one mode of being with the others but the co-presence of the others in the one" (ibid.). So besides the relations between the persons in the immanent Trinity, as the basis of differentiation, there is also a coinherence of the divine persons, the basis of God's unity.

Rehearsing Barth's doctrine of the Trinity here helps us in a few ways. First, not unlike Boethius, it is out of the livingness of God's triune

---

21. Following a discussion of *perichoresis* or *circumincessio*, Barth concludes that these terms imply "both a confirmation of the distinction in the modes of being, for none would be what it is (not even the Father) without its co-existence with the others, and also a relativisation of this distinction, for no one exists as a special individual, but all three 'in-exist' or exist only in concert as modes of being of the one God and Lord who posits Himself from eternity to eternity" (I/1, 370).

being, as expressed in difference and unity, that time is created and preserved. For Barth, that God's being is eternal does not mean that it excludes movement; rather eternity is the measurement of God's being that includes the perichoretic and electing life of the Father, Son, and Spirit. This eternal triune life Barth describes as divinely temporal and as such is the prototype and source of created time. This will become apparent in the next section of this chapter. Second, because there is a threefold order within the immanent life of God there corresponds a threefold pattern within the economy of God's works *ad extra*. There are times, then, appropriated to the eternal Father, Son, and Spirit (created, fulfilled, and ecclesial times). Third, moreover, corresponding to the perichoresis of the divine persons is a perichoresis of the trinitarian times. There is a coinhering or simultaneity of created, fulfilled and ecclesial time as the work of God in his movement towards the creature he has elected and loves.

ETERNITY IN *CD* II

Barth has two goals in his discussion of eternity in *CD* II/1. First, he wants to distinguish his definition of eternity from the traditional atemporal one, even while incorporating what he sees as its best insights. This includes the definition of eternity as pure duration, or the simultaneity of beginning, middle, and end. This will finally demonstrate that Barth does not reintroduce an atemporal view of eternity, whether expressed as timelessness or an eternal and static Now. He in fact makes true theological progress on this important and difficult divine perfection. Second, he gives a brief exposition of eternity as pre-, supra-, and post-temporality. This exposition in particular will demonstrate the positive relation between eternity and time that Barth envisions, a vision I argue that continues to unfold in volumes III and IV of the *Church Dogmatics*. It will be noted, moreover, that these formal concepts are only given life and impetus by the doctrine of the Trinity, and closely following Christology and pneumatology.[22]

22. In the last chapter we noted Hunsinger's excellent reading of this section. He suggests that the dialectical relation of the trinitarian concepts of *ousia*, *hypostases*, and *perichoresis*, found in *CD* I/1, are analogous to the dialectical relation of pure duration, "beginning, middle, end," and simultaneity, found here in II/1. My reading of this section is more straightforward, while Hunsinger is more concerned with the conceptual parallels of I/1 and II/1. Though it seems his insights are commensurate with the present summary, especially on the centrality of the Trinity.

Barth claims at the outset to take a different methodological basis in defining eternity. He does not want to discuss this perfection as an abstract philosophical notion. Rather, "like every divine perfection it is the living God himself. . . . This radically distinguishes the Christian knowledge of eternity form all religious and philosophical reflection on time and what might exist before and after time. . . . We have simply to think of God Himself, recognizing and adoring and loving the Father, the Son and the Holy Spirit. It is only in this way that we know eternity" (II/1, 638–39). For Barth, then, eternity cannot be defined apart from knowledge of the triune God. "For, rightly understood, the statement that God is eternal tells us what God is, not what He is not" (II/1, 613). Nevertheless, Barth's method is closer to traditional approaches than he admits. I will point out, for example, that Barth's defining of eternity fulfills the traditional notion of the *via triplex* in superb fashion. In the *via triplex* the *via positiva* or *via causalitatus* suggests a positive relation between God the world, a view that Christian theology has always supported. With the *via negativa*, however, God's ontological distinction from the world is upheld. This is something Christianity shares with Greek philosophy. But because Christianity claims to have true knowledge of God as Father, Son, and Spirit it may move toward the *via eminentiae*. So while God's eternity creates, preserves, and works in time (*via positiva*), it is still ontologically distinct from created time (*via negativa*). But because God's triune being contains life and movement it has a divine temporality (*via eminentiae*). This is evident in Barth's discussion.[23]

Eternity and the Critique of Atemporality

In the first half of the discussion Barth affirms, critiques, and incorporates elements of the traditional discussion. The affirmation rests on the conviction that it is necessary to distinguish eternity from created time. In this way, he affirms insights of Augustine and Aquinas. But distinguishing time and eternity is not enough; they must be brought into positive relation. To make this connection, Barth takes up Boethius' definition of eternity, but decisively moves beyond the sixth-century philosopher. The positive relation of eternity and time, moreover, is not

---

23. For a fuller comparison of Barth with some traditional views see Langdon, "Confessing Eternity."

based merely on philosophical reflection but arises from the doctrines of the Trinity and incarnation.

Barth begins in what may seem to be a traditional mode. He makes a sharp distinction between eternity and time by defining eternity as pure duration (*via negativa*). Eternity as "pure duration" means that "beginning, succession and end are not three but one, not separate as a first, second and a third occasion, but one simultaneous occasion as beginning, middle and end." This leads Barth to suggest that "Eternity is not, therefore, time" (II/1, 608). In fact, time "is distinguished from eternity by the fact that in it beginning, middle and end are distinct and even opposed as past, present and future. Eternity is just the duration which is lacking to time, as can be seen clearly at the middle point of time, in the temporal present and in its relationship to the past and the future" (ibid.). The point Barth is making is that whereas for humanity the past and future are separated from the present, thereby making the experience of time one of loss and anxiety, the same cannot be said for eternity. With eternity, there is no loss of the past and fear of the future. Eternity as pure duration overcomes the fleetingness of time. The sharp distinction of eternity and time resembles the traditional discussion. In fact, Barth positively quotes Augustine, Anselm, and Polanus to this effect. This distinction, moreover, is supported by the doctrines of divine constancy and unity, also perfections of the divine freedom.[24]

Nevertheless, as soon as Barth makes the necessary distinction between eternity and time, he notes that pure duration is not merely what is missing with beginning, succession, and end, but that "the duration of God Himself is *the* beginning, succession and end" (II/1, 610). This has the positive meaning that God's eternity possesses, "decides and conditions all beginning, succession and end. It controls them" (ibid.). So not only is eternity distinguished from time, but it is the basis of all past, present, and future, or beginning, succession, and end.[25] In fact, "God is both the prototype and foreordination of all being, and therefore also the prototype and foreordination of time. God has time because and as

---

24. Defining eternity in connection with constancy, or in traditional terms immutability, is reminiscent of the traditional approach. And as Barth states: "the reason why He is free to be constant is that time has no power over Him. As the One who endures He has all power over time" (II/1, 609).

25. Barth uses past, present and future interchangeably with beginning, succession, and end; both describe the unidirectional flow of time. Yet, as was noted in the introduction, these descriptions are based on different understandings of time.

He has eternity" (II/1, 611).[26] Barth moves from the negative distinction to the *via positiva*; eternity is the pure duration that controls the movement of time.

To support this positive relation, Barth takes up Boethius' famous definition of eternity from *The Consolation of Philosophy*: "*aeternitas est interminabilis vitae tota simul et perfecta possessio*" (V.6). He suggests that this definition goes beyond Augustine and Anselm who were "too occupied with the confrontation between eternity and time" (II/1, 610). While this was the most important definition of eternity in the middle ages, according to Barth it was not properly exploited, neither by Boethius himself nor Aquinas after him.[27] For Barth, Boethius' focus on the divine Now, which was a *nunc stare* (standing or still now), was defined in opposition to the *fluere* (flow) of time. But such an opposition cannot exist for Barth: "the concept of the divine *nunc* must not exclude the times prior to and after the 'now', the past and the future, nor may it exclude the *fluere*. On the contrary, it must include it no less that the *stare*" (II/1, 611). Barth defends his view of eternity not by reference to the negation of time, but because of the knowledge of God's unending possession of life.[28] That is, with knowledge of God's triune life.

Barth moves to the *via eminentiae* by finding support for the total, simultaneous, and perfect divine life in the doctrines of the Trinity and incarnation. First, eternity is not atemporality because God's eternal immanent being has its own order, succession and movement—its own time. This lengthy passage explains Barth's position:

> We are speaking about the God who is eternally Father, who without origin or begetting is Himself the origin and begetter . . . We are speaking about God who is also eternally the Son, who is begotten of the Father and yet of the same essence with Him . . . We are speaking about the God who is also eternally the Spirit . . . who as the Spirit of the Father and the Son is also undividedly beginning, succession and end, all at once in His own essence. It is this 'all', this God who is the eternal God, really the eternal

---

26. See II/1, 612 as well. This mirrors the idea that God's omnipresence is the prototype of created space (II/1, 613).

27. Barth has in mind here Boethius's *The Trinity*, Bk. 4 and Aquinas, *STh* I, q. 10, art I.

28. He even suggests that the traditional approach was close to the idea that if there is no time there is no eternity, since its definition of eternity depended on the negative distinction of eternity and time.

> God. For this 'all' is pure duration, free from all the fleetingness and the separations of what we call time, the *nunc aeternitatis* which cannot come into being or pass away, which is conditioned by no distinctions, which is not disturbed and interrupted but established and confirmed in its unity by its trinity, by the inner movement of the begetting of the Father, the being begotten of the Son and the procession of the Spirit from both. Yet in it there is order and succession. The unity is in movement. There is a before and an after.... If in this triune being and essence of God there is nothing of what we call time, this does not justify us in saying that time is simply excluded in God, or that His essence is simply a negation of time. On the contrary, the fact that God has and is Himself time, and the extent to which this is so, is necessarily made clear to us in His essence as the triune God (II/1, 615).

Second, Barth notes that God has time for humanity in the fulfilled time of Jesus Christ: "The fact that the Word became flesh undoubtedly means that, without ceasing to be eternity, in its very power as eternity, eternity became time. Yes, it became time" (II/1, 616). For these reasons, Barth rejects eternity as "pure timelessness" (II/1, 617). God is temporal both in the sense that his own being contains order and movement *in se*, even antecedent to the world, and in his action *ad extra*, exemplified in the incarnation. Barth can conclude, then, that God is both timeless and temporal. God is timeless in the sense that his eternity is not created time, but temporal in his own triune being and in his creating, reconciling, and redeeming activity within the temporal order.

There is an ironic double relationship between Barth and his classical predecessors. First, it is obvious that Barth is indebted to the western tradition. From the Greek philosophers he inherited both the strong ontological distinction between eternity and time and the idea of simultaneity. And from patristic, medieval, and post-reformation sources he learned to describe God's triune being. Yet, second, Barth uses the trinitarian description of God's being, as well as the incarnation, to redefine the perfection of eternity. In this way, Barth rejects notions of atemporality popular in classical sources. As Barth sees it, his predecessors did not fully exploit the livingness of God that was inherent within traditional theology itself. It is not as if Barth merely dismisses the tradition, constructing his view in opposition to others. Rather, in an important sense, he is being a faithful student of the history of Christian theology. It could be argued, that he is faithful to its most important insights and critical of its wrong turns.

Pre-, Supra-, and Posttemporality

With this threefold concept Barth describes God's eternity before, during and after created time. Pretemporality includes the being of God antecedent to the creation of the world; supratemporality includes God's creation and accompaniment of time; and posttemporality is God's eternity after the end of time. In this way God's eternity, Barth argues, encloses time on every side. "Eternity is in time, and time is in God's eternity" (II/1, 620). He also argues that this threefold division is essential for a proper understanding of the gospel. If God is not seen as active in relation to time, then the gospel is reduced to myth or it cannot be articulated in a credible way (ibid).

Pretemporality refers to the being of God antecedent to creation and the beginning of time. God exists as Father, Son, and Spirit in the fullness of his free and loving perfections. We begin to see the effects of Barth's developing doctrine of election when he suggests that in pretemporal eternity God elects the Son to become incarnate for the fellowship of God with the world.[29] Thus, in the freedom of God's pretemporal existence Barth evinces the christocentrism that will be characteristic of his theology (II/1, 622). In pretemporality there is also the anticipation of creation itself, all times therein, the church as the fellowship of believers, and the eschatological end. In his pretemporality God is ready for time, anticipating his work and activity in creating and acting within creation (II/1, 621–622).

With the concept of supratemporality, Barth immediately admits that the preposition "supra" is inadequate. He also suggests the terms "co-temporality" and "in-temporality" to explain what he means by this second form of eternity. All three of these prepositions will prove important for understanding his view. "Supra" emphasizes the ontological

---

29. While Barth's fuller version of election comes in *CD* II/2, it is quite evident here: "For this pre-time is the pure time of the Father and the Son in the fellowship of the Holy Spirit. And in this pure divine time there took place the appointment of the eternal Son for the temporal world, there occurred the readiness of the Son to do the will of the eternal Father, and there ruled the eternal peace of the eternal Spirit—the very thing later revealed at the heart of created time in Jesus Christ" (II/1, 622). On the development of Barth's doctrine of election see McCormack, *Barth's Dialectical Theology*, 453–463.

distinction between God's eternity and created time. "Co" emphasizes that God's eternity is temporal in a distinctively divine way and that eternity accompanies time. Whereas "in" points to the fact that the eternal God works in time, especially for Barth in the incarnation. All three descriptions, then, must be kept in view if God's eternity is not only thought of in distinction from, but also in relation to, created time.

Supratemporality is defined as the accompaniment of time by eternity. Time's "whole extension from beginning to end, each single part of it, every epoch, every lifetime, every new and closing year, every passing hour: they are all in eternity like a child in the arms of its mother" (II/1, 623). However, one is not to think of supratemporality, according to Barth, as a general law in which God is abstractly present in every now. While it is true that every created now is present to God, Barth does not want to construe this in terms of an abstract and immediate experience.[30] Rather, it must be kept in view that one is taking account of the "supratemporality of God the Father, Son and Holy Spirit," and thus "we are not to speak secretly of a timeless God or a godless time, again taking refuge in a desperate hypostatising of the 'now' of our time which cannot be hypostatised" (II/1, 625). When thinking of supratemporality, then, not only is God's creation and preservation of time in general taken into account, but also God's work in Israel, Jesus Christ, and the Church. It is with the later that the meaning of time in general is found (ibid.).

Barth then gives a discussion of Jesus Christ as the fulfillment of time, which is clearly the centerpiece of supratemporality. While this will be examined further in chapter 5, a number of comments are pertinent. First, Jesus Christ is the center of time, and all time past and future receive their meaning from his time (II/1, 626). Second, this turning from the past to the future, from the old aeon to the new aeon, from sin to salvation, is accomplished in his death and resurrection. With the

30. That is, supratemporality must be seen as coming from pretemporality (with the election of Jesus Christ) and moving toward the eschatological redemption of all things. If supratemporality is abstracted from pre- and posttemporality there is a danger of idolizing the human experience of "now" as that which is eternal. "And any conception of the relation of time and eternity is in error which tries to find eternity only in an immediate perpendicular connection with each moment of time, and does not see that the basis of time is also in the divine 'before' and 'after'. . . . A doctrine of God which consists and results in the hypostatising of our 'now' between the times, what we think we know as our present, or perhaps of our temporal consciousness, or in speculation on the connection of all times with God, is more the doctrine of an idol than the doctrine of God" (II/1, 624).

cross, Jesus Christ put to death the sin and disobedience of the old man and the sinful past. "He bore in His person the sin of Israel, thus bringing it under the divine forgiveness. He paid the debt of the human race" (II/1, 626). With the resurrection, moreover, Jesus Christ "brought to light and life in Himself the new man of the second sphere," and "led men upwards and forwards to the freedom in which man will no longer be a sinner or the slave of any fate. He made him the heir of eternal life. In Himself He brought the kingdom of God near for all who believe in Him" (II/1, 626–27). In Jesus Christ there is a turning from the past of sin toward the future of salvation.[31]

Third, turning to anthropology, human creatures participate simultaneously in the two times. As Luther stated, believers are *simul iustus et peccator* (II/1, 627). Though the two spheres do not have the same reality; for "in Him the equilibrium between them has been upset and ended. He is the way from the one to the other and the way is irreversible" (II/1, 628). Fourth, believers may look to the past and future differently. They do not need to look to the past with tears and complaints or yearning to live pasts again. Rather, they are to look to the work of Jesus Christ in the past. The future, moreover, is not to be anticipated with fear. "But the future is not this empty time. It is the coming new age with all its benefits for which we are set free in Jesus Christ. As men set free in this positive way we can look and move to the future—this is the meaning of the evangelical admonition not to worry" (ibid.). To live under God's supratemporality is to live in this real turning, to live "in the real time healed by God, the time whose meaning is immediate to God" (II/1, 629). So the accompaniment of time by God's supratemporality is not a general abstract concept. Rather, it is defined with reference to the salvific activity of God in Jesus Christ.

The third form of God's eternity is posttemporality. Posttemporality refers to the eternity of God after the completion of history and time in the eschaton. It includes the judgment and redemption of all time that comes before it (II/1, 630). As such, from this side of the eschaton, all time moves toward this end (II/1, 629). This will occur with the final revelation and unveiling of the kingdom of God. "God's revelation stands

---

31. "In the sense of the Old and New Testament witness, Jesus Christ is taken seriously only when we see that as He comes between the two spheres He makes the one really past and the other no less really future, constituting time itself the way from this past to this future" (II/1, 627).

before us as the goal and end of revelation. After time, in post-temporal eternity, we shall not believe in it. We shall see it. It will be without the concealment which surrounds it in time and as long as time continues" (II/1, 630).[32]

For Barth, then, eternity refers to the life of God antecedent to, accompanying, and completing time and history. Eternity is a description

---

32. Following his exposition of the three forms of God's temporality, Barth insists that the forms must not be abstracted from one another, giving emphasis to one form at the expense of the others (II/1, 631). At the end of the section he bases this on the fact that God is the living God, and beginning, middle, and end are distinct but not separable (II/1, 639-440). This is even analogous to the perichoresis of the divine persons. There is "a mutual indwelling and interworking of the three forms of eternity. *God* lives eternally. It is for this reason that there are no separations or distances or privations. It is for this reason that that which is distinct must be seen in its genuine relationship. In the future course of dogmatics we shall often have occasion to think of both the distinction and the unity of God's eternity" (II/1, 640).

Barth sees unbalance in different theological movements from the Reformation to his own theology. For their part, the Reformers were preoccupied with God's pretemporality, to such an extent that supratemporality and posttemporality were treated as appendixes (II/1, 631-32). More dangerous, however, was theology in the 18th and 19th centuries that tended to focus solely on God's supratemporality. Neglecting pre- and posttemporality meant a preoccupation with man in his time. This was expressed in Schleiermacher's "eternity in a single moment." But more dangerously "it became little more that an exclamation mark which had no positive content, so that it could be placed not only behind the word 'God' but behind any word at all denoting supreme value, even in the very last analysis, as we have seen under National Socialism, behind the word 'Germany'" (II/1, 633). Thus a focus on eternity in time, neglecting the other two forms, meant that God's presence and activity became a cipher for whatever would take it over. Lastly, posttemporality was rediscovered at the end of the 19th and beginning of the 20th centuries. This arises from not only the exegetical recovery of eschatology, but, closer to Barth, the ministry of the Blumhardts and their companions. This rediscovery of eschatology and hope, however, went astray when the coming Kingdom was tied to secular socialism and not to the return of Jesus Christ. In this connection, Barth states that the theological error of the elder Blumhardt was abstracting pneumatology from Christology (II/1, 633-34). These insights in the end led to a focus on supratemporality similar to pietism and liberal neo-Protestantism. Thus, there are always dangers lurking when one form of eternity is neglected at the expense of the others.

Barth admits as well that a sole focus on posttemporality is dangerous. It is in this context that Barth gives a rare piece of theological autobiography. He states his close association with and objections to theological liberalism, the Blumhardts, and socialism (II/1, 634-638). He admits that in the reaction against these influences he and his companions focused on posttemporality as "a pure and absolute futurity of God and Jesus Christ" (II/1, 634). Barth has in mind his own work in the *Romans* II. Though he recognizes the error in neglecting pre- and supratemporality he insists that the overemphasis was necessary at the time. Nevertheless, Barth seeks to strike a balance between the three forms.

of God's electing and perichoretic life as Father, Son, and Spirit, before, with, and in created temporality. The center of Barth's understanding is Jesus Christ, whose life, death, and resurrection is the work of the triune God bringing salvation to humanity. Consequently, believers may now look to the past and toward the future with hope and expectation.

The Beginning before Creation: Eternity and Election

In 1936 Karl Barth attended the international Calvin congress in Geneva where the papers of Pierre Maury and Peter Barth had important effects on his revision of the Reformed doctrine of election.[33] In terms of understanding the overall development of Barth's theology this revision was paramount for at least two basic reasons. First, as Bruce McCormack suggests, the doctrine of election was a major development in Barth's theology, a doctrine which would decisively shape the rest of his theology.[34] We begin to see the effects of this christocentric turn even in *CD* II/1 when Barth defines God's being as *actus purus et particularis*. God's being is defined as act and event because God's self-revelation in Jesus Christ is event and act. But antecedent to this revelation, God's triune being is living, active, and willing in itself (II/1, 257–72).[35] This continues into the discussion of eternity, as just noted, when pretemporality is understood with reference to God's choosing to become incarnate. Second, closely following this, Barth's doctrine of election more fully completes his "actualistic ontology." By "actualistic ontology" we mean an order of being and existence that is understood in terms of event, act, and history rather than substance and immutability. For Barth, God's being is defined with reference to the life, death, resurrection, and parousia of Jesus Christ. This actualism refers not only to God's self-revelation in Christ but antecedently to the being of Father, Son, and Spirit *in se*. The eternal divine life, for Barth, is the event of the Son proceeding from the Father, and the Holy Spirit spirating from the Father and Son. It is the eternal event of the Father electing the Son to become incarnate, and the Son receiving this election in the unity of the Holy Spirit. According to

---

33. For Barth's own account of the congress see II/2, 188–192.
34. McCormack, *Barth's Dialectical Theology*, 453–63.
35. See ibid., 461–63 as well.

McCormack, this actualism is more fully complete in *CD* II/2 when it is "pushed back into the eternal being of God."³⁶

Nevertheless, this section is specifically concerned with the relation of Barth's view of election to the perfection of eternity and its relation to time.³⁷ I will point out that the progress Barth makes in redefining eternity in *CD* II/1 complements his revolutionary doctrine of election in *CD* II/2. For example, Barth's doctrine of election fits into the threefold understanding of pre-, supra-, and posttemporality and a dynamic view of eternity. He does not need to fundamentally redefine eternity again. Nevertheless, in the doctrine of election there is significant development in filling out the content of pretemporality in such a way that will shape the rest of his *Dogmatics*. So while Barth will continue to speak of eternity using formal categories throughout the *Dogmatics*—eternity as simultaneity of past, present, and future, for example—the doctrine of election gives eternity definitive content and direction. I will demonstrate the development and continuity between *CD* II/1 and II/2 by first noting how pretemporality is deepened, and then demonstrate second how Barth uses a dynamic understanding of eternity in support of his doctrine of election.

The first major implication of Barth's revision of election is a decisive expansion of the content of pretemporality. While he has already stated in II/1 that God chooses to become incarnate in his pretemporal life, this is given fuller explication in II/2. Barth argues that the traditional Reformed view of election, which suggests God pretemporally elects some to salvation and others to damnation, needs to be fundamentally revised. It is not because it is improper to speak of God's predestination or sovereign grace, or that mercy and justice have no place in election, but because the traditional view is not founded on the concrete knowledge of God revealed in Jesus Christ. As Barth states, "the doctrine of election must not begin in *abstracto* either with the concept of an electing God or with that of elected man. It must begin concretely with the acknowledgement of Jesus Christ as both the electing God and elected

---

36. McCormack, "Barth's Historicized Christology," 213. For more on Barth's actualism see McCormack, "Grace and being" and "The Ontological Presuppositions of Barth's Doctrine of the Atonement," as well as Nimmo, *Being in Action*, 4–12.

37. For fuller discussions on the development of Barth's doctrine of election see McCormack, *Barth's Dialectical Theology*, 453–63 and Gockel, *Barth and Schleiermacher on Election*, 158–197.

man" (II/2, 76). So while Barth takes up a number of reformed themes, these are significantly revised.

Election is the pretemporal decision of God which precedes and shapes God's entire works *ad extra*. Even before the decision or actualization of creation, there is the election of Jesus Christ. Jesus Christ "is the beginning of God before which there is no other beginning apart from that of God within Himself. . . . He is the election of God before which and without which and beside which God cannot make any other choices" (II/2, 94, see 99–103 as well). There is nothing antecedent to this besides God's triune life, wherein each divine mode of being has a role in the electing:

> God anticipated and determined within Himself . . . that the goal and meaning of all His dealings with the as yet non-existent universe should be the fact that in His Son He would be gracious towards man, uniting Himself with him. In the beginning it was the choice of the Father Himself to establish this covenant with man by giving His Son for him, that He Himself might become man in the fulfillment of His grace. In the beginning it was the choice of the Son to be obedient to grace, and therefore to offer up Himself and to become man in order that this covenant might be a reality. In the beginning it was the resolve of the Holy Spirit that the unity of God, of Father and Son should not be disturbed or rent by this covenant with man, but that it should be made the more glorious, the deity of God, the divinity of His love and freedom, being confirmed and demonstrated by this offering of the Father and the self-offering of the Son. This choice was in the beginning. As the subject and object of this choice, Jesus Christ was at the beginning (II/2, 101–02; see 99–103 as well).[38]

---

38. There has been recent controversy surrounding Barth's doctrine of pretemporal election. McCormack has called for a critical correction on the relation between Trinity and election. For Barth, God's election does not begin with an unknown, the election of some to salvation and the election of others to damnation. McCormack correctly argues that for Barth, "He is a God whose very being—already in eternity—is determined, defined, by what he reveals himself to be in Jesus Christ; viz. a God of love and mercy towards the whole human race" ("Grace and being," 97–98). This election in eternity contains the death and God-abandonment of Jesus Christ by way of anticipation (ibid., 98). McCormack takes it one step further when he attempts a critical correction of Barth by giving the doctrine of election *logical* priority over the doctrine of the Trinity. He reasons: "The denial of the existence of the *Logos asarkos* in any other sense than the concrete one of a being of the logos as *incarnandus*, the affirmation that Jesus Christ is the second 'person' of the Trinity and the concomitant rejection of the free-floating talk of the 'eternal Son' as a mythological abstraction—these commitments require that we

It is easy to see, then, why election belongs to the doctrine of God for Barth. It is the irrevocable decision of God and is definitive for all of God's ways. And "Once made, it belongs definitively to God Himself, not in His being in and for Himself, but in His being within this relationship [to another]" (II/2, 6). In other words, election is "God's self-ordering of Himself" (II/2, 89).

To secure this christological focus, lest Jesus Christ become an instrument for a hidden will of God, Barth suggests that Jesus Christ is both the electing God and the elected human—the subject and object of election. He is the electing God insofar as the Father elects the Son, the Son is obedient, and the Holy Spirit is the bond that ensures this election. In this way, the divine Son is the subject of election (II/2, 102–04). But Jesus Christ is also the object of election as the purpose of the eternal election is to become this man: "in the pre-temporal eternity of God, the eternal divine decision as such has as its object and content the existence of this one created being, the man Jesus of Nazareth, and the work of this man in His life and death, His humiliation and exaltation, His obedience and merit. It tells us further that in and with the

---

see the triunity of God logically as a function of the divine election" (ibid., 103). And so, the "decision for the covenant of grace is the ground of God's triunity and, therefore, of the eternal generation of the Son and of the eternal procession of the Holy Spirit from Father and Son" (ibid).

In response to this, Molnar first argues that Barth does indeed have a positive, albeit limited, place for the *logos asarkos* in affirming God's freedom (*Divine Freedom and the Doctrine of the Immanent Trinity*, 71). Molnar points to the following passages: *CD* I/2, 168–171; III/1, 54; III/2, 65–6, 147–8.; and IV/1, 52. If the doctrine of logos *asarkos* is used to protect God's freedom and not used to undermine the view that the eternal Son is to be incarnated (*incarnandus*), then it has a positive dogmatic role to play. Second, Molnar calls into question the view that election is logically antecedent to the triunity of God. He argues: "For Barth, God exists eternally as the Father, Son and Holy Spirit and would so exist even if there had been no creation, reconciliation or redemption. Thus, the order between election and triunity cannot be logically reversed without in fact making creation, reconciliation and redemption necessary to God" (ibid., 63). Van Driel draws the same conclusion: "Trinity precedes election, and both make election possible, as well as gives it its peculiar character, namely by taking up the elect in the community of God" ("Karl Barth on the Eternal Existence of Jesus Christ," 52). According to Molnar and van Driel, not only does McCormack's suggestion misinterpret Barth but the logical outcome would also imply the necessity of creation and reconciliation for the being of God. To these rebuttals it may be added that in the doctrine of creation, for example, Barth consistently gives the immanent divine life of Father, Son, and Holy Spirit logical priority over the doctrine of election (in III/1 see 43, 45, 46, 48 and 97). For McCormack's response to these criticisms and his suggestion that there may be some ambiguity in Barth, see "Seek God Where He May be Found."

existence of this man the eternal divine decision has as its object and content the execution of the divine covenant with man, the salvation of all men" (II/2, 116). So included within this election is humanity's salvation and glorification. Its goal, which is an overflow of divine glory, is the fellowship of God and creatures. But because of human sin, the election of Jesus Christ includes the suffering of the cross, which is the judgment of God on human sin (II/2, 120–127, and 161–74): "God from all eternity ordains this obedient One in order that He might bear the suffering which the disobedient have deserved and which for the sake of God's righteousness must necessarily be borne" (II/2, 123). In this way, Jesus Christ takes on double election: he is the elected man who bears the rejection in order that there is only grace available for humanity.

In *CD* II/2, then, Barth gives definitive content to pretemporality. Jesus Christ, as the electing God and the elected human, is the beginning of all God's ways with created reality. In fact, all of God's works are included by anticipation in the doctrine of election—whether the positive works of creation, reconciliation, and redemption, or the permissive existence of sin, death, and hell. All these works are within the context of the gracious God who elects in Christ (II/2, 91–93).

The second major implication of Barth's revision of election for our discussion is that it is commensurate with a dynamic understanding of the eternity-time relation. So not only does election add decisive content to pretemporality but it seems that Barth's dynamic view of eternity supports the doctrine of election. When Barth moves from pretemporal election to the supratemporal activity, election is seen in dynamic terms as the eternal God continuously works within time and history: "The eternal will of God which is before time is the same as the eternal will of God which is above time, and which reveals itself as such and operates as such in time" (II/2, 156; see 155–61). The electing will of God is a continuous action, whether in creation, reconciliation, or redemption. This may be illustrated by examining the second major division of the doctrine of election "The Eternal Will of God in the Election of Jesus Christ."

In this section Barth seeks to draw out some general implications of this doctrine of election. The fourth and final implication focuses on Barth's actualism, the claim that the fulfilling of God's predetermination must be understood as "a divine activity in the form of the history, encounter and decision between God and man" (II/2, 175).[39] He constructs a polemic against the concept of an "isolated and static being" (II/2, 184) with reference to his dynamic understanding of Trinity and election. The origin of this is God's inner triune life: "From all eternity God is within Himself the living God. The fact that God is means that from all eternity God is active in His inner relationships as Father, Son and Holy Ghost, that He wills Himself and knows of Himself, that He loves, and He makes use of His sovereign freedom" (II/2, 175). And following this, "His being and activity *ad extra* is merely an overflowing of His inward activity and being, of the inward vitality which He has in Himself" (ibid.). Barth continues by expounding the encounter between God and humanity, where both divine and human freedom are maintained. The actualization of divine election does not exclude true individualism and autonomy since humans also elect God; which finds expression in faith, obedience, and gratitude (II/2, 177–80).

In a supportive small print section Barth discusses the term "decree," suggesting that if the term is to be employed it cannot be understood as a completed act in pretemporality but as a "living decree" (II/2, 183).[40] In expounding this Barth takes up his formal delineations of eternity. First, the threefold division of pre-, supra-, and postemporality supports his actualistic understanding of election: "The fact that from all eternity God has predetermined, elected and decided has, of course, all the weightiness of the eternal *perfectum*. It is something isolated and complete. . . . But in so doing, it has and is the life of God. . . . It has the character not only of an unparalleled 'perfect' but also of an unparalleled 'present' and 'future.' And it remains because it is eternally before time. It is not left behind by time, but as that which is above time (for there is only one eternity with God) it accompanies time, and as that which is beyond time it outlasts it" (II/2, 183). Second, eternity defined as simul-

---

39. The other points: first, epistemologically, election in Jesus Christ truly reveals God's will, it is not an absolute hidden will (146–154). Second, the eternal divine will which is revealed shows God's good pleasure and mercy (155–161); while third, the content of this will is establishing fellowship with humanity, which means that Jesus Christ must take on the divine judgment. Thus divine election contains Christ's rejection and our exaltation (161–175).

40. It is also interesting to note that in this small print section Barth seems to prefer to speak of God's "constancy" and "faithfulness," and is cautious in using "immutability" (181–83). For a fuller discussion of this in Barth's theology see McCormack, "Divine Impassibility or Simply Divine Constancy," 150–186.

taneity in *CD* II/1 suggests that all futures are anticipated, all presents synchronic, and all pasts are recapitulated by eternity. This also supports Barth's revision of election:

> It not only was but is and will be.... It is true, of course, that in that eternity there can be an 'earlier' as there can be a 'now' and a 'later,' for eternity is certainly not the negation but the boundary of time as such. But for that very reason 'then' cannot mean only 'earlier.' When we speak of God's eternity we must recognize and accept what is 'earlier' as something also present and future. God's predestination is a complete work of God, but for this very reason it is not an exhausted work, a work which is behind us. On the contrary, it is a work which still takes place in all its fullness today (II/2, 183; see 183–84 and 188).

So it is clear that when Barth revises election, and thereby develops his actualistic ontology, he draws on his previous discussion of eternity in *CD* II/1. He uses his redefinition of eternity to break free from earlier understandings of decree which would strait-jacket God's election to a pretemporal decision at the expense of his constant activity. Predestination is not hidden or "inaccessible" to the distant past, "But is an act of divine life in the Spirit, an act which affects us, and act which occurs in the very midst of time no less than in that far distant pre-temporal eternity" (II/2, 185).[41] It is a history and encounter which constantly "takes place" in "movement" (II/2, 186). For Barth, then, the formal definitions of eternity provide a secure basis on which to expound the content of his revised doctrine of election.

Barth's basic insights on the relation between eternity and time in *CD* II are found in later volumes. His view that eternity is the life of the Trinity remains, as does his christocentrism rooted in the doctrine of election, and the idea that humans can participate in fulfilled time. Nevertheless, there are important developments that deserve explication. This includes especially the creation and preservation of time appropriated to the Father, as well as ecclesial time appropriated to the Holy Spirit. He also deepens his view of fulfilled time and human temporality in general, not only with exegesis and theological reflection but also in dialogue with phenomenology. But even with this development Barth's

---

41. I am here capitalizing "Spirit" in this passage since Barth seems to be referring to the Holy Spirit, whereas the translators do not. On the previous page, however, they oscillate between capitalizing and not capitalizing "Spirit" in the phrase "divine life in the Spirit" (184). It is unclear why.

christocentrism is key: created and preserved time are understood only in relation to fulfilled time; fulfilled or reconciled time is the time of Jesus Christ; and the time of the community is the time of the Holy Spirit creating a bond between Jesus-history and the times of believers.

This complex nexus of trinitarian times may best be understood, I would argue, under the rubric of an *analogia trinitaria temporis*. This is evident as Barth continues reflecting on eternity and time in the rest of his *magnum opus*. That he has begun the trek to overcome the Babylonian captivity of an abstract view of eternity should be clear, but to see how far he advances will take us much further into the *Church Dogmatics*.

PART II
Barth's *Analogia Trinitaria Temporis*

THREE

The Theatre of the Divine Glory
The Father and Time

TRADITIONAL AND CONTEMPORARY DISCUSSIONS of the eternity-time relation generally occur in abstraction from particular doctrinal loci. With the predominate approach, beginning with Plato and continuing into contemporary analytic philosophy, time is defined first and then features of this definition are abstracted in order to define eternity. This *via negativa* has often lent itself to atemporal definitions of eternity. Even in contemporary defenses of divine temporality the discussion often revolves around definitions of time that are compatible with divine activity in time and not the fecundity of Christian doctrine per se.[1] The advantage of Barth's view over these approaches is the constant use of central Christian beliefs in approaching the issue.

Barth assumes common definitions of time in his construction as well. But rather than using these definitions to define eternity, whether atemporal or not, he subsumes them under the doctrine of creation, the work of the Father. This is the first loci of Barth's *analogia trinitaria temporis*. Within his trinitarian and covenantal ontology, common definitions of time, assumed to be the shared experience of creaturely existence, are incorporated. Such an approach has the methodological

---

1. Even in those who defend divine temporality (whether sempiternity, interventionism, or omnitemporality) there is only reference to the doctrines of the Trinity and incarnation tangentially, these doctrines are not central to the discussion. For example, in the Four Views book *God and Time*, ed. Ganssle, three of the four contributors (Padgett, Craig, and Wolterstorff) defend some form of divine temporality, contra timelessness (Helm), without central use of these doctrinal loci.

advantage of not defining eternity merely in its relation to time, but in terms of God's triune being and activity. What is more, Barth's view includes the particular and complementing times of the incarnate Son and the Holy Spirit, a material advantage. The important thing for Barth is not whether particular definitions of time lend themselves to either divine timelessness or temporality, but rather how it is that the being and activity of the triune God reconstitutes and redefines what one thinks time is for. The purpose of time is God's gracious movement toward the creature, first conceived in the pretemporal election of the Son, then unfolding in the work of creation and reconciliation, and finally in the completion of time in the eschatological redemption of all things. Therefore, time cannot be defined apart from the being and work of God—there is no secular or common experience of time in the abstract. For Barth, God's time is primary; it reconstitutes all other definitions and descriptions of time.

But what does this imply for the time of creature? The inseparable relation between the form and content of time is a key for understanding human temporality. Temporality is a basic *Existenzform* of the creature, as are the *imago dei* and the body-soul relation. The basic function of time is to allow humans to live a life, for there is no activity and relation with God and humanity apart from temporality, human existence must be lived in time. In this way, time is a gift (III/2, 520–522). Thus Barth can state, "Humanity is temporality . . . However we may interpret it, human life is that movement from the past through the present into the future. Human life means to have been, to be, and to be about to be" (III/2, 522). This is fundamental to the form of existence of the creature. Yet for Barth the Father creates and preserves creatures in their time for the primary purpose of covenantal partnership. This is the purpose and content of time, the qualitative dimension of what time "is for." Thus Barth makes the following distinctions. God originally creates humanity in their time to have fellowship with the creature, this is *created time*. The creature rejects this, however, and the purpose of time is lost, the creature's time becomes *fallen time*. The form of time remains, because it is constitutive of the creature *qua* creature, though the true purpose and meaning of time is abated. But because of God's fatherly goodness time is *preserved* so that the creature is given further time to respond to the reconciling activity of God. And this reconciling depends on the work of the Son and Spirit in time, *fulfilled* or *gracious time*. This is the time "of" God's reconciling and redeeming activity and presence. While the creature lives in fallen time, they may participate in gracious time simultaneously. Thus while the temporal *Existenzform* of the creature remains, the quality or experience of time depends on one's relation to God in this time.

Within this trinitarian narrative of time moreover some of the major issues concerning eternity and time are discussed. Barth criticizes Augustine's view of a timeless creation, for example, and provides an alternative to the discussion of divine foreknowledge and future contingents, so important in traditional discussions. He also provides a profound theological response to the individual's movement toward death, so important in modern phenomenology. Nevertheless, I will suggest that more attention to the nature of time in general would have prevented him from suggesting that temporal existence ends in the eschaton. For example, Barth's brief discussion of the objective time of the cosmos correctly points out that it is the context wherein human temporality is embedded. But further reflection on the relation between objective and subjective time in general would help discern the need for a more robust view of eschatological temporality. This will be hinted at in this chapter and explained more fully in the next.

To explicate these distinctions and to demonstrate that the Father creates and preserves the creature in their time this chapter will first outline some of the basic features of Barth's doctrine of creation, especially the relation of creation and covenant. The rest of the chapter will expound created, preserved, and fallen time as found in volumes III/1– III/3 of the *Church Dogmatics*. It will become evident that although Barth does note the reality of objective time his focus is clearly on human temporality, especially as the Father creates and preserves human time for covenantal purposes.[2]

BARTH'S DOCTRINE OF CREATION AND PROVIDENCE

Barth thoroughly seeks to Christianize his doctrine of creation.[3] This Christianizing creation and providence is summed up in the axiom that

---

2. Barth's anthropocentrism is questioned by Torrance, *Karl Barth*, 132. See as well Gunton, who suggests that Barth does not appreciate creation in and of itself but more as an instrument, *The Triune Creator*, 165.

3. On the relation of covenant and creation in Barth as his attempt to Christianize these, see Tanner, "Creation and Providence," 111–126.

the covenant is the internal basis of creation, and creation is the external basis of the covenant (§ 41.2–3). God created the universe with its own history and time in order that he may enact the covenantal history with humankind within it. For Barth, echoing Calvin, creation, history, and time are the *theatrum gloriae Dei*.[4] Yet this axiom is based upon a number of other presuppositions arising from the Trinity and election. Briefly summarizing these presuppositions will enable a clearer understanding of Barth's discussion of eternity and time in the doctrine of creation. They reveal that he is not working with views of creation or time apart from dogmatic loci or the Christian narrative. These presuppositions can be summarized in two basic clusters. The first concerns how the life of the immanent Trinity is reflected in the work of creation; the second concerns basic distinctions of God's external works in creation and providence.

The themes of the first cluster include the appropriation of creation to the Father, the analogies of relation between the triune life and God's relation to creation, the perichoresis of persons *in se* and work *ad extra*, and the critical doctrine of election. These ideas secure the conviction that the work of creation is first an intra-divine decision before it is actualized.

Within the immanent Trinity the Father is the basis of origin, source, and authorship, since he generates the Son and, with the Son, spirates the Spirit. Thus creation and preservation are appropriated to the Father.[5] The possibility and actuality of God creating is based on the inner divine life: "It arises out of a self-grounded and self-reposing possibility in God. It is—and all this is to be regarded as an intradivine relation or movement, as *repetito aeternitatis in aeternitate*" (I/1, 393–94). The doctrines of creation and providence, then, are not a reflection on general world occurrence as such, whether a scientific cosmology or a philosophy of history, but the recognition that God's providential care

---

4. In III/3 Barth suggests a number of metaphors to describe the sustaining of the creature and creation by God, such as servant, instrument, material, and mirror. His favorite metaphor, however, is creation as a theatre. Creation as the *theatrum gloriae Dei* meets the requirement of understanding creation as the external basis of the covenant. The metaphor of theatre suggests that creation provides the time and space for divine and creaturely activity, making possible the communion between God and humanity (III/3, 44–49).

5. See III/1, 49 and III/3, 28–29.

is based on his fatherly love expressed in the revelation of Jesus Christ (III/3, 20).[6]

Barth also forms analogies between the eternal relations of Father, Son, and Spirit and God's relation to the created order. The most predominant analogy of relation is between the relation of Father and Son and the relation of God and the created order. This follows from the appropriation of creation to the Father. As Barth states: "There is an affinity between the relation of the Father to the Son on the one hand and the relation of the Creator to the creature on the other. In both cases, though in a sense which differs *in toto coelo*, we are concerned with origination. In respect of this affinity it is not merely permitted but commanded that we ascribe creation as a *proprium* to the Father and that we regard God the Father *peculiariter* and specifically as the Creator" (I/1, 397).[7] The eternal basis of God's fatherly care, moreover, is rooted in "what has taken place from all eternity, and then in time, between God the Father and the Son" (III/1, 49). Thus the eternal relation and love between Father and Son is the source of God's fatherly creating and preserving. A second analogy occurs between the eternal role of the Holy Spirit as the "communion and self-impartation" between the Father and the Son, and the Spirit as the principle of the creaturely existence and preservation (III/1, 56). The Spirit ensures the difference and unity between the Father and the Son; just as the relation of the Father and the Son is the principle of "otherness" in the divine life, so the Spirit is the principle of "connecting" or "communion" in this otherness. Following this, Barth argues, "it is in God the Holy Spirit that the creature as such pre-exists. That is to say, it is God the Holy Spirit who makes the existence of the creature as such possible, permitting it to exist, maintaining it in its existence, and forming the point of reference of its existence" (III/1, 56).[8]

Following the analogies is the doctrine of perichoresis in relation to the divine life *in se* and work *ad extra*. While creation is generally appropriated to the Father it is also the work of the Son and the Spirit (I/1,

---

6. For Barth's polemic against a philosophy of history being the subject of providence see III/3, 21–24. It often goes unnoticed, however, that Barth does leave room open for something of a partial Christian "worldview," if it is not static but constantly open to being reformed by the work of the Holy Spirit. See III/3, 55–57.

7. This *analogia relationis* is repeated in III/1 as well, 14 and 50. For a discussion of the *analogia relationis* in III/2 with particular reference to Barth's ethics and its implications for an ethics of the family, see Deddo, *Karl Barth's Theology of Relations*.

8. See 46.2 "The Spirit as Basis of Soul and Body," III/2, 344–366, esp. 355–66.

394). For it "is only an appropriation to the degree that it does not also express the truth of perichoresis, of the intercommunity of Father, Son and Spirit in their essence and work" (I/1, 396). So while the difference in the divine life leads to the naming of the Father as Creator, the unity of the divine life suggests that the Son and Spirit are present in the work of creation as well.[9]

The last feature of pretemporal life to note is divine election. Given Barth's view of election in *CD* II/2, he can state that God creates because of the election of the Son (III/1, 50–51). In fact, the eternal decree and will before creation compels God to create. As Barth reasons, "If God willed to give His eternal Son this form and function, and if the Son of God willed to obey His Father in this form and function, this meant that God had to begin the act as Creator, for there could be no restraining His will" (III/1, 56).[10] Thus the decision to create arises from the primal election of the Son to take up human nature to reconcile God and humanity. The pretemporal basis for both creating and preserving time is found therefore in the relation between the Father and Son, especially in the eternal election of the Son.

A second cluster of themes are concerned with God's external work in creation and preservation. First, conceptually following supralapsarian election is Barth's thesis that the covenant is the internal basis of creation and creation is the external basis of the covenant.[11] For Barth,

---

9. See I/1, 394 and 397, as well as III/1, 48–49. Despite these stated trinitarian themes, it remains unclear how the Son and Spirit are *agents* in the action of creation. When relating the Son and creation, for example, Barth speaks of the being and decision of God antecedent to the creation of the world but does not suggest how the Son or Word, as the second divine person, is an agent in the act of creation itself; on this see Gunton *The Triune Creator*, 158. For Gunton's own view of creation "through" the Son and "in" the Spirit see *Christ and Creation*, 75–79. To put the question simply: does the eternal Son do anything at the initial act of creation? Torrance also asks whether Barth's doctrine of creation is sufficiently trinitarian and wonders why he neglected speaking of the cosmos. See *Karl Barth*, 132.

It is noteworthy that Barth refuses to take up a discussion of the Spirit in relation to creation in his exegesis of Genesis 1:3 (the Spirit or wind swept over the waters). For comment on this see Gabriel, "A Trinitarian Doctrine of Creation?," 44–47. For examples of pneumatological agency in the doctrine of creation see Pannenberg, "The Doctrine of the Spirit and the Task of a Theology of Nature"; and Gunton, "The Spirit Moved Over the face of the Waters."

10. See III/1, 18 as well.

11. For discussions of election and covenant see McCormack, "Grace and being"; Cochrane, "Karl Barth's Doctrine of the Covenant"; and Whitehouse, "Election and

the history of the covenant takes priority over the history of creation. In fact, covenant history is the presupposition and content of creation history and its time. That is, it is the true content of history and time in general (III/1, 59). The covenantal purpose of creation is repeated in the doctrine of providence as well. On the relation of God's eternal decree and providence, Barth argues that providence "belongs to the execution of this decree. It is eternal, divine providence to the extent that it is grounded in this decree" (III/3, 5). Conversely, covenant history, which is the goal and presupposition of providence, needs providence as an external basis (III/3, 7).

A second distinction is the one between creation and providence. This is based on the two forms of divine activity in the doctrine of creation: the initial act of creation and God's preserving, accompanying, and ruling what has been created.[12] Providence ensures that creaturely being has a "permanence and continuity" (III/3, 68 and 71). Or in relation to temporality, "The act of creation takes place in a specific first time; the time of providence is the whole of the rest of time right up to its end" (III/3, 8).[13] The distinction between these two activities is based on the direct and indirect activity of God. "In creation God acts directly, i.e., without the intervention of other things, for other things could enter in only as the product of His creative activity and not as the co-efficient of it" (III/3, 64), which is likened to God's direct creative activity in the covenant of grace.[14] The providential work of God, in distinction from creation and covenant, is indirect, concerned with preserving the creature and creation in its total environmental nexus (III/3, 64–67).[15]

Covenant." The prominence of the doctrine of election in III/1 follows from Barth's exposition of it in the doctrine of God. On the development and importance of this see McCormack, *Karl Barth's Dialectical Theology*, 453–67.

12. "As distinct from creation, providence is God's knowledge, will and action in His relation to the creature already made by Him and not to be made again. Providence guarantees and confirms the work of creation. And no creature could be if it did not please God to continually confirm and guarantee and thus to maintain it" (III/3, 6). See as well Tanner "Creation and Providence," 122; and Webster, *Karl Barth*, 94–112.

13. For Barth's rejection of a continuous creation see III/3, 68.

14. From the calling of Abraham, to the resurrection of Jesus Christ, to the calling of individuals by the Holy Spirit, these activities have "the very same immediacy as the act of creation itself" (III/3, 64).

15. Here Barth admits he is following Aquinas, see small print section, ibid., 66–67.

Third, this work of the Father in creation and providence is hidden from humanity in general. While God's fatherly providence is revealed in the actualization of God's eternal election in the covenant with humanity, this is still hidden from general world history. This is reflected in the providential theme that the particular history of the covenant is a thin line in general world history, even while it is the "starting-point or goal" that fulfills all of history (III/3, 36). Conversely, knowledge of this particular history leads to faith in God's general preserving and sustaining. Moreover, while God's providence is known now through the covenant of grace, it will be fully revealed in the new creation (III/3, 37–39). Thus the hiddenness of God's providential work will end with the universal unveiling of the reconciliation between God and humanity in Jesus Christ. However, before this future unveiling, creation history, upheld in God's providence, co-ordinates or co-operates (albeit asymmetrically) with the unfolding of covenantal history; there is "a positive, material and inner connection between the two series" (III/3, 40). That is, for the creature there is a real freedom and activity; "in its continued existence the creature may serve the will of God in His covenant, grace and salvation, it does this in the individuality and particularity given it with its creation by God, in the freedom and activity corresponding to its particular nature" (III/3, 43).

But what have these distinctions to do with Barth's trinitarian reading of time? Concerning the role of the Father, it may first be noted that the creating and preserving of time is appropriated to the Father, while the distinction between creating and preserving time is based on the two modes of creative activity. The analogies of relation between the divine modes of being and God's creative activity demonstrate that Barth was thinking of the God-world relation via analogical categories. To suggest, then, that there is an analogy between eternity and time in the *CD* is commensurate with Barth's thought. Moreover, Barth's supralapsarian Christology and doctrine of election not only compels God to create and informs the axiom that creation is the external basis of the covenant, and vice versa, but is also reflected in Barth's view that the fulfilled time of Jesus Christ is not merely a response to fallen time, but in fact the prototype and goal of created time itself. Just as the incarnation is not primarily a response to human sin but God's will for fellowship with humanity, so gracious time is not merely a response to fallen time, but the goal of created time itself.¹⁶ The last point, that the history of the covenant is the secret of history in general, will become more obvious throughout these last three chapters as it becomes clear that the gracious time of the Son and Spirit are the eschatological goal of time and history itself. Lastly, the theme of asymmetrical co-operation is important for understanding the relation between divine and creaturely freedom, which Barth takes up in the discussion of preserving time. With these distinctions in mind, created, preserved, and fallen time may be explicated.

THE CREATION OF TIME

Time is a basic form of existence (*Existenzform*) of the creature, along with the *imago dei* and soul-body relation, which serves as the basis for the covenantal relations with God and fellow humanity.¹⁷ Barth favors two descriptions of time in his discussion. The first is the rational-linear concept of time—time as the succession of past, present, and future—and the second is allotted time, one's lifetime (III/1, 67–68, cf. 71).¹⁸ Again, these forms of time need to be filled with human and divine activity. Barth only briefly takes up the objective time of creation, which he discusses in his exegesis of Genesis 1, particularly vv. 1 and 4: the creation of the first day and the creation of the luminaries. The exposition of time beyond human existence however is a concern for Barth because it provides the context for human historicity. In this way, cosmic time is the indirect basis for covenantal time.¹⁹

---

16. On Barth's supralapsarian Christology and view of election see van Driel, *Incarnation Anyway*, 63–124.

17. It must be noted in passing that time, as the *Existenzform* of the creation, is fundamental to Barth's understanding of a universal human nature. Although Barth's anthropology is christologically focused, he still presupposes a universal form of human existence (this can be seen especially in volume III/2, wherein each section of this part volume begins with a christological section and then proceeds to discuss humanity in general); see McLean, "Creation and Anthropology," 127; as well as Krötke, "The humanity of the human person in Karl Barth's anthropology." Thus while Barth reads anthropology christologically, beginning with the particular, this is not at the expense of a universal human nature.

18. Barth assumes these standard descriptions of time are the way in which God created the creature in the cosmos. Other subjective views of time in the western tradition include the cyclical-mythical or the escapism of mystical experience; on these see Achtner, et al, *Dimensions of Time*, 27–53 and 102–8.

19. Aside from this Barth hesitates to describe the nature and reality of objective time. This is a result of his view that the Bible does not give insight as to the inner re-

At the outset of his discussion of time in *CD* III/1, Barth reiterates that time is a creation of eternity, which has its own particular temporality. This clearly evinces the analogical relation between eternity and time. In discussing the attribute of eternity in II/1, it was noted that God's eternity is not in opposition to time, but is rather an inner readiness of God to create time. More specifically, God's eternity can be considered divine "time" because there is movement and succession between the divine persons (II/1, 615 and 660). Barth repeats these ideas in III/1, where it is claimed that eternity is "the source of time as it is supreme and absolute time" (67). In fact, God's eternity "is the prototype of time, and as the Eternal He is simultaneously before time, above time, and after time" (ibid).[20] In Barth's view not only does eternity contain its own "history" or "temporality," but it is also the source of all time.

This positive and analogical relation between eternity and time is readily apparent in Barth's dialogue with Augustine. Barth emphasizes two points concerning the initial creation of time in dialogue with the church father. First, time begins with creation, and second, creation occurs in time (III/1, 68). The first point that time begins with creation is not uncontroversial for Christian theology; the second point is. In answering objections concerning *creatio ex nihilo*, in contrast to the eternity of the world, Augustine argues for the beginning of time with creation in his *Confessions*. The sceptical question "What was God doing before creation?" was meant to weaken the Christian view by placing a certain arbitrariness into God's being.[21] It was asked, "Why did he not make the world sooner," or if he decided to make the world would this "decision" not imply change in God? (Bk. XX.10). Augustine responds to such questions by pointing out that they imply a "before" and "after" which is not applicable to a situation before the creation of the world—

---

lationship between God and creation, unlike the relation of God to humanity. As such, objective time is only examined as it relates to time of humanity, Barth does not fully work out the embeddedness of human time in cosmic time. On the embeddedness of subjective time within objective see Achtner et al., *Dimensions of Time*.

20. "He is not non-historical because as the Triune he is in his inner life the basic type and ground of all history. And he is not non-temporal because his eternity is not merely the negation of time, but an inner readiness to create time, because it is supreme and absolute time, and therefore, the source of our time, relative time. But it is true that in this sense, in his pure, divine form of existence [*göttlichen Existenzform*], God is not in time, but before, above and after all time, so that time is really in him" (III/1, 68).

21. *Creatio ex nihilo* could be considered orthodox Christian belief at this point; on the development of the doctrine see May, *Creatio ex Nihilo*.

since God is timeless. That is, time comes with the creation of the world and one cannot ask what God was "doing," because there is no activity or movement in God (ibid.). Following this, creation is thought to be a timeless act.[22]

While Barth agrees that time began with creation, he questions Augustine's claim that creation is a timeless act. He does so for three basic reasons. First, God's eternal being has its own divine time, and thus any act of God *ad extra*, whether the initial act creation or subsequent acts in time, will be the work of this divine temporality. Second, the works of God in the history of the covenant and Jesus Christ are historical and temporal. Thus, if the character of God's work as covenant partner is the same as his work as creator, then divine creating is not atemporal (III/1, 14–15, 60–61, 68).[23] Third, the Genesis narrative itself implies that not only did God create time but also that he created *in* time: God continued to create in the seven days. Therefore, to say that creation is timeless is to deny both that God has his own divine temporality and to miss the historical character of divine activity. Rather than beginning the discussion in an apologetical mode like Augustine, then, Barth constructs his view with reference to what he considers the positive revelation in scripture. In this way, creaturely time is a creation of God's eternity.

The difference between Augustine and Barth then is Barth's insistence that eternity is not timeless. While for Augustine God acts within time, this does not lead him to suggest that eternity has its own distinct temporality.[24] In contrast, for Barth God's eternity has a distinct temporality because God is triune and acts within time.

---

22. Augustine's basic answer was that such questions did not apply because time means movement, and before creation there was no movement because God is unmoving and unchanging. For further analysis of this in Augustine see Knuuttila, "Time and creation in Augustine," 105–7.

23. As Barth argues: "According to scripture there are no timeless truths, but all truths according to scripture are specific acts of God in which He unveils Himself; acts which as such have an eternal character embracing all times, but also a concretely temporal character" (III/1, 60). For references to the historicity of God's work in *CD* III/1, see 15, 16, 125, 183, 216, 217, 218, and 223.

24. This is not to say that Augustine refuses to see God working in time. A fuller examination (including not only Genesis commentaries and the *Confessions* but *The City of God*) would reveal that Augustine does see God working in time. In *The Trinity*, Augustine even suggests that the temporal missions of the Son and Spirit are founded upon eternal triune relations (IV.25–32). Yet he does not go so far as Barth to suggest that there is a distinct temporality in God's eternity. Augustine's apologetical concerns

Objective Time and Human Historicity

Further along in III/1 the creation of time resurfaces in Barth's exegesis of Genesis 1. Similar to some classical theologies of creation, the core of III/1 is a theological exegesis of the first two chapters of Genesis. In subsection 41.2, "Creation as the External Basis of the Covenant," Barth examines Genesis 1 arguing that it gives an ordered account of God's creating the cosmos and humanity that is directed to the covenant. This culminates in the creation of humanity in the *imago dei* and God's Sabbath rest. Thus Barth maintains that Genesis 1 establishes creation as the theatre (III/1, 99, 101) or house (III/1, 181) of God's covenantal works. Conversely, in subsection 41.3, "The Covenant as the Internal Basis of Creation," Barth exegetes Genesis 2 arguing that the covenantal relation between God and humanity is "prefigured" when humanity is given a place to live and an opportunity to respond to God's word and command (III/1, 232). Barth's exposition of these two chapters supports his view that "Creation is one long preparation, and therefore the being and existence of the creature one long readiness, for what God will intend and do with it in the history of the covenant" (III/1, 231).[25]

Embedded within the exegesis of Genesis 1 is the oft-neglected discussion of objective time. In fact, Barth seems only to note it in passing. For Barth, as for many commentators, the first three days are concerned with the creation of light, sky, and land, while the next three days "fill" this space with luminaries, birds, fish, animals, and humanity.[26] That is, while the first three days describe the creation of time and space, providing the home for creatures, the last three days describe "the furnishing of

---

likely prevented him from moving in this direction.

25. Barth, however, does not claim that these texts are historical the way in which other scriptural texts appear. On the one hand, he refuses to view Genesis 1 as a revealed scientific cosmology to be taken literally. Yet, on the other, he is unwilling to view it as pure mythology, although it contains myth. For Barth, myth implies a story constructed to tell timeless truth (III/1, 84–87). Creation and creation history, however, are not timeless truths. The logic here is important: since God the Creator is also the God of the covenant, and it is clear that God acts historically and temporally in his dealings with humanity in the covenant, then the Genesis texts are not timeless mythology. They refer to historical action by God. The term Barth attaches to this genre is *saga* (III/1, 81). Thus, Genesis points to the theological reality of creation, which is at the same time historical actuality. Though it is obviously not observed and recorded history in the modern sense. Given this particular genre, then, there is interplay between a natural description of creation and symbolic interpretation.

26. See, for example, Wenham, *Genesis*, 6–7.

the cosmos" (III/1, 156). On the first day, God calls into existence light, which is followed by darkness, and thus creates the first day, while on the fourth day, the luminaries of the sun, moon, and stars are created to mediate the light of the first day and thus make measured objective time a possibility. Yet the units of time created by God (day, week, etc.), are created for human historical existence. In this way, human historicity is embedded within cosmic time.

Barth explains the commencing of time with the creation of the first day as the first of God's historical works *ad extra*, when eternity creates time.

> Time as such came into being, and was at once made a day, the first day. It is the naming which characterised God's accomplished work as an historical act, as the first in the series of all God's other historical acts. It was not in an instant of an eternal moment, nor in an indefinite time, but in a day limited by an evening that the *opus Dei ad extra* became an event. It is in such a day that it obviously wills to become and will again become an event. It is this fundamental act of the divine compassion and condescension which becomes apparent in the fact that God not only has eternity but also time, and that now He also gives time to His creatures as the living-space appropriate to them; that he not only wills to act uninterruptedly, in accordance with the constancy of His own nature, but that He also wills, as He is able, to do so interruptedly in individual, concrete and, of course, finite acts, in accordance with the finitude of the created reality distinct from Himself (III/1, 130).

This passage points out not only the emergence of time, co-existent with the creation of light, and thus the first of God's works, but also the character of God's work's *ad extra*. As noted already, creation is not a "timeless act" for Barth, since God creates and acts only historically and concretely in time. Also important to note is the twofold manner in which God acts toward creation: uninterruptedly and interruptedly. God in his constancy will preserve creation uninterruptedly and in his freedom act interruptedly, in concrete ways. Yet most significant for the present discussion is the appropriate "living space" created for human existence, the gift of human historicity.

Furthermore, contrary to views that would take the creation of "day" in Gen. 1: 3–5 only figuratively, Barth argues that these verses speak of real objective time. "God created time: not just time in general, but our time, the actual time in which each creature actually lives; or concretely time as a unit, i.e., the day, and time as a sequence, i.e., the week; and that He created it by giving to light the name day" (III/1, 125).[27] Though the passage speaks in the form of saga Barth insists it is concerned with the reality of days and week, the objective time that is meant for the creature. Note that Barth's description is quite minimal—there is the unit of day and the sequence of week. He does not explain the connection between time and the cosmic processes. He argues instead that the objective reality of time is a creation of the Word of God (III/1, 129).

The exposition of objective time is found again in the exegesis of the fourth day of the creation narrative. Genesis 1: 14-19 states that God called forth the sun, moon, and stars so that they may govern the sky during the day and night. The luminaries then act as the objective measurement of time, allowing humanity to make their way in time. Barth states that they "are the objective measure of time and space; the objective clock and objective compass with the help of which man can orientate himself and thus be capable of history" (III/1, 162). He explains this at length, stating that the luminaries control the shape of time to include days, months, seasons, and years, which has both cultural and historical significance. For Barth then, the luminaries control the plurality of times associated with biological and cultural life: weather, navigation, agriculture, as well as the historical existence of human life (III/1, 158 and 162). In this way, there is an integration of objective and subjective time. The days, seasons, and years are created by God in order that humanity may live in time, and thus historically. The anthropocentricity here is unmistakable. The luminaries prepare man "for his activity as the earthly subject of the history appointed for him by God" (III/1, 162). Thus their ruling is to allow humanity to be not only aware of its natural existence as such but to be open to history and, more importantly, the history in which humanity will be encountered by God.[28] In fact, the "proceeding works all aimed generally at man, or rather at God's relationship with man. But from this point onwards everything aims particularly at man's interested partnership in his relationship with God" (III/1, 157).[29]

---

27. Barth insists this is in reference to real objective time; see III/1, 125–26.

28. See III/1, 156–63, where he makes the point in various ways.

29. Barth defends his anthropocentric interpretation by critiquing both ancient and modern cosmologies, which tend to ignore the purpose of creation: the relation between God and humanity. In the first place, Barth sees a certain demythologization

Barth's view of the creation of exogenous or objective time may be summarized with the following comments. In the first place, the articulation of objective time is a theological one. That is, he is concerned not merely to argue that time is an objective reality, but to state the theological function of time. God creates time and space in order that the human creature may exist historically, which is the external basis wherein covenantal history is actualized. Moreover, Barth presupposes that objective time is a part of the cosmic process. Within the discussion of the first and fourth days he points out that time is objectively measured and a part of the natural order. The luminaries created on day four (the sun, moon, and stars) are positioned by God to be objective measurement of time. Since Barth only gives an exposition of objective time in its relation to the time of humanity, however, there is no consideration of how eternity relates to cosmic time. While the present interpretation will demonstrate the triune pattern of eternity's relation to human temporality, there is little construction of how the triune God relates to the created order and its time. Barth presupposes that there is a *direct* relation between God and non-human creation, but he suggests that there is no biblical knowledge of how this relation is to be understood. Thus theologically, Barth reasons, the internal relation between eternity and subjective time can be discerned but not the internal relation between eternity and objective time.[30] It may be asked of Barth, however, does not all of creation, and thus its times, have a place in the reconciliation and redemption of the world through Christ and the Spirit (Rom 8:18–25)?

---

of ancient views of the luminaries as deities in their devaluation to mere instruments in the service of God (III/1, 159–160). Modern cosmology, moreover, in its tendency to examine the cosmos without reference to the purposes of God, exhibits the same refusal to acknowledge anthropocentricity via the covenant (III/1, 160). According to Barth, then, both ancient and modern cosmologies, either in deifying creation or ignoring its relation to the covenant, misplace or ignore a proper anthropocentrism.

30. As Barth states in III/2: "We do not know what time means for animals or plants, or for the rest of the universe. We live in constant relationship to the rest of the universe. Therefore, since we ourselves are in time, we may conclude or suspect that time is the form of existence of everything created. At any rate, the mode of existence of the earthly cosmos as observed and conceived by us shows countless analogies to our own to support this view.... Moreover the biblical accounts of creation, especially the first, seem clearly to imply that time was created simultaneously with the universe as its form of existence. Like man the whole universe is in time as created by God and therefore real" (521). Nevertheless, he concludes that "we do not know what it means for beings in the earthly cosmos to be in time. We have no means of observing or conceiving of their temporality. But we can observe and conceive our own" (ibid.).

This reluctance to reflect more on the relation of objective and subjective times will surface in the next chapter when Barth's view of time in the eschaton is questioned. He suggests that time ceases to exist in the eschaton, which is not only problematic for humanity but for cosmic time as well. It will be suggested that a more rigorous attempt to think of subjective and objective times together would aid a better eschatological understanding of time.

PRESERVING TIME

Theologically following the act of creating time is that of preserving it. Barth discusses the preservation of time in the doctrine of providence in III/3, which contains two pertinent and related themes. First, the eternal God preserves creaturely time in anticipation of covenantal encounter, and second, this encounter preserves and protects both the freedom of God and the freedom of the creature. The first theme will serve the next section of the chapter, as God preserves the creature even in its allotted and fallen time for the possible participation in gracious time. The second theme is Barth's alternative to the problem of divine foreknowledge and future contingents. This problem has often governed the problem of eternity and time, at least since Boethius and it is even found in the work of Augustine. Typically the discussion has focused on the formal problem that if God knows all future times then this implies they are fixed and therefore the freedom of the creature is illusory.[31] While Barth does not altogether neglect such formal questions, he defends a version of prescience in II/1 (558–60), his focus in III/3 is the encounter of God and humanity in covenantal partnership. Thus the terms of the debate are superceded by Barth's actualistic ontology. God's will and purposes are pursued in the course of time and history as he graciously pursues the creature in every temporal moment. God's eternal election of humanity through Christ does not preclude the actual becoming of history, but includes it, and in such a manner that protects the autonomy and freedom of both God and humanity in their relation and encounter in

---

31. Of course, the traditional answer is no, foreknowledge does not imply a fixed future. Of the vast amount of literature, see for example Zagzebski, "Omniscience, Time, and Freedom"; Or, Hasker, *God, Time, and Knowledge*, who argues for an "openness" of God and the future. Barth's approach has the advantage of a dynamic view of God's work in time and history which positively moves beyond the philosophical conundrum.

time and history.³² For Barth, the eternal God encounters humans in their time—even in the limitations of allotted time—in a way that preserves their freedom as creatures.

In the doctrine of providence Barth makes use of a threefold rubric adopted from Protestant scholasticism: divine preserving (*conservatio*), accompanying (*concursus*) and ruling (*gubernatio*). With these divisions Barth argues for both divine and creaturely freedom and the necessity of their interaction. The point of the divine preserving (*conservatio*) is the "upholding and sustaining [of the creature's] individual existence—the existence which He gave to it as the Creator and which is different from His own existence—and by giving to this existence its continuity" (III/3, 58). Conversely, the point of divine accompanying (*concursus*) is that God exists alongside and with the creature even as he gives them its proper time and space. While the life of the creature has a limited time span, allotted by God, the divine being lives before, during and after the limited time of the creature.³³ The third theme, divine ruling (*gubernatio*), qualifies the other two. While preserving and accompaniment focus on the autonomy of the creature and God respectively, divine ruling focuses on the purpose and direction of divine providence. God does not preserve and co-exist with the creature and creation without a particular *telos*.

---

32. See, for example, Colwell's comments on the inclusion of human participation in divine election in *Actuality and Provisionality*, 28.

33. While Barth cannot be described as panentheistic he does make a strong case for the close relation between God and creation. Yet he continuously maintains that this is an asymmetrical relation and that God is not a part of creation. He states: "In Him, and not somewhere near Him, we live and move and have our being, and not on the basis of our self determination, or of the determination of a field of force within which, or a system of norms under which, we may happen to find ourselves" (III/3,130). For Barth, in similarity to some of the church fathers, it is equally correct to say that creation is in God as it is to say that God is present in creation. In the discussion of God's omnipresence, Barth develops the concept of God's spatiality (*CD* II/1, 466–474). So in Barth's view it is incorrect to think of God as distant from creation, since God is the prototype of all space and the universe is present to him in this containment. When God creates the universe it is *in* the divine space and time, "so that time is really in him" (III/1, 68). For references in some of the church fathers see Theophilus of Antioch, *Theophilus to Autolycus*, Bk II, chap. III. In *Ante-Nicene Fathers*, Vol 2; Irenaeus, *Against Heresies*, Bk II: chaps. I.1; II.3; V.4; XXV.2 and 4 in *Ante-Nicene Fathers*, Vol 1; and Hilary of Poitiers, *On the Trinity*, Bk I, chap. 6; Bk II, chaps. 6 and 20, in *Nicene and Post-Nicene Fathers*, 2nd Series, Vol. 9.

On the first theme, the general preservation of time, four interspersed points can be extracted. In the discussion of divine preserving (*conservatio*) Barth first states that the preservation of time is the continuation of created time. "But the statement that God preserves the creature means much more than that He gave it time. When he created it, He might well have given it time in order not to preserve it indefinitely.... But if He really sustains it, this means that He gives it more time, that He confirms it in its being in time" (III/3, 61). This preservation, second, encompasses the full multiplicity of times in the created order, both subjective and objective (III/3, 84). And third, humanity in its time, along with all creaturely species, and even history itself, is preserved with limits (III/3, 61). Barth rejects both the immortality of the creature and the eternality of creation.[34] This allotted time, however, does not mean the life of the creature is "partial, transitory or imperfect" (ibid) or "an evil necessity, an obscure fate" (III/3, 85) but that even in its limitation there is an opportunity to respond to the covenant of grace. Fourth, the divine preserving of the creature in allotted time is the result of God's eternity. In discussing the divine accompanying, which surrounds the time of the creature, Barth states that it is the work of the eternal God:

> God is eternal. It is as the eternal God that He acts in time. And this means that He acts not merely before the work of the creature as this work occurs within the limits of its own time, not merely contemporaneously with it, but also after this work is concluded, and therefore after the time allotted to it has come to an end. God was, and was at work, even when the creature had not commenced its work. God is, and is at work, in the accomplishment of this work. God will be, and will still be at work in relation to this work, when the creature and its work have already attained their goal (III/3, 151).

Here eternity as pure duration ("was," "is," and "will be") surrounds the time of the creature. God was before the creature, accompanies it, and will be after the life of the creature ends. Since this enveloping of time will be examined with fallen time, it is suffice to note that the eternal God in his fatherly providence proceeds, accompanies, and follows the allotted time of the creature.

---

34. On Barth's rejection of the soul's immortality see Nielsen, "Karl Barth on Time and Eternity," 12–14.

This description of God's preserving of time—since his eternity is pure duration—is complemented in the doctrine of providence with the discussion of divine and creaturely encounter in time. This second theme is Barth's alternative to the problem of divine knowledge and future contingents. Instead of considering whether or not humans are free in light of divine foreknowledge, he variously argues for the autonomy and freedom of God and the creature in their covenantal encounter and final fellowship in the eschaton.

At times the argument takes on a formal tone. Under the discussion of divine accompanying (*concursus*), for example, he argues for three interrelated themes. First, God co-exists with the creature as the living God, in all the richness and particular activity of the divine being (III/3, 92). Second, the divine accompaniment is a co-operation. When God works he does not bypass the activity of the creature. "Just as He Himself is active in His freedom, the creature can also be active in its freedom. God Himself can guarantee this to the creature. It is His creature. And even the freedom in which it can work is His gift" (III/3, 92). Yet, third, this co-operation is asymmetrical since God accompanies as Lord (III/3, 93). God is the creator and sustainer of the creature and so it is not just any form of accompaniment. Similarly, a major portion of the discussion of divine ruling (*gubernatio*) makes a formal argument for preserving both the freedom of God and the freedom of the creature (III/3, 157–175). Here there is sustained attention given to the divine permission bestowed upon the creature. God controls creaturely activity by sustaining and permitting the creature to exist within its own sphere (III/3, 165–166). Barth argues that the creature has its own dignity and activity even under God's ruling; there is no contradiction between the ruling of God and the freedom of the creature. God's ruling gives the creature time and space for its own free activity.[35] So the basic argument is that God's providential activity ensures that both God and the creature co-exist in a way that preserves the freedom and activity of both, even while God is still Lord over the creature. This basic argument, to use a phrase of Kathryn Tanner, is a "non-competitive relation" between God and humanity.[36]

---

35. See III/3, 165 and 168–170.

36. Tanner, *Jesus, Humanity and the Trinity*, 2, see 2–4. See as well her earlier work, *God and Creation in Christian Theology*, especially chapters 2 and 3.

The success of Barth's proposal, however, relies on dogmatic content. He admits that his reflections rest on the first article of the creed, on the "Father, Almighty, Creator of heaven and earth" (III/3, 176 ff). Or, the subject of general world providence is the same subject revealed in the covenant. The "King of Israel is the King of the world" (III/3, 176), and the "I am" who concretely reveals himself in the Old and New Testaments is the subject of world governance. More specifically, the foundation of this ruling is the eternal decision of the triune God to graciously turn in love toward humanity (III/3, 183 and 187). The basis of his answer to the problem of divine and human freedom resides in the living God of scriptures, which is coupled with the actualistic language of encounter.

For example, when reflecting on the actualization of God's eternal divine will, Barth highlights that this is a relational and dynamic concept. It is not to be thought of as a secretly "fixed plan which precedes the creation of the world and therefore all temporal occurrence" (III/3, 164). Rather:

> The plan of God is, and consists, and is divine, in the fact that He actually carries it out, that by His power His decision continually becomes an event. This is its essence and content. The divine activity in time is identical with His willing, so that the divine willing is not somewhere behind this activity but has to be perceived and adored within it, and the activity cannot be a later fulfillment of His willing, nor can it be understood as such. It is in the temporal activity of ordering that the divine order is realized, and it is because God causes it to be realized in time that it is eternal (III/3, 164-165).

Based on Barth's actualistic ontology, this passage argues for the dynamic unity of God's pretemporal will and its actualization within time. This ordering, moreover, is "a continuing operation by which an occurrence in time takes place in accordance with a definite plan, and is determined and formed and directed through constantly changing situations and stages... The rule of God is the order of God in this active sense, His ordering of all temporal occurrence" (III/3, 164, cf. 188.). God's eternal will, for Barth then, is not a fixed plan that mechanically predetermines all times, but rather is constantly working through all times to bring this will to completion. Toward the end of the discussion on divine governance, Barth finally makes reference to the concrete encounter between

God and humanity found in the scriptures: "If we look at this factual relationship, and therefore at the rule of the God of Israel, we see that it is actually true that in the world-governance of God everything has to be and is absolutely under God, and yet everything attains in freedom to its own validity and honour" (III/3, 189). The argument for divine and human freedom rests on the encounter between God and humanity as attested in the scriptures.

This encounter has a particular end, moreover. God ultimately directs all creaturely activity toward an end that includes both the glorification of God and the eschatological glorification of the creature. While humans have a particular goal in mind for their action, "it is God who decides where and how it will actually culminate, what will be its upshot. . . . And this is true both when the culmination and effect correspond more or less to the creaturely activity and also when either by its non-existence or its different form and bearing it is a complete surprise in relation to it" (III/3, 167). Even while human freedom may be directed to a particular end, ultimately God judges and decides on the final effects of human action.[37] The goal of God's ruling, finally, is both the glorification of God and the creature (III/3, 168).

God follows his pretemporal will in encountering the creature in its own time and space. While the creature's action may not follow God's will, he determines the final outcome of the creature's history in his eschatological judgment. This occurs, Barth argues, in a way that maintains the freedom of God and the creature, even while God is Lord. So besides the more general view that God preserves the creature in its time in order to have covenantal partnership, Barth's defense of divine and human freedom supplants the traditional discussion of divine foreknowledge and future contingents. Not only does Barth discuss the creation of time, then, but he is also concerned with God's preserving it, in all its variety and complexity, so that the covenantal history and fellowship may occur. However, the human partner, in his freedom, refuses the divine intention and created time becomes fallen time. But for Barth, God preserves the creature even in its fallen time.

---

37. This is evident earlier in the section when discussing God's eternal preservation of time. In the eschatological recapitulation of all times God judges and preserves the times of creation; see III/3, 87-90.

LIFE IN FALLEN TIME

While the divine purpose for created time and its preservation is covenantal fellowship, humanity refuses this and its time becomes fallen. The *Existenzform* remains, as humanity still lives in the flow of past, present, future, and within the limit of allotted time, though the being and activity therein is one of human sin. Consequently the experience of time is fundamentally one of insecurity and fear, insecurity in light of the fleeting present and fear in the face of inevitable death. Thus the qualitative difference of fallen time arises from the lived "content" of sinful existence. Yet, as shall be demonstrated, Barth insists that God preserves the creature in its fallen time as to provide it with an opportunity to respond to his gracious call. Barth first makes mention of fallen time at the beginning of III/1, in relation to created and gracious time, though the most substantial exposition of it occurs in III/2, where there is a full-fledged phenomenology of fallen time.

At the center of Barth's definition of fallen time is the creature's failure to see time as a gift. It occurs when the creature "is not content to enjoy and treat it as something loaned to him, but tries to possess and use it as his very own, as the predicate of his thinking, willing and existence" (III/1, 72). In *reality* time is a gift to the creature to be in relation to God and humanity, but its *appearance* (time as a human phenomenon) is transformed into a flux, riddle or hypothesis.

> It is the time whose flux has become a flight. It is the time in which there is no real present and therefore no real past and future, no centre and therefore no beginning and no end, or a beginning and end only as the appearance of a centre which is in reality the one and only thing and in one respect or another is not true and proper time. It is the time which, like an insoluble riddle, seems as though it must necessarily be finite as well as infinite, but no less necessarily cannot be either the one or the other. It is the time of which—although it is our only time—it can unfortunately be maintained only as a hypothesis that it is even related to a real absolute time as its origin or goal or secret content, thus having the character of reality. It is time without any recognizable ground or meaning in eternity (ibid., cf. as well III/2, 525–526).

So while the form of creaturely time remains—whether the flux of past, present, and future or allotted time—its content is that of fallen humanity lived apart from eternity. It is a time then without its true purpose, meaning, and centre.

Besides this basic definition, it is important to note that fallen time does not negate the reality of created time. For Barth God created humanity with a universal structure: *imago Dei*, ensouled bodies, and existence in time. Within Barth's anthropology these three features of the human being are not destroyed by sin. Since God has determined humanity for fellowship with himself in Jesus Christ, any attempt to deny the purpose of God for humanity (sin) is ultimately an impossibility.[38] In the case of temporality, it is clear that time as the *Existenzform* of the creature remains despite sin. It is only that the purpose of time, as fellowship with the creator, is unacknowledged, ignored, or turned away.

Following in III/2, Barth provides his exhaustive phenomenology of fallen time. Here he weaves together a complex discussion that answers both ancient and modern concerns of human temporality while employing both phenomenological description and theological response. The ancient problem is distilled in Augustine's *Confessions*. Humans only experience time in the present, yet this present is illusive and constantly slipping away (Bk.XI.20). Barth describes this as time from the *inside*, concerned with the conscious experience of past, present, and future. The individual subject experiences this as memory, intuition and expectation. The question here is how do humans live in the transitory now?

In modern phenomenology another problem for human temporality comes to the fore. While not neglecting discussion of the fleeting present altogether, the authentic experience of time (to use Heidegger's terms) is related to the anticipation of death.[39] Barth terms this allotted time, time bracketed by birth and death, with a focus on the movement toward death. Barth terms this problem as time from the *outside*. The

---

38. As Webster explains: "To decide for sin is not to decide for a possibility which, however dreadful it may be, is equally as real an actualization of human being as the life of obedience to God. To decide for sin is to negate what one inescapably is as a human being, and therefore to adopt an impossibility as it were merely one more way of being a creature," *Karl Barth*, 102. See as well Krötke, "The humanity of the human person in Karl Barth's anthropology," 165–66.

39. On the role of temporality in modern phenomenology see Dostal, "Time and phenomenology in Husserl and Heidegger." He argues that the experience of time is a foundational problem in modern philosophy, running through Kant and Husserl into Heidegger, though it is never properly resolved. On the importance of death for Heidegger's schema see Hoffman, "Death, time, history: Division II of *Being and Time*."

concern is not the fleetingness of the present but that one comes from non-being and will return to non-being. The question here is how do humans live knowing their time is limited? Barth answers both problems with reference to the eternal God and his temporal work.

In the doctrine of creation Barth has generally avoided dialogue with other disciplines.[40] Yet in these subsections, as mentioned, Barth sees fit to present phenomenological and theological discussions together.[41] As will be evident, the phenomenon of time must be understood, critiqued, and appropriated to theological concerns, but nonetheless Barth does present a sustained phenomenological description. As Nielsen explains:

> Barth does not use the term 'phenomenology' but speaks of '*Erscheinung*', appearance, which may be assumed to mean the same thing. Phenomenology is not an approach Barth avails himself of under normal circumstances and closer scrutiny reveals that nor does he here. It figures, rather, as one strand in a more complex structure which aims at showing that a purely phenomenological analysis ends in a theological aporia, i.e. an irresoluble knot. The implication, in other words, is that a theologically acceptable approach to the problem of time needs to be informed by a component quite distinct from the phenomenon of time itself.[42]

---

40. Earlier in III/2 (71–132) Barth presents a sustained discussion of the phenomenon of humanity (he takes up naturalism, idealism, existentialism, and theistic anthropology) though he critiques these approaches for a failure to relate humanity to the authentic humanity found in Jesus Christ. The difference here in III/2 is that Barth himself uses a phenomenological method and is not merely critiquing the use of it by others.

41. The term phenomenology is being used here in a general sense. Barth does not explicitly take up any of the methodological issues found in phenomenology as such (description, reduction/bracketing, essence, intentionality, etc.). But his approach does fit into Merleau-Ponty's general description of phenomenology: it "tries to give a direct description of our experience as it is, without taking account of its psychological origin and the casual explanations which the scientist, the historian, or the sociologist may be able to provide" ("What is phenomenology?," 13).

42. Nielsen, "Time and Eternity," 9. Or, as Barth explains his method: "Always against the background of God's eternity, we have tried step by step to isolate human time—the time created and given by God—from its distorted and obscured manifestation, and to study and present it in and for itself. We began with an analysis of time in the distorted and sinister form we know only too well. . . . We then proceeded to analyse time in the reality in which it may be seen as the time given us by God" (III/2, 551).

Eternity and the Fleeting Now

Like Augustine before him, Barth relates the problem of the transitory and fleeting present to God's eternity. Unlike Augustine, however, who views time as something to be ultimately escaped in the goal of union with God,[43] Barth sees the temporal "now" in light of God's accompanying presence and argues it as an opportunity for covenantal relation with God. The fleeting now is not to be escaped but is to be seen as an opportunity. Barth's main assertion is that time is not a monstrosity but a gift of God's fatherly goodness. And again like Augustine, this experience of the present contains reflection on memory and anticipation, which, when used properly, empowers the creature to live in time with confidence and hope.

Barth first reviews "the phenomenon [of time] as it presents itself to us," which is "our own movement from the past through to the future, of the fact what we were yesterday and are today and will be tomorrow" (III/2, 512). The past "is the time which we leave and are in no longer" (ibid), while the future "is the time which we do not yet have but perhaps will have" (III/2, 513). Both the memory of the past and the anticipation of the future are problematic since they are an elusive substitute for their reality. Even the present, which ought to provide the most certainty, is presented by Barth as "a step from darkness to darkness, from the 'no longer' to the 'not yet,' and therefore a continual deprivation of what we were and had in favour of a continual grasping of what we will (perhaps) be and have" (III/2, 514). For Barth, reflecting on the phenomenon of time shows the ambiguity, darkness, and enigma surrounding the human experience. Philosophical reflection on time can only lead to the conclusion that time is an uncertain riddle (III/2, 514). In fact, such reflection on time without christological moorings is merely a description of *sinful humanity in time*. "The man who lives in that monstrous situation . . . is the man who is alienated from his Creator and therefore from himself, from his creaturely nature, and who has to pay for his rebellion against God by living in contradiction with himself, in contradiction with his God-given nature" (517). Such a contradiction is exposed in Jesus Christ, according to Barth.[44]

---

43. See Kirby, "Time in the *Confessions* of Augustine."

44. "In the existence of the man Jesus it is decided and revealed that God did not at all create man in that state of falling 'from cliff to cliff'; that it is not at all His will which is manifested in the fact that our being in time is very different from the creaturely

Therefore, time as the form of existence of the creature must be thought of in correspondence to God's eternity and be seen as willed by God from eternity for covenantal relation (III/2, 526–27). Given the analogical relation between eternity and time, Barth reflects again on the phenomenon of the past, present, and future, relating the temporal modes to God's eternity, and thereby re-describing them anew. This means that the response of anxiety in the face of the ambiguity, even monstrosity, of temporality is replaced with a response of faith and gratitude. In the following interaction between the phenomenon and gift of time, eternity is defined as the *simul* of past, present, and future. In this definition of eternity all times are related to eternity by anticipation, synchronicity, or recapitulation.

The phenomenon of the present is experienced subjectively between recollection and expectation, but this way between past and future is hardly secure (III/2, 527–528). The insecurity of the present can be overcome however by realizing that the elusive now of the present is under and with God's now: "Primarily, however, it is not we who are now but God who is now: God who created us and is in the process of rescuing and preserving us; God who is not dismayed at our sin, and does not cease to be for us, nor reverse our determination to be for Him and in mutual fellowship; God in all the defiance of our unfaithfulness and His own faithfulness. He is now primarily; and we secondarily" (III/2, 529). Barth goes on to describe God's presence in our now with reference to the *simul* of eternity. He suggests that God's eternity is truly present to the human now even while transcending it, since eternity anticipates, is synchronic, and recapitulates all times. "He is now as Creator. But this means that there is first a divine stepping from the past to the future. This is His present. We speak of His eternity, in which the past is not 'no longer' nor the future 'not yet,' in which therefore the Now has duration and extension. It is in His eternity that God is now. But we do not speak of God's abstract eternity, but of the eternity of His free love, in which He took and takes and will take time for our sakes, in which He wills to be for us and also wills that we should be for Him and therefore in mutual fellowship" (III/2, 530). The present, then, is a stable reality for human experience because God accompanies it in his love and grace.

---

nature given by Him; and that He is determined to vindicate and protect His right as Creator and ours as His creatures in face of the monstrous perversion and corruption in which we exist" (III/2, 517–518).

This implies, moreover, that the present is not a neutral existence, but an opportunity for fellowship and encounter with the covenantal God and other human beings. "What is this transition, then, but the offer, the summons, the invitation, to be with God now, to be present with Him, to make this transition with Him, recognizing that He always precedes us, not without us, but for us and on our behalf" (III/2, 531). The present therefore is an opportunity to fulfill one's created purpose.

While Barth admits that the past may possibly continue in the present, since humans are made up of their past—"I am still the same person I was yesterday" (III/2, 533)—he suggests that there is no guarantee of this continuity; the past in fact ceases to exist. The unreality of the past, then, casts a shadow over the present and future, for they too are doomed to pass into this unreality.[45] Overcoming the problem of the past is attempted either by remembering, keeping the past alive in various histories, or trying to forget the past, often manifested as belief in progress, a turn to the future. Yet, the attempt to remember the past carries no guarantee and the desire to forget it is irresponsible. Humanity, according to Barth, usually lives with a combination of both (III/2, 534–535).

But again Barth contrasts the problems associated with the past to God's eternity, which contains the coinherence of past, present, and future, and thus its own past and remembrance (III/2, 535–36). Thus, one's past is not lost to God, even as it stands under his judgment. According to Barth, because God preserves all pasts in his eternity: "Our being in time with its regressive duration and extension not only was real but is real. It is not lost. . . . We are in our whole time, in the whole sequence of its parts, and not just in the one part we call the present. For our time is the dimension of our whole life. If our whole time is the gift of God, then God also pledges to maintain its reality as whole" (III/2, 537). This reality of the past, which makes up the sequence of each lifetime, is in fact guaranteed by God: "We are really the persons we were in the whole duration and extent of our past,

---

45. "And this raises the disturbing suspicion that even our present and future are hastening towards the past; that that fatal line will be drawn again and again; that our present and all our future being are incontrovertibly condemned to undergo that transformation and therefore to become past being in the sense described, and as such to be no more. From this standpoint again it would seem as if we have no real time" (III/2, 524).

because in it we are before God, to whom we owed everything but were also responsible for everything" (III/2, 538).

Since lives can be seen as a whole, as a gift of God under his preservation, the solutions of recollection and forgetfulness can be seen in a new light. With regard to remembering, on the one hand, one ought to look back in gratitude and try not to escape the past; while on the other hand, humans ought not to be trapped in the past, confined to its grip (III/2, 539-40). In the same way, the phenomenon of forgetting is balanced in light of God's eternity. Forgetting is a positive aspect of our consciousness; it "is a good thing that God draws this veil over the past even without our asking. In so doing, He allows us to live today for tomorrow with just the few memories we need of what was" (III/2, 540). Yet one does not have to forget all in order to live: "There is every reason to think that it is God's good purpose that these fragments of the past should belong to our life in the present and the future" (ibid).

Like the phenomenon of the past, Barth admits that the future is not real as such, as it is only anticipated.[46] Yet the experience of anticipation is also wrought with difficulty. There is in fact much insecurity in anticipating the future, not only in whether one's plans will work out, but in the end of individual existence in death. The human response to this uncertainty and insecurity, according to Barth, is again twofold. One may posture themselves in an unreflective, frivolous, optimistic, and activist mode; not concerned with the end or uncertainty of the future. Or, one may take a reflective, preoccupied, pessimistic, and quietist mode; preoccupied with the certain end and uncertain ends of the future. Neither of these options is appropriate for Barth. To be purely unreflective is naïve and careless, while being purely reflective and preoccupied with the future is paralyzing (III/2, 542-544). The way out of this dilemma is again by reflecting on the eternal God, whose life has a genuine future.[47]

46. "As we are, we anticipate the future. We project ourselves into the future. We see and will ourselves as we shall be. We act as though our future being had already arrived. To this extent we are determined by it. Our thoughts, feelings, actions and reactions are coloured by specific hopes and fears. All our human activity, but also all our human experience and suffering, hastens towards a *telos* . . . . At any rate, whether we are conscious of it or not, the present is always openly or secretly pregnant with the future" (III/2, 541).

47. "But between Him and us there will be a connection, for in His eternity—it is the eternity of the living God—there is also a genuine Then. . . . But this eternal God will guarantee the reality of our future too (however long or short it may be), just as He guarantees it even now and has always done so. He will give it to us as the dimension of

The eternal God, with his future, accompanies and guarantees each future, which is part of each lifetime seen as a whole. Thus humanity must not live in either a mode of naïve unreflecting or anxious preoccupation with the uncertain future, but rather live in gratitude and responsibility in the allotted time that is given to each individual (III/2, 547–550).

Barth, then, sees the problem of the fleeting now —variously experienced as remembering, perception, and anticipation—in light of God's eternity. The problems associated with recollecting and forgetting the past and reflective and unreflective anticipation of the future are resolved by relating them to the simultaneity of past, present, and future in God's eternal life. For Barth, this realization of God's divine accompanying—with its genuine past, present, and future—creates in the human subject the ability to see her life as a whole, to see it as an opportunity for covenantal fellowship with God, in gratitude and faithfulness. Like Augustine then, the problem of human temporality is resolved with reference to God's eternity. For Barth, though, God's eternity is analogously related to all modes of time and reconstitutes the subjective experience of time. Unlike Augustine, human temporality is not something to be escaped then, but the possibility of encounter with God.[48]

Jesus Christ and the Movement toward Death

While Barth does not cite Heidegger in III/2, he was obviously familiar with his work—especially through his conversations with Bultmann[49]—and definitely takes up the philosopher's concern on the limited time of individuals. As Piotr Hoffman summarizes Heidegger: "Dasein's authenticity requires the lucid acceptance of one's own death, it is precisely because Dasein's totality can be revealed only in its being-toward-death."[50] Yet Barth's ontology is fundamentally different than his contemporary's and so his answer to the problem of individual movement toward death is not the totalizing force of the movement toward death. Rather, the totalizing force of individual existence is the God who has reconciled humanity to himself in the cross of Jesus Christ. Individual death, in Barth's view, is reduced to a sign of the "second death" or wrath of

---

the life which He has appointed for us" (III/2, 545).

48. Kirby, "Time in the *Confessions* of Augustine."
49. See Busch, *Karl Barth*, 161.
50. Hoffman, "Death, time, history," 196.

God. Death therefore is not to be feared but to be met with confidence since God, who is the Lord of death, lovingly meets one at their end.[51] Barth continues his phenomenological and theological conversation. But instead of describing time from the transitory present, the focus is on individual allotted time having a definite beginning and an ever-approaching and inevitable end.[52]

The last three subsections of §47 are concerned with this allotted time. The last two, "Beginning Time" and "Ending Time," will be the focus of more sustained attention. In "Allotted Time," the first subsection, Barth defends this form of time as the good and natural way in which God created human existence by rejecting unending duration in time and immortality. Humans, created in the image of God, are constituted to live in relation to God and fellow humanity, and so unending time could allow them to perfect these relations (III/2, 556–57). Barth, however, first argues negatively that it is not necessarily the case that limitless duration would guarantee the perfection of humanity's relation to God and one another (III/2, 559–561). A long or limitless duration would only mean limitless opportunity, not fulfillment; The creature "would be condemned to perpetual wanting and asking and therefore dissatisfaction. Could there be any better picture of life in hell than enduring life in enduring time?" (III/2, 562).[53] Yet positively, the limits of one's life

---

51. In the history of Christian thought there have been two main ideas concerning humanity and death. The first and most dominant, closely following Greek thought, is concerned with the immortality of the soul. Death in this view is the release of the immortal soul from the body. The second and more recently accepted is that humans are created with a finite boundary and death is natural (see Jüngel, *Death*, 41–42, and Nielsen, "Time and Eternity," 13–14). Barth argues for the second option, that death is the natural end of human existence and there is no "part" of the human person that exists subsequent to death. Barth does not indicate here how he understood the continuity of human existence after death, during the intermediate state. Nielson suggests that for Barth an individual's time is preserved in God's eternity, though he is unsure if and how this relates with a temporal, future eschaton; see "Time and Eternity" 18–19. Barth seems to suggest such an "intermediate preservation" of individual times in God's eternity until the final eschaton (III/3, 87–90).

52. "His time is the allotted span, i.e., the limited space, which he needs for this fulfillment [of his life] and which is given him for this purpose. This span begins at a certain point, lasts for a certain period and finally comes to an end. Man is, therefore, in this span, and not before or after it. It is only in this way, as allotted time, what time is his time" (III/2, 554).

53. Or, "No infinity of space or everlasting time can achieve or even guarantee this negation [of everything which negates], this removal of restrictions, this realization, which consists in the perfection of the relationship to God and fellow-man which it

are placed there by God and are not abstract limits. That is, God is the neighbor on all sides (III/2, 562–66). And in this surrounding of humanity, there is a possibility for a real encounter "in speech and action" (III/2, 565). Not only within one's allotted time, but also outside of it: "There is no part of our time which is not as such also in His. It is, so to speak, embedded in His eternity. But as we are thus in God's time, He limits ours. He appoints its beginning before which we were not, and its end after which we shall be no longer. And in this he is to us in a particular way the gracious God. This is shown in the fact that the very points where we emerge from non-existence and return to non-existence, we are confronted in a particular way by the gracious God. For at these points we are referred wholly and absolutely to the fact that He is our gracious God" (III/2, 568). Thus the idea of allotted time, in contrast to an unending duration in time, is appropriate for the life of human beings. There is no guarantee that unending life would bring the result of proper relations with God and fellow humans. In fact, Barth argues, God gives humans an allotted time in order to respond to his gracious call.

Allotted time has a beginning and end. In terms of phenomenological description, because both the beginning and end of life point to one's origin and return to non-being they create perpetual anxiety for the human subject, constantly relating one's existence to non-existence. Given this plight, it is difficult to see how allotted time is a gift from God. As Barth suggests: "We have described our being in time as a flight from our non-being from which we come, a flight which is finally destined to be futile if we must ultimately die and again find ourselves confronted by non-being. Is there any other way of seeing and putting it? Obviously this is the only way we know of. But if our life is a flight, and a futile one at that; if it is a story of fear and failure; if it is therefore a twofold terror, how can it be the good creation of God?" (III/2, 594). Reflecting on the limitations, Barth argues, only leads one to conclude that life is a flight lived in fear, failure, and even terror.

While he admits that one's beginning is not as problematic as one's end, not casting the same shadow over the individual, there is still darkness and uncertainty concerning it: "our being is bordered by our non-being . . . our non-being behind and before is a most terrible threat to our being" (III/2, 572). In fact, Barth argues that uncertainty and non-being in relation to our beginning "carry and bring with us

---
aspires" (III/2, 561).

from our beginning a lurking terror which in virtue of the irreversible direction of our life and our time takes the opposite form of fear to our end, but which in both its latent and patent form is essentially one and the same fear of the term set to our life, of the allotment of a fixed span for our time" (III/2, 573).[54] Similar to his previous reflections on the past, the human response to the shadow of the past is often one of historical searching at both individual and collective levels (III/2, 575–76). Though Barth admits there are legitimate reasons for remembering, it can also be "a passionate attack on our allotted span of time" (III/2, 576). The answer for Barth to the shadow carried forward is once again found in the gracious God. "We certainly come from non-being, but we do not come from nothing. We do not come from an abyss which has spewed us out only to swallow us up again. God is not nothing nor chaos" (III/2, 576). The beginning of allotted time, then, is only problematic without knowledge that the gracious God goes before and with each life (III/2, 577). Thus the shadow of non-being in the beginning is overcome with knowledge that the electing, perfect, triune God was before us.

The more pressing issue for Barth, however, is the movement toward death that monopolizes allotted time. He now asks the question of whether or not death is a natural and good end to human life as it is created and determined by God. The problem is first analyzed by phenomenological description and discussing pertinent biblical material. Through this, it is concluded that death as the end of human life seems unnatural and unsuitable for the creature made in the image of God. But after distinguishing between two views of death found in scripture (what Barth terms "death as a sign" and the "second" or "eternal" death), and relating the discussion to the cross, resurrection, and final return of Jesus Christ, Barth eventually affirms that death is the appropriate and good end for a human life.

Beginning with phenomenological reflection and description, Barth suggests death is more urgent than the beginning of one's life for two basic reasons: first, life desires life, and second, each life moves forward toward death. Life itself is a phenomenon that seeks to survive,

---

54. In connection with this, Barth has little time for some of the attempts to speculate on the origin of the soul and its beginning (the topic of a small print section, III/2, 573–574), but simply states that in "the terms of a more biblical view of man, there was a time when I myself as the soul of my body, I myself as the unity and totality of my psycho-somatic existence, did not yet exist, but I began to be" (III/2, 574).

flourish, and reproduce itself. "And the real disquiet arising from the fact that our existence in time comes to an end consists in the fact that the point will come when, still alive and therefore still involved in that flight from non-existence, still hungering and thirsting after further life, we shall not be able to live any further" (III/2, 587). This forward movement and natural drive for life however is overridden with anxiety because of the inevitability of death. Our "life in time – irrespective of whether we are conscious of it—is in fact a time fraught with anxiety and care. It is overshadowed with death" (III/2, 588). Compounding this general experience of anxiety is religious guilt. If allotted time is created for fellowship with God and fellow humans, then it follows that humans fail terribly in this designation. Since this is the case, allotted time and its end in death can only mean accumulated guilt and judgment before God (III/2, 596–97). For these reasons, Barth leads his readers to think of death as unnatural and evil, especially in the face of God's judgment.

He responds to the problem of death by arguing that individual death is a *sign* of God's judgment, not the judgment itself. This is the core of Barth's argument in this section. While the movement toward death brings the prospect of judgment, "there is a possibility of our being spared this death because Another has suffered it in His death for us" (III/2, 597). Barth argues that Jesus Christ took upon himself the "eternal judgment" or the "second death" on the cross in order that humanity would not have to suffer it (III/2, 600, 603). Jesus Christ, as fully God and fully human, is not only the judge but also the judged. He takes on the eternal judgment that humans deserve in light of their sin and guilt. In Christ "infinite suffering is imposed upon the creature which God created and destined for Himself, when God reacted against this creature as it deserves. It is, of course, true that this man is the Son of God. In Him God Himself suffers what guilty man had to suffer by way of eternal punishment" (III/2, 603). Death as the end of each individual life, as the sign of judgment, is to be distinguished from death as the judgment that Jesus Christ took upon himself. Death as the end of allotted time, according to Barth, is not the full judgment for which our sin and guilt calls.[55]

55. The idea of Jesus assuming the wrath of God on the cross has often been questioned in contemporary theology, especially in light of God's love. Lauber, however, argues that the idea of Jesus Christ taking on the second or eternal death on the cross must be understood within the overall context of Barth's doctrine of the atonement in which God is motivated by love and not wrath. See Lauber, *Barth on the Descent into Hell*.

The term "second death" (δεύτερος θάνατος), found in Rev. 20 vv. 6 and 14, refers to a "lake of fire" which is to consume Death, Hades, and those whose names are not found in the "book of life" (vv. 14-15). Augustine in the *City of God* (XXI), whose interpretation of hell has had a significant influence in western Christendom, takes this reference literally to refer to a description of an eternal and everlasting punishment.[56] Yet Barth suggests the second death to be something that Christ takes upon himself. Thus he maintains the meaning of the biblical passage only in the sense that there is an ultimate judgment of God on death and humanity, but states the cross is the place of this and not an end-time event. Barth's view of individual judgment in the eschaton is a purifying judgment.[57]

As a sign of judgment, however, individual death still carries meaning. Barth makes three points in this connection. First, death exceeds, overshadows, and calls into question human greatness and grandeur. There is no one exempt from death. Even the incarnate Son of God is not exempt from the end of his allotted time (III/2, 601-2). Second, the death to which each individual moves implies the threat of eternal corruption and judgment (III/2, 602-4). Though no human is to experience the judgment of the second death, the end of each is a sign that points to our guilt and to the cross. Third, "death is the goal which is the appropriate reward for the life of man as it is actually lived" (III/2, 604). Humanity's estimation of itself cannot come from a measuring stick based on experience and reflection, no matter how pessimistic or optimistic, for the cross implies that humanity is guilty of sin (III/2, 605).[58] In these three negative points, death is nevertheless only a *threat* to human existence.

---

56. For a comparison of four views on hell and eternal life (eternal punishment, universalism, annihilationism, and reverent agnosticism), see Hunsinger, "Hellfire and Damnation." He describes Barth's view under reverent agnosticism. That is, Barth refuses to choose between "all are saved" and "not all are saved," 242-48; On Augustine's view see 229-34.

57. See Hunsinger, "Hellfire and Damnation," 246-47. For a brief statement of this see Karl Barth, *Dogmatics in Outline*, 134-36. For example: "the judge is not primarily the one who rewards some and punishes the others; he is the man who creates order and restores what has been destroyed. We may go to meet this judge, this restoration or, better, the revelation of this restoration with unconditioned confidence, because we come from His revelation" (ibid., 135).

58. In connection to this, it is interesting to note that Barth makes his only references to Martin Heidegger and John Paul Sartre in connection with this discussion of

After reflecting on the cross, Barth interprets the allotted end with reference to the resurrection and second coming—the heavenly session being conspicuously absent. With the resurrection of Jesus he argues there is a relativization of death: "Even the sentence of death which seems to have been already pronounced serves only to drive the Christian as never before to trust and hope in God as the One who raises the dead. The question now is not where God is, but what has become of the victory and power of death (I Cor. 15: 55). Man can now look back and down, not upon a past life overcome by death, but upon defeated death itself" (III/2, 620). The Christian community, which lives in the light of the cross and resurrection, is aware that it is living in the last days, awaiting the final and general revelation of Jesus Christ (III/2, 622). Believers await this final and general revelation that will also be their own glorification (III/2, 623).[59] What is more, echoing an earlier section, Barth reasons that if Jesus Christ has accomplished salvation for humanity by taking on death in its different forms and believers await their eschatological glorification, then the completion of his work in humanity requires finitude for this to be effective. An infinite temporal existence for humanity could only mean that humanity "should only be able to sin infinitely and even quantitatively multiply our guilt on an infinite scale" (III/2, 631). For faith in Jesus Christ to take effect human life must end, only then could one throw oneself "conclusively and definitively and exclusively on God and therefore concretely on Jesus Christ as our deliverer from the wrathful judgment of the second death" (III/2, 630). Thus to "belong to Him we must be finite and not infinite. Finitude, then, is not intrinsically negative and evil. There is no reason

---

law, Jewish or otherwise, as a yardstick to measure humanity's sin. The point is that existentialism is merely another attempt to define human fallenness apart from the revelation of the gospel and its definition of sin (III/2, 605).

59. Barth makes the connection between the cross, resurrection, and second coming in the following way. The cross is the "event in which man's sin and guilt and consequent death are abolished and time is fulfilled," while the resurrection is the "preliminary indication of this event establishing faith in Jesus as the Deliver from death" (III/2, 623). There is also a relationship between the resurrection of Jesus as "the preliminary indication inaugurating the last time and establishing the Church and its mission and His *return in glory* as the conclusive, general and definitive revelation of the event" (ibid.). The faith of humanity in response to the being and work of Jesus Christ means the relativization of death and the ability to look down and back to it; not forward in fear. Thus humanity, as it is awakened to faith in Jesus Christ, is gathered around him and looks upon death without fear (III/2, 607–25).

why it should not be an anthropological necessity, a determination of true and natural man" (III/2, 631). For these various reasons, death as the end of human life and death as the punishment of God are not to be equated. Death as the end of human life can be viewed as a natural end created by God (III/2, 628–30).

Barth begins with the phenomenological description, suggesting that life desires life and that death seems to be the unwelcome end to human existence. Jesus Christ however has taken on the second death and thus the death of the individual is relativized.[60] Those who live by faith in the Christian community look back and down on death because its power has been defeated in the death and resurrection of Jesus Christ. But they also look forward, because the resurrection points to the second coming and the final fulfillment in the eschaton. This relativization of death means that death in the negative sense and death as a natural phenomenon are not identical. In fact, Barth argues, the end of human life provides one the opportunity to throw oneself on the grace of God. Given the revelation of the eternal God in time and history, one's life is not to be overshadowed and defined by the movement toward death. Rather, life provides an opportunity to know and encounter the loving God. This will become clearer in the next two chapters.

The experience that fills and constitutes fallen time is merely a penultimate description, whether its the anxiety of the transitory present or the fear in moving toward death. Anxiety and fear ought to be overcome

---

60. For a discussion of death deeply influenced by Barth (as well as Jüngel and Moltmann) and yet intersecting with personal experience, see Lewis, *Between Cross and Resurrection*, 404–435. See as well Jüngel, who takes up different meanings of death including natural death, death as a curse, and the second death. He eschews any reference to the second or eternal death if it means an everlasting punishment and suffering of individuals (*Death*, 88–94). For a thorough critique of Lewis' work see Weinandy, "Easter Saturday and the Suffering of God." For Weinandy's fuller discussion of impassibility see his *Does God Suffer?*

More recently, Balthasar's view of Holy Saturday has come under critique. Pitstick argues that Balthasar consciously breaks with the Catholic tradition when he interprets Holy Saturday in terms of the Son suffering further judgement. On this, see the lively discussion between her and Oaks, "Balthasar, Hell, and Heresy: An Exchange" and "More on Balthasar, Hell, and Heresy." For Pitstick's fuller argument see *Light in Darkness*. It cannot be doubted that Balthasar departs from the traditional Catholic doctrine. The question remains however what type of status does the descent have and does this constitute heresy if there is less uniformity of the doctrine in the tradition than Pitstick assumes. For a discussion along these lines, see Griffiths, "Is there a Doctrine of the Descent into Hell?"

in light of the presence and activity of the eternal God. In the first case, God is present in all three modes of past, present, and future; while in the second, the Christian believer realizes there is no need to fear death at the end of allotted time. Death is merely a sign of God's true judgment enacted on the cross. Barth answers phenomenological problems of time, from both the inside and outside, with reference to "totalizing force" of God's eternal being and activity. Allotted time for Barth is not a problem, but is the opportunity and possibility to encounter the triune God in covenantal partnership. This is why God preserves the creature in fatherly goodness and patience even in their fallen time.

CONCLUSION

While it was once commonplace to suggest that Barth leaves no room for human temporality and history, given his unrelenting focus on God's life and revelation,[61] it has been demonstrated that this is not the case. Barth's theology of the first article in fact includes a complex understanding of time that takes great care to protect the reality, necessity, and appropriateness of human time. In the first place, time is a good creation of the Father intended for covenantal partnership. This includes time as the succession of past, present, and future, and allotted time. There are even hints that Barth understood human temporality within the context of the rest of creation, though this is not thoroughly fleshed out. Time created is also time preserved. And so in the doctrine of providence Barth takes care to articulate God's preserving of time in order that covenantal activity may take place. The creation and preservation of time correspond to the Father's eternal role in the divine life and reflect his goodness and patience. The human creature rejects the true purpose of time, however, and the forms of time are filled anew with his sinful activity. The experience of the present "now" is the source of anxiety rather than opportunity, and the movement toward death creates fear rather than hope and promise for eternal life. But even in fallen time the eternal God is present and active, and so the succession of time can be experienced as an opportunity and the end of allotted time with hope. But this is only possible because God does not leave humanity alone in its fallen time.

61. See Roberts, "Barth's Doctrine of Time," 143–146; and Brandenburg, "Der Zeit – und Geschichtsbegriff bei Karl Barth," 358.

Following created time and its preservation by the Father is the gracious response of another time. The being and activity of God in response to fallen time retrieves the purpose of created time and heals fallen time in the expecting time of Israel, the fulfilled time of Jesus Christ, and the responding time of the Church. This gracious time is the "time of" renewed communion and the fulfilling of God's purposes for temporality itself. Barth's focus on Jesus Christ fulfilling time and the human response enabled by the Spirit in ecclesial time will be the foci of the next two chapters.

FOUR

Anticipatio et Recapitulatio
Christology and Time

EVIDENCE OF BARTH'S CHRISTOCENTRISM abounds in his discussions of time. He makes some of the perplexing claims concerning Jesus Christ and time, for example: "The *raison d'être* of all time, both past and future, is that there should be this fulfillment at this particular time" (III/2, 459); Jesus Christ is the "Contemporary of all men" (III/2, 440); and past, present, and future are not "an absolute barrier" but "for Him in His time a gateway" (III/2, 464). While it is clear that Christology is central for Barth's view of the eternity-time relation, it is less clear whether or not it can be coherently understood and what meaning and implications flow from it. In explicating the second major loci of Barth's *analogia trinitaria temporis*, this chapter suggests that Barth does have a coherent and meaningful view of Christology and time, even if it is at times opaque and there are features of his exposition that may be questioned.

There seem to be two related ways to proceed in this chapter. For Barth, Jesus Christ, as the God-man, participates in both eternity and time in a unique and final way. One may explain Barth's view either formally or by way of narrative. Formally, one can relate Jesus-history to eternity defined as simultaneity.[1] Though eternity is ontologically

---

1. The term Jesus-history is used by Farrow in *Ascension and Ecclesia* (6) as shorthand for the life and work of Christ, considered both in its ontological integrity as the expression of his person and in its functional, episodic diversity. The term will be used in a similar way here, without prejudice to the issue of Farrow's differences from

distinct from time it is related to all times by way of anticipation, synchronicity, and recapitulation. Since the fulfilling time of Jesus-history participates in eternity it is anticipated by eternity, synchronic with all times subsequent to it, and will recapitulate all times in the eschaton. In this chapter, however, we will proceed with the use of narrative instead, though the formal understanding is presupposed.²

In order to distil a coherent interpretation from the pertinent sections of *CD* III and IV, the categories of *anticipation* and *recapitulation* will be employed. This will enable the narrative explication. Similar to the use of anticipation in the discussion of *simul*, this refers to the anticipation of the Christological fulfillment of time in pretemporal election, created time, and the history of Israel. The doctrine of ἀνακεφαλαίωσις or *recapitulatio*, which has its origin in Paul and was used more systematically by Irenaeus, refers to both the retrieving and redirecting of time. Jesus-history retrieves the original intent of created time—that is, proper covenantal relations—and in so doing heals fallen time. But his filling of time is not static; Jesus-history continues in the flow of time and history on the way to the eschaton. In fact, the movement of Jesus Christ redirects all time and history toward their eschatological completion. The various episodes of Jesus-history are included in this redirecting: the resurrection and forty days, the ascension and heavenly session, and his return in the eschaton.

The Son's particular "filling" of time includes this retrieval and redirecting activity. His time, moreover, not only presupposes the creation and preserving of time by the Father, but is also the answer to fallen time and the basis of ecclesial time. Thus Barth's christological reading of time must be considered within the full breadth of the analogy between eternity and time. For Barth, because the eternal Son (in his sonship, *filiatio*) is the intra-divine basis of "manifestation" and "revelation" (I/1, 363) and following this is elected to be incarnate, he takes up human temporality in the incarnation. The fulfilling of time by the Son is analogous to his eternal role within the divine life and a result of his eternal election. Since he is begotten by the Father, and with the Father

---

Barth (ibid., 241–54). The term "God-man" is also used in the present work, in a fully Chalcedonian sense, Barth's concern about the use and abuse of this term notwithstanding (*CD* IV/2, 115).

2. It may be noted that both the formal and narrative descriptions include the full scope of God's pre-, supra-, and posttemporality.

spirates the Spirit, he is sent into time and subsequently sends the Spirit to awaken believers to his contemporaneity.

Nevertheless, to say that Barth has a coherent and meaningful understanding of Jesus Christ as Lord of time is not to suggest there are no concerns; some of them were noted in chapter 1 above. There is a general concern that Barth's christocentrism is so emphatic that he leaves little room for the time of the creature. That this is not a major problem in Barth should be evident by now, especially after the discussion of the last chapter. Another criticism, however, is that Barth describes the forty days after the resurrection in such language as to suggest it as the fulfillment of eternity in time, a description better suited for the final return of Christ. There are also tendencies in Barth to downplay the ascension of the risen Jesus as a concrete event and ambiguities surrounding his understanding of human temporality in the eschaton. All of these issues will be dealt with in turn.

These concerns should not distract us however from one of the major issues Barth himself is concerned with. In *CD* IV especially, Barth's explication of Christ's contemporaneity is aimed at the modern problem of faith and history. It is often asked how is it that believers today can relate to an event that occurred over two thousand years ago. To paraphrase Lessing, there is a wide chasm between the necessary truths of reason and the contingent truths of history. How do modern Christians deal with this problem? Barth answers this within is understanding of fulfilled time.

ANTICIPATION

Viewed under the first theme of this interpretation, the fulfilled time of Jesus Christ was anticipated in the pretemporal election of the Son to become incarnate. And just as the covenant is the internal basis of creation, so the time of Jesus Christ is the prototype of created time and the purpose and meaning of the history of Israel. In places, Barth even views the pre-resurrected life of Jesus as anticipating his fulfilling of time beginning in the resurrection. The fulfilling of time by the Son is anticipated in these various other times. "Time may seem to move into the void but it is actually moving towards this event" (III/2, 459). This is evident in various discussions of *CD* III/1 and III/2.

As noted in the last chapter, given Barth's view of election he argues that God creates because of the election of the Son. In a sense, this eternal decree and will before creation compels God to create. This is reflected in Barth's view that gracious or fulfilled time is the prototype and ground of created time. Just as the incarnation is not primarily a response to human sin but of God's will for fellowship with humanity, so gracious time is not merely a response to fallen time but the goal of created time itself. Barth reasons the following in *CD* III/1: "If it is true that the world and man are created in Jesus Christ, . . . then creation does not precede reconciliation but follows it. . . . In this case, too, the first and genuine time which is the prototype of time is not the time of creation but that of the reconciliation for which the world and man were created in the will and by the operation of God" (III/1, 76). While created time was first in the sequence of times actualized by God, it was not first in the eternal determination of God's will. The time of grace, centred on the incarnation, is first in God's eternal decision.

This is more fully developed in III/2, § 47.1 "Jesus, Lord of Time." In this important subsection Barth is seeking to ground the reality of human temporality—defined both as the flow of past, present, and future, and allotted time—in the time and history of Jesus Christ. The basic purpose is to set the temporal *Existenzform* of the creature on christological moorings, which follows the basic method of his anthropology. Barth argues that if Jesus Christ participates in these forms of temporality then their reality is established and they can be viewed as a good gift of the Creator. The human creature was created in time to live out its existence in the twofold and reciprocal relation with God and other humans. Jesus Christ lives out this twofold relation, but as *vere Deus* and *vere homo* he is the true representative of God to humanity and humanity to God (III/2, 438–40). The being and activity of the Son incarnate thus fills anew created temporality even while participating in God's eternity. In expounding this, § 47.1 is divided into two basic sections, Jesus Christ in relation to time from the "outside" (allotted time) (III/2, 439–462) and from the "inside" (the experience of past, present, and future) (III/2, 462–511).[3] It is within the discussion of Jesus and the past that anticipation is made clear.

---

3. The discussion of Jesus Christ and allotted time is further divided into the first history of Jesus Christ, from his birth to death (III/2, 440–41), and the second history of Jesus Christ, his subsequent history following the resurrection (III/2, 441–462). Following this, Jesus Christ in relation to present, past, and future is expounded (III/2, 462) following the order of Rev. 1:8: "I am the Alpha and the Omega . . . who is and who was and who is to come, the Almighty." The three divisions of the main text end with a

Barth articulates his reflection on Jesus and the past from the perspective of the NT community during Easter-time, the forty days. He looks back to the pre-Easter history of Jesus, the history of Israel, initial creation, and the pretemporal eternity of God. To reverse the order, fulfilled time is anticipated in the following modes: it was elected in pretemporal eternity, was the internal basis of created time, expected and prefigured in Israel, and began, albeit hidden, with Jesus' incarnation and lifetime.

Barth first takes up the pre-Easter or first history of Jesus: his death on the cross, the parting from his disciples, his going up to Jerusalem, the journey into Galilee, words and deeds during his lifetime, and a few glimpses from his infancy and boyhood. The fulfillment of time secretly begins with the life of Jesus, "the great dividing line is secretly but very really drawn which marks off the new age from the old. Here there lives and moves and acts and suffers the Lord who reveals Himself as such at the resurrection, and then in the power of this revelation builds, maintains and rules his community until the new age is consummated" (III/2, 474). The lifetime of Jesus both inaugurates and anticipates the christologically filling and fulfillment of time. In a fine print section Barth discusses the transfiguration, baptism, and infancy narratives, describing them as anticipating the time of Easter, just as Easter anticipates the final *parousia* (III/2, 478).[4] In the pre-Easter lifetime of Jesus the fullness of time is present, though concealed, awaiting the second history of Jesus Christ beginning with the resurrection.

Barth gazes further back from the forty days to the history of Israel. For the "appearance of the man Jesus from 1 to 30 A.D. is not to be taken as an arbitrary intervention of God" (III/2, 475). Jesus-history was expected and prefigured in the history of Israel, and is thus its fulfillment (III/2, 475ff). To think of the relationship in a reverse manner, the time of Israel moves toward the time of Jesus Christ. "Hence, although in and of itself this time was not His time, in virtue of its content as the history in which He was prefigured and expected it was His time. He

---

reference to Rev 1:8 (III/2, 468, 478, and 493).

4. Describing the function of the transfiguration, Barth states "its purpose in the pre-Easter period is obviously to demonstrate that even in this time, although in concealment, He was actually and properly the One He was revealed to be in His resurrection. And even this time was not without transitory indications of His true and proper being" (ibid., 478). Both the baptism and infancy narratives, as well, anticipate who Jesus *is*, even before he completes his work (ibid., 479–480).

was the Lord of this history too, because He was the goal and meaning of this time before" (III/2, 476).[5] Later in the section, when discussing the second history of Jesus Christ, Barth reflects on the biblical idea of "appointed times" (καιροι ἰδιοι, Titus 1:3) found in the OT; sabbatical year, jubilee year, and the weekly Sabbath. These are "the times which God has adopted for His purpose and therefore made his own" (III/2, 456).[6] The most important of the OT appointed times, the weekly Sabbath, is an appointed time to share in God's freedom, festivity, and joy as reflected in the Sabbath of Genesis 1 (III/2, 456). For Barth, the Sabbath and the other appointed times point to the greater fulfillment in Jesus Christ. While the Israelites did not see this fulfillment, the apostolic church did in Jesus-history (III/2, 458).

Next, Barth relates Jesus Christ to the beginning of time itself in the act of creation and primal history. Based on the relation of covenant and creation, he states that the New Testament community "saw in the man Jesus, prophetically prefigured and expected in Israel, and finally appearing in His own time, the real object of God's foresight and foreordination in the creation and ordering of reality distinct from Himself" (III/2, 476-477). In connection with this, Barth insists that the logos or Son of God is not to be thought of in abstraction from Jesus of Nazareth, thus reaffirming his rejection of an abstract *logos asarkos*. One is not to think of the eternal Son apart from the *incarnandus* and from fulfilled time.[7] The time of Jesus Christ is anticipated then as the presupposition and goal of created time and creation history.

---

5. Cf. the "Time of expectation" in I/2, 70-101.

6. Lying behind this, as Barth admits a few pages later, is a view of time as an empty vessel needing to be filled. Time is "empty in both the negative and positive sense: empty of this content and empty for this content" (III/2, 461). This is commensurate with what was said in the Introduction and last chapter in which time as the form of existence of the human creature is created in order to be filled with the encounter with God and with other humans.

7. Barth reflects on the following passages: John 1:1, 1 John 1:1; 2:13 f; 1 Cor 8:6; Col 1:15-17; 2:10; Heb 1:2; 1:10; and Rev. 3:14. As he explains: "the whole wisdom and power of the Creator at the beginning of all being were concretely the power and wisdom which appeared and were revealed in the man Jesus: that He was the purpose and ground of the divine creative action at the beginning of all times. It was in this way, not abstractly in His Son, but concretely in the giving of His only Son, in the unity of His Son with the Son of Man Jesus of Nazareth (Jn. 3:16), that God willed to demonstrate His love to the world, having already loved it in creating it" (III/2, 483). Barth's view of the *logos asarkos* was discussed above in Chapter Three. Although Barth's caution on the use of the *logos asarkos* is important, it was still asked if Barth could have given

Barth completes the gaze back with pretemporal eternity. Here he simply argues that just as the fulfillment of time was concealed in his lifetime, expected in the time of Israel, the internal basis of creation, so too "He had been in the counsel of God before creation and therefore before all time" (III/2, 477). He rhetorically asks, "How can it be denied that in God's free plan and resolve He was before the beginning of time and all things, and therefore that He was really, supremely and fully, that He divinely was?" (ibid.). In the plan and purpose of God's pretemporality, in the commission of the Father and the obedience of the Son, the fulfilled time of Jesus Christ was anticipated. In explaining this, Barth carefully protects both the anticipation of Jesus-history in pretemporal eternity and its historical actuality and particularity in time. Anticipation does not negate actualization. First, based on the *simul* of past, present, and future,[8] Barth states that the "man Jesus is in this genuine and real yesterday of God's eternity, which is anterior to all other yesterdays, including the yesterday of creation" (III/2, 484). Second, this anticipation of Jesus Christ in pretemporal eternity does not diminish the singularity involved in first century Palestine (III/2, 484–85). The predestination of Jesus-history does not exclude the *becoming* inherent in the eternal Son taking up flesh, and thus time, in the incarnation. This becoming is present in God's pretemporality by way of anticipation.[9]

RECAPITULATION

Anticipation claims that Jesus-history is the fulfillment of what comes beforehand. But how exactly does Jesus fulfill time? To explicate this difficult discussion I will use the concept of recapitulation.[10] While Barth does not exploit recapitulation in the discussion of Christology

---

a fuller account of the Son's agency in the initial creation. In this way, Barth's view is important critically, yet less developed constructively.

8. "This eternity included not only the present and future, but also the past. God's eternity does not invalidate past, present and future, and therefore time; it legitimates them. In it they have their origin and true character. In it yesterday, today and tomorrow are one, and in their unity genuine and real" (III/2, 484).

9. As mentioned in the first chapter, Roberts sees a contradiction between eternal election and its realization in time ("Karl Barth's Doctrine of Time," 118–19). This does not take account of the movement from pretemporal election and decision to supratemporal becoming and actualization.

10. Farrow briefly suggests that Barth's doctrine of time contains his version of recapitulation; see *Ascension and Ecclesia*, 231, and "Ascension and Atonement," 78.

and time, he clearly saw the recapitulating work of the Son to include the summing up of all times. He considers recapitulation in his reflection on Ephesians 1:10:[11] "The One who wills and accomplishes and reveals the *anakephalaisis* also wills and accomplishes and reveals the 'fulfillment of the times.' It is with the summing up of all created being in Christ as its Head that the καιροί – the individual times of individual created things – are not cancelled or destroyed but fulfilled. None of these times moved into the void. They all moved towards this goal, this event, and therefore this particular time" (III/2, 459). It will prove to be a useful schema from which to view his discussions found in both § 47.1, "Jesus, Lord of Time," in III/2, and § 59.3, "The Verdict of the Father," in IV/1.[12]

The first theologian to make extensive use of ἀνακεφαλαίωσις or *recapitulatio* was Irenaeus of Lyons (c.130–c.200). In his context, ἀνακεφαλαίωσις was a formal term of Greek grammar and rhetoric referring to the "summary or recapitulation of a narrative."[13] While Irenaeus was likely trained in Greek rhetoric his use of the term is materially controlled by his theological concerns, using the biblical narrative with special reference to the being and work of Jesus Christ.[14] As John Lawson states, Irenaeus develops the doctrine that the activity of Jesus Christ was a "going over the ground again."[15] He "went over the same ground as Adam, but in the reverse direction. He placed Himself in the same circumstances as Adam, and was confronted with the same choices. At every point where Adam weakly yielded, slipping down to destruction, Christ heroically resisted, and at the cost of His agony retrieved the disaster.... The benefits of this victory can pass to mankind, because Christ was acting as the Champion of humanity."[16] Important to note in Lawson's description is what may be called the logic and movement of

---

11. The passage reads: "With all wisdom and insight he has made known to us the mystery of his will, according to his good pleasure that he set forth in Christ, as a plan for the fullness of all time, to gather up (ἀνακεφαλαιώσασθαι) all things in him, things in heaven and things on earth" (vv. 8b–10, NRSV).

12. Admittedly, this is a limited selection, but it does provide sufficient material to demonstrate the present interpretation and further exposition would only supplement this. For example, § 69.2 "The Light of Life" will not be taken up.

13. Grant, *Irenaeus of Lyons*, 50.

14. Ibid., 52–53.

15. Lawson, *The Biblical Theology of Saint Irenaeus*, 143.

16. Ibid., 144–45. For further discussions of recapitulation see Rowe, "Myth and Counter-Myth"; Trevor Hart, "Irenaeus, Recapitulation and Physical Redemption."

retrieval and *redirection*. Jesus Christ goes over the same ground again as Adam, though resisting instead of yielding, and then becomes the champion whose benefits "can pass to mankind." Similarly, Douglas Farrow states that Irenaeus's version of recapitulation has a "reduplicative force—the logic of *transformation* as well as of *headship*," wherein the christological movements of descent and ascent "do not cancel, but *restore* and *consummate*, human existence."[17]

In the rest of this chapter the reduplicating force of "transformation" and "headship" will be explained under retrieval and redirecting. The fulfilling-time of Jesus Christ retrieves the true purpose of created time, as the locus of covenantal relations between God and humanity, and redirects all time and history on the way to the eschaton. All other times find their true meaning in the particular time "filled" with the being and activity of Jesus Christ.

Retrieval

Through his mediating history Jesus Christ retrieves and restores the original purpose of created time and heals fallen time. As already maintained, temporality as an *Existenzform* of the creature is meant for covenantal relations with God and others, but this has been obscured and corrupted by sinful and fallen existence. Therefore, the particular history of Jesus Christ, his being and activity in time, renews the communion between God and humanity and thereby retrieves the original intent of created time and heals fallen time. For Barth this particular history qualifies what we think we know about time.

The clearest expression of this retrieval is found in the discussion of time in III/1 where Barth relates fulfilled or gracious time to created and fallen time. In fulfilled time, the forms of time are filled anew with the gracious activity of the triune God, centering on the work of the Son in reconciliation but also including human participation by the work of the Holy Spirit. In the first place, fulfilled or gracious time is the answer to

17. *Ascension and Ecclesia*, 56, italics added. Or, in temporal terms, "creation time and fallen time—though quite distinct—are brought together in Christ, and that the conflict between them is overcome at his own expense" (ibid., 58). He summarizes Irenaeus' view with two other foci: 1) there is a focus on the particular dispensation of Jesus Christ, from which the rest of creation is to be understood; 2) from this particularity not only is the integrity of Jesus Christ preserved but the integrity of every other particular (ibid., 53–56). These two points of recapitulation are also found in Barth's christocentric reading of time.

the problem of fallen time. Barth suggests that "Within 'our' time, i.e., the time of the man who has fallen into sin and is isolated from God, there is initiated with God's acceptance of man in grace the new time which God has for us and which, now that we have lost the time loaned to us, He wills to give to us again as the time of grace" (III/1, 73). And while our fallen time "was condemned to perish as lost time" in Jesus Christ it was "exalted as a new and true and fulfilled time, i.e., a time ruled by God" (ibid.). In fact, both gracious time and created time are time in fellowship with the creator. Concerning created time Barth states that "at its divinely ordained centre stands in a clear, definite relation to God's own, absolute time; which from this centre has also realty and stability" (III/1, 75). He correlates this with gracious time: "In this way the time of grace, the time of Jesus Christ, is the clear and perfect counterpart to the time of creation. Like it, and in contrast to 'our' empty time, it is fulfilled time" (ibid). Barth even suggests that created and fulfilled time "are undoubtedly identical in nature, and the meaning and content of the time of grace are unquestionably those of the preparatory time of creation" (ibid). Yet while created time is a "commencing time," and it begins with the initial act of creation, the same cannot be said of gracious time, as it is a response to fallen time (ibid). Fulfilled or gracious time is actualized in the covenant of grace culminating in the revelation of Jesus Christ.

Clearly for Barth, then, the Son's mediating history retrieves the original intent of created time, "time for" fellowship with God, and in so doing heals fallen time. They are similar in content since created and fulfilled time are both times of fellowship, while different in sequence and responsibility. Created time is first in sequence—it originates at the initial creation—while fulfilled time occurs in Israel, Jesus Christ, and the Church. Yet fulfilled time is not only the response to fallen time but also the prototype and purpose of created time itself, and thus carries a different responsibility. Created time is the theatre for covenantal partnership, while fulfilled time is the actual drama—why the theatre was built in the first place.

Redirection

If Jesus Christ is the Lord of time, then not only does he retrieve the original purpose of created time, but is the contemporary of all subsequent times. As such the particular history of Jesus Christ redirects all times as they move toward the eschaton. Time "may seem to move out of the void, but it is actually moving from this event" (III/2, 459). The full narrative of Jesus-history—his life, death, resurrection, ascension, intercession, and final return—constitutes this redirection. Given the full episodic dimension of redirection this section will be much more exhaustive than the previous.

The basic anatomy of Barth's view is that the resurrection demonstrates that Jesus Christ is the living One and thus contemporaneous with all subsequent times. He lived an allotted life like all others but his resurrection inaugurates a new and eternal history in which, as the God-man, he is contemporary and present in all subsequent times, although his presence and activity varies depending on the episode under consideration. During the *forty days* Jesus Christ was immediately and visibly present as God the reconciler in a particular, limited, and proleptic way. With the *heavenly session* he is mediately and invisibly present in a particular, limited, and proleptic way by the work of the Spirit (especially in word, sacraments, and spiritual gifts). Finally, in the *eschaton* he will be immediately and visibly present to humanity in a universal, unlimited, and final way. The being and activity of the incarnate Son fills and fulfills time in these modes. In expounding this redirecting of Jesus-history pertinent sections of III/2 and IV/1 will again be examined.

While all episodes in Jesus-history contribute to this redirecting, there are some critical questions to be asked of Barth's view. As noted in the first chapter, Ford suggests that Barth's description of the forty days as the final fulfillment of eternity in time is unwarranted. The resurrection appearances rather belong to a series of events that point forward to a final fulfillment in the eschaton; they signify promise as much as fulfillment. Farrow follows this by suggesting that the theological reason for such finality during the resurrection time is Barth's view of the cross. The cross for Barth is the completion of salvation, where the Judge is judged in our place. The resurrection is then viewed as the unveiling of this completion. Farrow argues, especially in regard to *CD* IV, that this soteriological completion is a result of, first, Barth identifying the states of humiliation and exaltation with the descent of God and the ascent of humanity respectively on the cross; and second, of a basic negative correlativity between God and creation that requires reconciliation in God himself, which is then manifested on the cross. Farrow, rejecting these two themes, argues that the two states be seen as the movement of the *God-man* and suggests that the ascension, heavenly session, and final eschaton be given fuller soteriological import.

From these critiques two basic concerns arise. First, articulating the time of Jesus Christ must protect the successive nature of Jesus-history, with each episode in its sequential relation to the others. In other words, one episode of Jesus-history is not to carry emphasis or meaning that is due another. Within this concern, the proleptic nature of Jesus-history needs to be maintained; as Ford suggested, the episodes of Jesus-history point forward to eschatological fulfillment. Second, Jesus-history must be soteriologically related to the time of humanity. The contemporaneity of Jesus Christ must direct, condition, and transform all other times, so that human temporality is understood in relation to his particular history. In this way each episode of Jesus-history constitutes the true meaning and content of concurrent time and history. Barth generally takes up these two concerns, though there are problems.

Jesus' Pre-Easter Life

As mentioned above, for Barth the life of Jesus in one sense anticipates the fulfilling of time during the forty days. Yet he also suggests that it is the beginning of fulfilled time itself. In other places, moreover, Barth is simply content to state that Jesus had an allotted lifetime like every other human (III/2, 440–41). So while Barth does not emphasize the soteriological significance of Jesus' pre-Easter history—except for the cross, of course—he does view it as the beginning of fulfilled time in a hidden and proleptic way.

When expounding the time of Jesus Christ with reference to the idea of "appointed times" (καιροὶ ἴδιοι, Titus 1:3), Barth suggests Jesus' pre-Easter history inaugurates fulfilled time. For example, in examining Galatians 4, Barth makes two important points. First, when the Son of God "entered the temporality which is that of each and every man" the "'fullness of time'" arrived (III/2, 459). Second, given this, all other times are relativized, either moving toward or away from this one fulfilled time (ibid, see 461 as well). After discussing the Pauline passages, Barth turns to the Gospels, particularly Mark 1:14–15, which contains the statement of Jesus at the beginning of his ministry: "The time is fulfilled (πεπλήρωται 'ὁ καιρὸς), and the kingdom of God has come near; repent and believe in the good news" (1:15). Barth notes a tension between time being "fulfilled" (πεπλήρωται) and "is at hand" or "has drawn near" (ἤγγικεν). The first term "implies that the eschatological salvation is no longer just a future expectation, but a present reality" (III/2, 460), while the second "implies that the irruption of the kingdom into history is imminent" (ibid.), that is, still to come.[18] Thus for Barth the life and ministry of Jesus inaugurates the fulfilment of time but mainly in a way that anticipates Easter-time.

What becomes clear in these discussions however is that the pre-Easter life of Jesus, his first history, carries little soteriological effectiveness (except for the cross). But this episode of Jesus-history contributes to the redirecting of time as the historical beginning of a life that will *eventually* retrieve and redirect all times; it is generally viewed as proleptic and anticipatory of Easter-time.[19]

Resurrection and Easter Time

The resurrection has various functions in Barth's theology. Dale Dawson, in his study spanning from *The Resurrection of the Dead* (1924) to *CD* IV/3 (1959), notes not only the role of the resurrection in unveiling Jesus Christ as the Son of God, but also "that the resurrection is the event, the way and the power, of the turning of Jesus Christ, in all he had accomplished for us, to us. . . . [The] resurrection for Barth has to do with the movement of Jesus Christ in the fullness of his reconciling work from the christological sphere to the sphere of other human beings."[20] The redirecting force of recapitulation begins for Barth, then, with the resurrection and Easter time. While there is much evidence for the unveiling function of the resurrection, our concern here is that Christ's second history is inaugurated, and as the living One Jesus Christ

---

18. Evidence of the fulfillment of time, for Barth, is seen in Jesus casting out demons and his miracles, while the kingdom's coming is evidenced in the messianic secret.

19. Of course, it may be the case that Barth elsewhere bestows more soteriological importance on the pre-Golgotha life of Jesus, but its importance is fairly lean here. Irenaeus, in contrast, includes not only the cross but suggests the birth (corporeality) and temptations (obedience) of Jesus as effective for salvation as well (see, for example, Boersma, *Violence, Hospitality, and the Cross*, 124–25. In *Against Heresies*, see III.18.7, III.21.10, and V.21.1–3.). In part III of *Summa Theologica*, there is much reflection by Aquinas on the life of Jesus Christ. His baptism is to lead others into baptism (q. 39.2.1); his temptation strengthens, warns, exemplifies, and leads believer to overcome temptation (q. 41); the miracles confirm his union (q. 43); while his transfiguration is a sign of his future work to come (q. 45). See, as well, some of his reflections on the ascension and heavenly session (qq. 53, 56, 58, and 59).

20. Dawson, *The Resurrection in Karl Barth*, 3; see 4 as well.

is contemporaneous with all subsequent time and history. The resurrection and Easter time get sustained attention in both III/2 and IV/1.

Yet his contemporaneity is differentiated for each episode following the resurrection. Easter time is the first *parousia* of Jesus Christ, the time of his immediate, visible, and audible presence as the Son of God and Reconciler between God and humanity. This presence is known only by the disciples and early church through his appearances during the forty days. While Barth often uses language that suggests a finality during the forty days suitable only for the eschaton (especially in III/2), he nevertheless argues that it is a proleptic episode, anticipating ascension time and the final *parousia*, and sees it in sequential relation to the other episodes of Jesus-history. But we must not neglect to highlight Barth's own critical concerns. This includes not only defending the resurrection as an event in history but also critiquing the so-called modern problem of faith and history.

In III/2, when relating Jesus Christ to allotted time, Barth views the resurrection and forty days as the beginning of a "Second History" beyond the "First History" (III/2, 441–62). [21] In the first place, he argues, contra Bultmann and others, that the resurrection is an event that occurred in a particular time and place, and that the resurrection and forty days are really Easter *history* and Easter *time*.[22] Belief in the resurrection was not the product of apostolic preaching but was the result of "the recollection which concretely created and fashioned this faith and preaching, embraced this time, the time of the forty days" (III/2, 442). Barth defends the historicity of the resurrection again in IV/1, stating

---

21. Also important for Barth here is that the resurrected One is the basic epistemological presupposition of the first Christian communities. "All the other things they know of Him, his words and acts, are regarded in the light of this particular event, and are as it were irradiated by its light" (III/2, 442).

22. Barth critiques the views of Kümmel, Cullmann, and Bultmann. Kümmel, in Barth's view, simply neglects the resurrection. Cullmann marginalizes it to the end of his book on time and suggests that the NT has a particular conception of time; "an ascending line with a series of aeons" (III/2, 443). For Barth, however, the NT writers begin with the particularity of the resurrection and only move from there to general conceptions of time—if they even had any. But clearly it is Bultmann whom Barth has in his sights. According to Barth, for Bultmann belief in the resurrection is explained with reference to the rise of faith as a result of NT preaching (See Bultmann, "New Testament and Mythology," 40–44), for Barth it is the opposite, faith "in the risen Lord springs from His historical manifestation, and . . . not from the rise of faith in Him" (III/2, 443). To counter Bultmann, Barth exposes and critiques five of Bultmann's "dogmatic presuppositions" (III/2, 444–47).

that it is an event in time and space, an act of God, and thus historical (IV/1, 333–342). It is of course different than the cross in that there is no direct account of its occurrence; there is the sign of the empty tomb and the appearances of the risen Jesus to the disciples. As such, it cannot be viewed as historical in the same way as the cross, and in relation to the criteria of modern historical research it is clearly not historical (IV/1, 334–36). Since it is an act of God beyond human observation and agency, moreover, it can be termed a "saga" or "legend," analogous to the original creation.[23] Yet it is truly an event in time and space, and central in understanding Jesus-history (IV/1, 336).

After critiquing Bultmann in III/2, Barth explains the significance of the resurrection for the time of Jesus. While Barth notes this as the time of the man Jesus,[24] his emphasis lies more on the *vere Deus* of Chalcedon—the resurrection is the unveiling of Jesus Christ as God.[25] He states that "the *man* Jesus was manifested among them in the mode of *God*" (III/2, 448). While previously his deity had been "veiled," during the "forty days the presence of God in the presence of the man Jesus was no longer a paradox. . . . He has been veiled, but He was now wholly and unequivocally and irrevocably manifest" (III/2, 449, cf. 451). Barth continues: "There takes place for them [the disciples] the total, final, irrevocable and eternal manifestation of God himself. God Himself, the object and ground of their faith, was present as the man Jesus was present in this way" (III/2, 449). It is for this reason that in the NT the title of *Kyrios* is applied to Jesus (III/2, 450).[26]

The language Barth uses to describe this unveiling ("total, final . . . eternal manifestation of God") surely cannot be justified if the further history of Jesus and the Church are to be seen in their successive

---

23. For a brief discussion of this see chapter 3 below.

24. This is evidenced in the anti-docetic fine print discussions; see IV/1, 441, 448 and 455.

25. This is commensurate with Barth's focus in *CD* I/1 where he views the resurrection of Jesus Christ as the "unveiling" of the second person of the Trinity. Barth consistently connects the resurrection of Jesus Christ with unveiling, especially as it initiates the self-revelation of Jesus Christ, by the Spirit, to believers. Again, Dawson's work makes this point clear, *The Resurrection in Karl Barth*. For his discussion of III/2 see chapter 6.

26. In connection with this, Barth states that Easter time illuminates the whole life of Jesus as salvation history, previous to the resurrection, for the recollection of the church (III/2, 454–455). Clearly for Barth, then, the resurrection is the unveiling of the identity of Jesus Christ as fully God.

integrity. As Ford comments on this section in III/2: "The distortion is that the content of the Gospel accounts of the resurrection appearances does not bear out Barth's claim that they represent a unique fulfillment and completeness, a manifestation of eternity in time. They have more the character of 'sendings' into the future, and there is at least as much promise as fulfillment."[27] Barth's description, then, distorts the view of the forty days as but one episode of the Son recapitulating time.

Yet why does Barth construct his view in this way? Ford's suggestion that Barth moves beyond the literary function of the forty days is only descriptive. I would argue that the veiling-unveiling-imparting schema is combined here with Chalcedonian ontology (*vere Deus*) to alter the NT narrative. As noted in the second chapter, Barth's discussion of revelation in I/1 uses this schema to argue for the self-revelation of God as Father, Son, and Holy Spirit. In this view, the resurrection is the unveiling of the identity of Jesus as the Son of God, and this unveiling must have the sense of finality because the unveiling is identified with *vere Deus*.[28] But by identifying the moment of unveiling in revelation solely with the fully God of Chalcedon, Barth imposes an interpretation of the forty days not suggested by the narrative. To explain this critique Colin Gunton's distinction between the saving activity that is revealed and the God who reveals this may be noted:

> [W]hile it is undoubtedly true that God identifies himself through the action of the Spirit to be the Father of our Lord Jesus Christ, the focus of that action, as is shown by those confessions on which the New Testament centres and which its writers receive and transmit to others, is the salvation brought by Jesus of Nazareth. *The centre is not divine self-identification but divine saving action.* Thus it is preferable to say that revelation is first of all a function of that divine action by which the redemption of the creation is achieved in such a way that human blindness and ignorance are also removed. To that extent the doctrine of revelation should be understood to be a function of the doctrine of salvation.[29]

---

27. *Barth and God's Story*, 145.

28. On Barth's view of revelation as a triune event see Hart, "Revelation." On Barth's early use of the veiling-unveiling dialect see McCormack, *Karl Barth's Dialectical Theology*, 269–70, 274, and 327–28.

29. Gunton, *A Brief Theology of Revelation*, 111, italics in the original.

Thus while Barth is correct in maintaining that God is revealed through the resurrection of Jesus Christ, its function as unveiling the identity of the Son cannot inhibit one from understanding the soteriological purpose of the resurrection. So while "there seems little doubt that the resurrection is, from an epistemological point of view, the revelatory event *par excellence*, confirming as it does the revelations of the previous narratives," it "is an eschatological event, and as such an anticipation of final revelation."[30] It seems, then, that Barth's description of resurrection time as the final fulfillment of eternity in time is unwarranted if its proleptic function is to be preserved; and there is evidence of this in Barth as well.

The resurrection and its relation to time are taken up again in *CD* IV/1, though the context here is the doctrine of reconciliation and the concern is the resurrection's relation to the cross. In IV/1 not only does the resurrection inaugurate a new history, as in III/2, but also the emphatic language of final fulfillment is absent. The unveiling function of the resurrection shifts to the atonement achieved on the cross and not merely Jesus' identity as the Son of God (epistemology follows soteriology). This enables Barth to appreciate the proleptic nature of the resurrection and forty days and view it in its successive relation to other episodes of Jesus-history.

The most focused discussion of time in IV/1 is found in discussing the resurrection's relation to the cross in the "The Verdict of the Father," § 59.3.[31] In this subsection Barth has two basic concerns. The primary concern is to explain the resurrection as the necessary complement to the crucifixion.[32] While it is clear that the reconciliation between God and humanity is complete on the cross, Barth now wishes to show how

---

30. Ibid., 116.

31. Even before this, the opening of § 59 immediately evinces Barth's concern with time and history: "The atonement is history. To know it, we must know it as such. To think of it, we must think of it as such. To speak of it, we must tell it as history" (IV/1, 157). It is a particular history, but it is "the most basic history of every man" (ibid.).

32. In § 59 Barth expounds the first of three forms of the doctrine of reconciliation. The obedience of the Son of God occurs as he takes up human flesh and dies on the cross. The first subsection, "The Way of the Son of God into the Far Country," focuses on the condescension of the eternal Son in humble obedience to the will of the eternal Father. As Barth summarizes: "The passion of Jesus Christ is the judgment of God in which the Judge Himself was the judged. And as such it is at its heart and centre the victory which has been for us, in our place, in the battle against sin" (IV/1, 254). The discussion of the resurrection and the time of Jesus Christ, therefore, are based on the incarnate Son's death on the cross as the satisfaction for sin.

this is unveiled to and appropriated by humanity. This is the transition paragraph from Christology to anthropology.[33] The secondary concern is the problem of faith and history.[34] The distance between *Christus pro nobis tunc* and *Christus pro nobis nunc* is reflected in Lessing's dictum that there is a separation between the necessary truths of reason and the contingent truths of history. As quoted by Barth, "this is the gaping and wide chasm which I cannot cross, however often and seriously I have attempted the leap" (IV/1, 287). The usual attempts to overcome this problem include mediation in not only existential religious experience, as in Bultmann and Herrmann, but also in recollection through tradition and scripture, which can be assumed to refer to Roman Catholicism and forms of Protestantism (IV/1, 287–88). Such attempts to bridge Christ "then" to Christ "now" are critiqued by Barth, forms of what may be termed pseudo-contemporaneity. According to Barth, this modern problem and its religious counterparts have "more the character of a technical difficulty" than "that of a spiritual or a genuine theological problem" (IV/1, 288). The distance between Jesus Christ and the rest of humanity is in reality a harmartological separation; "on the one hand it is God for man, on the other man against God" (IV/1, 290).[35] In other words, Lessing's problem is one of sinful humanity in its fallen time.

But how is Jesus Christ contemporaneous with all humanity in its times? First, Barth reiterates that Jesus Christ was the one representative on the cross and that there has occurred a real objective alteration of the situation between God and humanity (IV/1, 289). This was the point of his previous two subsections of IV/1. Second, the transition into the anthropological sphere is enabled by the resurrection. The resurrection is the event and occurrence that inaugurates the second history of Jesus Christ beyond that of death. In what follows, Barth argues that true contemporaneity is found in Jesus Christ, the living Saviour, and not the pseudo-contemporaneity from human recollection or experience (though mediation does play a role during ascension time). Barth's

---

33. As he puts it: "There is a great gulf between 'Jesus Christ for us' and ourselves as those who in this supremely perfect word are summoned to regard ourselves as those for whom He is and acts" (IV/1, 286).

34. One can discern at work Barth's "intensive, although for the most part quiet, debate with Rudolf Bultmann" (IV/1, ix).

35. The genuineness of Lessing's problem arises from "a very genuine need: the need to hide ourselves (like Adam and Eve in the garden of Eden) from Jesus Christ as He makes Himself present and mediates Himself to us" (IV/1, 292).

secondary concern of faith and history is answered then with reference to the primary focus of the subsection: the relation between the cross and resurrection.

Barth's exposition of the resurrection in its relation to the cross includes five points, though it is points three and five that are important for the present discussion.[36] With the third point, Barth expounds the meaning of the resurrection in its relation to the cross (IV/1, 309–33). While assuming the alteration of the human situation on the cross, in which there is a new creation and ultimate *telos* for human existence and time, the resurrection is the unveiling of the atonement made there and inaugurates the further history of the crucified and living Saviour.[37] This is articulated with reference to the twofold *parousia* of the forty days and the final eschaton, along with the interim time of the Church (IV/1, 333). Barth sees this as the crux of the subsection, which is concerned with the transition from the ontic to the noetic.

To reflect on this transition Barth again takes up the problem of time, now issuing a clearer response. He has already rejected views that suggest the relation of faith and history is fulfilled anthropologically— whether by religious and existential experience or recollection through

---

36. Briefly, 1) the resurrection must be by the same God who judged humanity in Jesus Christ; 2) The resurrection must be clearly distinguished from the cross. While it is the revelation of the work of Jesus Christ on Golgotha, it is also the vindication of the work of the cross. It is not merely the revelation and declaration of the positive content of the cross, but is also the Father's declaring the justification of the Son, the verdict of the Father; 3) It must stand in a meaningful relationship with the cross; 4) It must have the character of a particular event that has taken place in time and space; 5) This second act must form a unity with the first (IV/1, 300–57).

Also important in this section is Barth's description of the resurrection as a trinitarian event (IV/1, 304). At the end of a small print section he gives a brief exposition of the Spirit's agency in the resurrection (IV/1, 308–09). He also speaks of the Spirit coming on the human Jesus. That is, the work of the Spirit is briefly mentioned beyond Pentecost, which is generally the place where the Spirit is discussed. This insight however is not exploited by Barth, a concern that was noted in chapter 1.

37. "It is an existence in the presence of the One who was and will be. He is its *terminus a quo* and its *terminus ad quem*. It is an existence in that alteration, that is, in that differentiated relationship between the death and the resurrection of Christ. . . . This means that the event of the end of the world which took place once and for all in Jesus Christ is the presupposition of an old man, and the event of the beginning of the new world which took place once and for all in Jesus Christ is the goal of a new man, and because the goal, therefore the truth and power of the sequence of human existence as it moves toward this goal. The world and every man exist in this alteration" (IV/1, 311–12; and see 316).

the mediums of scripture, preaching, and tradition. Such attempts are a form of pseudo-contemporaneity. For Barth, the problem of contemporaneity is only solved with reference to the risen and living Jesus Christ, who is Lord of time. As "the One who was in [his allotted time] He became and is the Lord of all time, eternal as God Himself is eternal, and therefore present in all time" (IV/1, 313). The resurrection reveals "His eternal being and therefore His present-day being every day of our time" (ibid.). As the one mediator between God and humanity he is "active and at work once and for all" (ibid.). In fact, "His history did not become dead history. It was history in His time to become as such eternal history—the history of God with the men of all times, and therefore taking place here and now as it did then. He is the living Saviour" (IV/1, 314).

The fifth and last point Barth makes is that the resurrection must form a unity with the cross and the rest of redemptive history (IV/1, 342–46).[38] The unity of the cross and the resurrection arises, first, from the unity of God and his election *in se* (IV/1, 343–43). Second, the unity of God's work *ad extra* is found in the full redemptive history of Jesus Christ. Here the recapitulating work of Jesus-history is clearly evident: "the death and resurrection of Jesus Christ are together the history of Jesus Christ, and as such the redemptive history to which everything earlier that we might call redemptive history in the wider sense moved and pointed, and from which everything later that we might call redemptive history in the wider sense derives and witnesses" (IV/1, 343). The life of Jesus Christ may retrieve and redirect all times moreover because it is an eternal history: "the life of the Resurrected as the life of the Crucified, as it began in that Easter period, and needs no new beginning, is an eternal life, a life which is also continuous in time. And that means that God, and we too, have to do with the Crucified only as the Resurrected, with the one event of His death, only as it has the continuing form of His life" (IV/1, 343–44).

In the discussion of the resurrection and time in IV, there is little indication that the resurrection is the fulfillment of eternity in time, as found in III/2. The emphasis of the unveiling function of the resurrection shifts to the atoning work of the cross and not the identity of Jesus Christ as the Son of God, the focus is soteriological rather than epistemological. There seems to be more attention to the narrative sequence

---

38. In the fourth point of the subsection, Barth argues as in III/2 that the resurrection is an event in time and space, an act of God and thus historical (IV/1, 333–342).

of the cross and resurrection (and to be seen shortly, the ascension and eschaton), and not on the Chalcedonian identity of Jesus Christ as the *vere Deus*. Yet in both III/2 and IV/1, the resurrection and forty days inaugurate the second history of Jesus Christ which demonstrates that he is the living One. As the living One he continues to be active in time and is contemporaneous with all subsequent history. The mode of his presence during the forty days, more clearly noted in III/2, is that of his immediate, visible, and audible presence as the Son of God and mediator between God and humanity.

Ascension and Heavenly Session

The ascension and heavenly session are the time of Christ's invisible presence and activity to the community mediated by the Holy Spirit, especially in word, sacraments, and other spiritual gifts. This episode of Jesus-history has a distinct mode of Christ's contemporaneity and thus fills time in this way. In comparison to the resurrection and forty days, however, the ascension and heavenly session receive sparse treatment. There is even a tendency for Barth to deny the ascension as an event. The reason for this seems to be his focus on the cross and resurrection and a general uncertainty as to the nature of the ascension. The result is that Barth uses the dialectic of visible-invisible to describe the christological mediation during the heavenly session and not presence-absence.[39] Following this, as will become clearer in the next chapter, the Spirit's mediating work through ecclesial practices is less than robust. Despite these problematic features, Barth's description of the ascension and heavenly session do uphold this as a separate episode and its proleptic nature is noted, though the soteriological importance of it is downplayed. Thus it is fair to say that Barth has an underdeveloped theology of the ascension and heavenly session in both III/2 and in IV/1.

Barth's treatment of the ascension in III/2 is found in two places: first, in the discussion of the "Second History" of Jesus Christ in relation to allotted time, and, second, in discussing Jesus Christ in relation to the present. In the first discussion, Barth gives an exposition of the ascension and the concept of "appointed times" (καιροι ἰδιοι) in relation to the forty days. In a fine print exposition, Barth views the ascension, along with the empty tomb, as *signs* of resurrection time: "the ascension—Jesus'

---

39. For criticism of this "invisible presence" in Barth see Farrow, *Ascension and Ecclesia*, 250–54.

disappearance into heaven—is the sign of the Resurrected, not the Resurrected Himself" (III/2, 453). The empty tomb and ascension "mark the limits of the Easter period, at one end the empty tomb, and at the other end the ascension, . . . they are both indicated rather than described; the one as an introduction, the other as a conclusion" (III/2, 452). He also adds that some gospel writers "do not refer to the ascension as a concrete event" (III/2, 453). Undoubtedly Barth is correct in stating that the empty tomb is a sign,[40] but surely he is mistaken to deny that the ascension is an event in Jesus-history. Even his description of the ascension does not support this claim.

In a review of Andrew Burgess's *The Ascension in Karl Barth*, Benjamin Myers criticizes the idea of the ascension as a spatial event.[41] He reasons: "So on the one hand, Christian theology has a right and a responsibility to re-think the concepts of 'space' and 'time' from the standpoint of Jesus' resurrection and ascension. But on the other hand, the account of space and time that we thus formulate cannot simply be a mythology; as a minimal requirement, it must cohere with what we already know from other sources about the nature of space and time."[42] He makes reference to Barth for his case: "[To] say that Jesus is ascended is to make a *theological* statement about God's exaltation of the crucified Jesus. It need not be regarded as a quasi-historical description of Jesus' movement through space, or as a statement about the 'physical location' of Jesus. Rather, and more straightforwardly, it is (in Barth's words) the confession that the crucified and risen Jesus 'went to God.'"[43] Yet cannot the ascension be seen as both a spatial-temporal event and a theological statement? To deny the ascension as a spatial-temporal event is to submit theological mysteries to philosophical and scientific problems

---

40. As he reasons: "The empty tomb is not the same thing as the resurrection. It is not the appearance of the living; it is only its presupposition. Hence it is only the sign, although an indispensable sign. Christians do not believe in the empty tomb, but in the living Christ" (III/2, 453).

41. Myers, "Andrew Burgess: The Ascension in Karl Barth." He writes: "to conceive of this 'agency' in terms of an ascended physical body seems rather problematic. I wonder whether it is intelligible – either scientifically or theologically – to speak of the risen Jesus as though he were simply removed to a different spatial location? What does it mean to say that Jesus 'departs 'physically' in the event of the ascension' (p. 26)? Or that 'Jesus is 'physically' located somewhere other than the church and sacraments' (p. 187)?"

42. Ibid.

43. Ibid.

Anticipatio et Recapitulatio 145

(which, nonetheless, ought to be dealt with) and miss the theological import of Christ's absence. If the ascension is denied as a spatial event does this not mean that Barth finally succumbs to Bultmann's criteria that theological statements must adhere to a modern worldview (which for Bultmann implied a Newtonian worldview, a closed mechanical nexus of cause and effect)? [44] But nonetheless Myers' reading of Barth may not be totally accurate.

While Barth focuses on the ascension as a sign he still *describes* the ascension as an event in Jesus-history, even if he *suggests* it is only a sign. He begins by describing the ascension as Jesus' disappearance into heaven. Heaven is defined as the "sum of the inaccessible and incomprehensible side of the created world" (III/2, 453).[45] When Jesus ascended "He entered the side of the created world which was provisionally inaccessible and incomprehensible" (III/2, 454). But oddly, this disappearance is not described as an event; rather it is the sign of Jesus' "hidden presence," evidenced for Barth in the biblical language of clouds surrounding the ascension story (Acts 1:9) (ibid.).[46] Barth also points to the unique role and identity of the ascended one: "who . . . lives on the Godward side of the universe, sharing His throne, existing and acting in the mode of God, and therefore to be remembered as such, to be known once for all as this exalted creature, this exalted man, and henceforth to be accepted as the One who exists in this form to all eternity" (ibid.). What is more, the proleptic function of the ascension is noted as well: "He reveals Himself not only as the One who according to Mt. 28:20 will be with them in this heavenly mode of existence all the days, even to the consummation (συντέλεια) of the age, but also as the One who will come again to usher in this consummation. The ascension is the proleptic sign of the *parousia*, pointing to the Son of Man who will finally and visibly emerge from the concealment of His heavenly existence and come on the clouds of heaven (Mt. 24:30)" (ibid.). While Barth suggests the

---

44. For a defense of the historicity of the ascension see Farrow, *Ascension and Ecclesia*, chapter 2; and for an attempt to deal with the physical problem of Jesus' bodily absence see van Driel, *Incarnation Anyway*, 167–170; on the general importance of the ascension see N. T. Wright, *Surprised by Hope*, especially chapter 7.

45. He continues: "so that, although it is not God Himself, it is the throne of God, the creaturely correspondence to his glory, which is veiled from man, and cannot be disclosed except on His initiative" (III/2, 453).

46. The visible/invisible distinction rather than the presence/absence distinction will become important when Barth defines the *parousia* further in *CD* IV.

ascension is merely a sign, he does seem to give it positive content. The resurrected Jesus Christ disappeared to the God-ward side of creation and is now hidden and present to his followers. The ascension also indicates that he will come again ushering in the eschaton, thus its proleptic nature. In other words, the ascension focuses believers upward and forward. Perhaps the criticism that may be brought against Barth in this passage is the failure to differentiate between the empty tomb and the ascension. Both may be signs of the resurrected one, but the empty tomb is a spatial location whereas the ascension is something that happens to Jesus; it is an event in Jesus-history.

Barth also takes up the ascension in III/2 when discussing Jesus Christ and the present. Here he gives this episode in Jesus-history fuller content with reference to the gift of the Holy Spirit and the sacramental life of the church. Ascension time or the heavenly session is time "for" the activity of the risen and hidden Lord by his Holy Spirit. Barth again states that for the NT community "the man Jesus is really but transcendentally present" (III/2, 467). His time overlaps "objectively as it were the present time of the apostles and their communities. . . . These men do not make or feel or know themselves the contemporaries of Jesus. It is not they who become or are this. It is Jesus who becomes and is their Contemporary" (ibid.). Barth argues that the transcendent and hidden presence of the exalted man Jesus is the foundation for the life of the church. The time and history of the church is lived in the presence of the ascended One, who is truly Lord over all time. Following this, the church is to make known to the world the reconciliation completed in the cross and resurrection (III/2, 467).

Jesus Christ's presence and agency is distinct, however, from the contemporaneity of other humans. His presence is not immediate but mediated through the work of the Holy Spirit, which includes preaching, sacraments, and other spiritual gifts. "The fact that He lives at the right hand of God means that even now He is absolutely present temporally. And to His own on their further journey into time, in and with the witness continually to be proclaimed and heard by them, He has given them His Spirit, the Holy Spirit" (ibid). Following this, the hidden presence of Christ occurs with the sacraments, but it is not limited to them, or through the gifts of the Holy Spirit (III/2, 467–68). Although there is minimal development here,[47] Barth does present an ascension and

---

47. While Barth is developing a theology of ascension here, oddly the fine print

ecclesial time as "filled" with the activity Christ by his Spirit—in word, sacrament, and other spiritual gifts. So in the present time, the time of the community before the eschaton, Jesus is contemporaneous by the work of the Holy Spirit.

A discussion of the ascension in connection to the resurrection is found in "The Verdict of the Father" in IV/1 as well. Immediately after declaring the risen Christ Lord of time, Barth provides a fine print section on the intercession or ascension time.[48] Here he reflects on a number of NT passages, eventually focusing on Hebrews, which includes statements on Jesus as high priest, whose sacrifice has power forever and who gains an eternal redemption.[49] The activity of the ascended Lord also includes making intercession for the Church (Heb 7:25). This is summed up in the temporal language of Hebrews 13:8: He is "the same yesterday, today and forever" (IV/1, 314). The intercession, in fact, is related to the main question of the subsection, "How does the atonement made then and there come to us and become our atonement?" (ibid.). The answer lies in recognizing that the Living Lord "is in eternity and therefore today now, at this very hour, our active and effective Representative and Advocate before God and therefore the real basis of our justification and hope" (IV/1, 314-15). So rather than being caught up in the problem of the necessary truths of reason and the contingent truths of history, believers are to realize the reality of their present moment under Christ: "There is no moment in which this perfect tense is not a present. There is no moment in which He does not stand before God as our Representative who there suffered and died for us and therefore speaks for us. There is no moment in which we are viewed and treated by God except in light of this *repraesentatio* and *oblatio* of His Son" (IV/1, 315). The human response is not to be preoccupied with questions of how

---

section that provides exegetical support focuses almost exclusively on the forty days. His discussion of Paul's conversion, for example, is likened and grouped with the forty day appearances and is followed by a discussion of the Emmaus road encounter (III/2, 470-72). One might expect a discussion of Hebrews instead, as in IV/1. For a discussion of ascension in the NT see Farrow, *Ascension and Ecclesia*, chapter 2, as well as NT references to the ascension and a brief diagram of the structure of Hebrews in appendix A (275-277 and 279-280).

48. As he states: "He not only did but does stand before God for us," and "he who died, yea rather, who is risen, is at the right hand of God" (IV/1, 314).

49. These include Rom 8:34; I John 2:1; the high priestly prayer of John 17, and Hebrews 4:14, 5:6, 6:20, 7:17, 7:24, 8:1, 9:12, and 10:14, 19.

Christ is made relevant, but rather to offer "prayer in the name of Jesus" (IV/1, 314–15). Though he does not provide a more detailed exposition of the intercessory activity, it is evident Barth holds it as a basic dogmatic presupposition.

Despite this brief exposition of the intercession, the structural problem of *CD* IV as a whole in relation to the *triplex munus* still remains. That is, following a Chalcedonian logic rather than the descent and ascent of the God-man, the role of High Priest corresponds to the descent of God, King to the ascent of man, and Prophet to the God-man. Jesus Christ as high priest in this schema is reserved for the cross and a full exposition of the ascended high priesthood is undeveloped.[50] Nevertheless, for Barth, the contemporaneity of Jesus Christ, and consequently the solution to the problem of faith and history, is based on the ascended Lord and his representative work.

After making clear the basis of contemporaneity in the resurrected and ascended One, Barth moves to the anthropological sphere. Here it is the time of the community that corresponds to the reality of the crucified, risen, and ascended Christ. The beginning of this time occurs with the end of the forty days in the ascension. As in III/2, the ascension is viewed as a sign. But the focus here is not the ascension as the signification of the end of the forty days, but as the "sign of His exaltation to the right hand of God, to eternal life and rule; of this transition to a presence which is eternal and therefore embraces all times" (IV/1, 318). There begins, then, another form of his *parousia*, which is characterized "as a time in which He was no longer, or not yet again, directly revealed and visible and audible and perceptible (as He had been) either to the disciples, the community, or the world" (ibid.). And as in III/2, this intercession time of his invisible presence needs mediation in the corresponding time of the community. While Barth earlier rejected proclamation, tradition, and recollection as mediation in IV/1, if they are understood as the human effort to bridge the historical horizons of present and past, he now views them under the mediating work of the Holy Spirit: "He was and continues to be and ever again will be directly present and revealed and active in the community by His Spirit, the power of His accomplished

---

50. According to Torrance, after he pointed out the lack of exposition of ascension activity in *CD* IV to Barth in their last conversation, Barth suggested that Torrance rewrite parts of *CD* IV to supplement this! See *Karl Barth*, 133–35. See as well Farrow, "Karl Barth on the Ascension," 141–143.

Anticipatio et Recapitulatio 149

resurrection (although not, of course, without that mediating ministry)" (IV/1, 318).[51] The work of the ascended Lord by the Spirit necessarily includes these forms of mediation. Within this time of the community, moreover, there is the human response of repenting, believing, and accepting the altered situation between God and humanity. This provides the basis and telos of the community. Thus, Christians exist in the activity of receiving the gift of salvation in faith and then making it known to the rest of humanity (IV/1, 317–19, 345).

This time of the Church and its faith is based moreover on the outpouring of the Spirit. Later in the subsection Barth states more explicitly the importance of the outpouring of the Spirit for the faith of the community. Again, in contrast to Bultmann and others who would have belief in the resurrection as a predicate of apostolic faith or preaching,[52] Barth insists that the resurrected One is the foundation of the community's faith and the work of the Spirit is the actual cause of this faith (IV/1, 338). The foundation of the forty days and his ascension thereafter only become real in faith for the disciples through the work of the Holy Spirit. Thus Pentecost is fundamental for understanding the beginning of the interim time. As found in I/1, the Spirit completes the movement of God by impartation; which will be the subject of the next chapter.

It seems Barth struggles with the ascension and the heavenly session. They are only discussed in relation to the resurrection and often in fine print sections. Clearly for Barth, the resurrection is the focal point in the redirecting work of recapitulation. There are various reasons for this. There is the basic focus on the resurrection and forty days because this is the first episode in the second history of Jesus Christ, which is denied by Bultmann and others. Yet it is also clear that the resurrection functions as an unveiling event. In III/2 it unveils the identity of Jesus Christ as the Son of God, and in IV/1 it unveils the atonement for humanity completed on the cross. Following these functions, the resurrection takes on the temporal role of a transition event. It is the

---

51. In a note on scripture, in particular, Barth argues that the believer cannot expect to look at the texts assembled by the NT community as typical historical sources since they are the instrument of the living Lord as he reveals who he is to the community (IV/1, 320). For a description of this mediation, with a focus on scripture, see Burgess, *The Ascension in Karl Barth*. For a bibliology that places scripture within the ontological context of God's self-revealing work see Webster, *Holy Scripture*.

52. Barth here critiques views that try and do away with the historical character of the resurrection, in particular Schleiermacher, Seeberg, and Biedermann, IV/1, 340–41.

transition to the further history of Jesus Christ that includes the appropriation by believers of the completed work on the cross. Only in light of this defense and exposition of the resurrection do the ascension (as a sign) and heavenly session receive attention. The nature of ascension time, moreover, is a veiling, the time of the hidden presence of the risen Lord who mediates his presence to believers in word and sacrament by the agency of the Spirit.

The Eschatological Completion of Time: Hints, Problems, and Suggestions

The redirecting of time by Jesus-history is completed with the glorious return—or, as Barth prefers the unveiling—of the resurrected and ascended One. The recapitulating history of the incarnate Son culminates in the final return of the Son in glory to judge the living and the dead. What was anticipated in pretemporality, and actualized supratemporally, will come to completion posttemporally.

It has been suggested thus far that time formally understood is something of an empty vessel that needs to filled. For Barth, I have argued, the Father creates time for covenantal relations (created time), while sinful humanity rejects this and uses time for rebellious activity and existence (fallen time), but God graciously intervenes in the history of Israel, Jesus Christ, and the Church. Following this interpretation, with the completion of time one would expect Barth to suggest how the being and activity of the Son fills time anew in the eschaton, thus allowing humanity to share in eternal life as redeemed creatures; implying some sort of eschatological temporality suitable for this eternal life. While there is some indication that Barth thought of Jesus Christ filling and fulfilling time in such a manner, there is also evidence that for Barth time as the *Existenzform* of creature ceases to exist. If this is the case, it is unclear how the reciprocal, asymmetrical, and covenantal relations between God and humanity are fulfilled in the eschaton. That is, it is difficult to conceive of eternal *life* for humans in their eschatological existence without some form of temporality. To explain this unresolved tension in Barth, both passages suggesting Jesus Christ finally fulfills time and those suggesting the cessation of temporality in the eschaton need to be examined.

The final return of Jesus Christ in glory to judge the living and the dead will mean his visible, immediate, and universal presence. Thus

Barth makes it clear that the redirecting movement of Jesus-history will include this future completing activity. There are numerous indications of this in the discussions of time being examined.[53] In III/2, for example, Barth discusses Jesus Christ in relation to the eschatological future. He makes clear that his being in time is not confined to the past but includes "a being in the future, a coming being" (III/2, 485). Looking from the Easter time of the NT community, Barth peers ahead to Jesus Christ as the Judge, Consummator, and new Creator. In this section, however, there is little exposition of what this final eschaton entails but focuses on Jesus Christ as the foundation of Christian hope and the proleptic nature of the ecclesial time before the final, general, and universal revelation of Jesus Christ (III/2, 492). Thus Christian hope is not based on a "progressive immanent development" or a future "Utopia" (III/2, 486), but rather on the visible manifestation of the risen Lord (III/2, 489). While Barth admits the NT does not always speak consistently in its eschatology, he argues it always speaks consistently "in all dimensions and relationships christologically" (III/2, 486). In fact, although what the apostles and their community witnessed was nothing short of the conclusive, definitive, and general revelation of the glory of Jesus Christ in the resurrection, this is merely a "foretaste" or "glimpse" of the eschaton (III/2, 487–88). And while Jesus' resurrection and his final return in glory appear to be two separate events, they are already one event for the resurrected One because he who *was* is he who will *come*.[54] Therefore the Christian is not to think of the last things without thinking of the last One. The final resurrection, judgment, restoration, and perfection of eternal life are predicates of his return. Thus the foundation of Christian hope rests on the final return and universal unveiling of the one who was resurrected and disappeared into heaven.[55]

53. Unfortunately, the fine print discussion supporting posttemporality in II/1 (631–38) is more concerned with Barth's reading of and relation to eschatological thought since the Reformation, though it is full of important bibliographic material and valuable in this way.

54. For "Him they are a single event. The resurrection is the anticipation of His *parousia* as His *parousia* is the completion and fulfillment of the resurrection" (III/2, 490).

55. Similarly, when summarizing the Gospel of John, Barth states that the successive events of Jesus-history are to be viewed in their connection as one event. "In fulfillment of the promise: 'I will not leave you comfortless; I will come to you' (Jn. 14:18), Easter, Ascension, Pentecost and *parousia* are here seen as a single event, with much the same foreshortening of perspective as when we view the whole range of the Alps from the Jura" (III/2, 497).

Part II: Barth's *Analogia Trinitaria Temporis*

There are also glimpses of the final fulfillment of time in the discussion of IV/1. Here again the focus is on the risen Lord as the foundation of eschatological hope for the community. The community not only looks back to the life, death, and resurrection of Jesus Christ as altering the human situation before God, but also forward to the final and general manifestation of this in the eschaton, the final *parousia* of Jesus (IV/1, 323). The final *parousia* will mean a definitive unveiling not only for Christians but for all of humanity: the manifestation of the judge, the revelation of their sonship, and a general resurrection of the dead (IV/1, 326).[56] The community is not to look at what is not yet but look to its living Lord who was, is, and will be—the coming Lord (IV/1, 327–28). This includes the general resurrection, final judgment, and the release of creation from bondage. This consuming work will result from a final, irrevocable, and universal unveiling of his presence.[57] There is ample evidence, then, for what might be called the eschatological filling and fulfilling of time.

Yet inconsistencies arise when Barth actually reflects on the nature of time in the final consummation. The tension is seen when comparing the previous passages with his brief discussion of the eternal preservation of all times in III/3.[58] Here Barth wants to make the point that the

---

56. For some comments on the general resurrection see IV/1, 329–30; here Barth discusses the hiddenness of the final resurrection in relation to the faith found in the interim period and the sight to be known in the final eschaton.

57. Despite hinting at the final judgment and resurrection of the dead, Barth still insists that the difference between the penultimate and ultimate *parousia* is one of manifesting what has occurred on the cross: "The one crucified and risen Jesus Christ is the object of New Testament faith and the content of New Testament hope. There can, therefore, be no question of understanding the alteration as more real and complete in its final form and less real and complete in its provisional" (IV/1, 328). Though Barth hints at the eschatological judgment, resurrection, and the salvation of non-human creation in general, this does not include, in his view, an alteration! For Barth, it seems, these final events will be but a manifestation of what has already occurred on the cross. This is problematic. Surely one must see here evidence to support the critiques of Ford and Farrow. Farrow's, in particular, highlights the problems of viewing the atonement as completed on the cross with no expectation of future soteriological alteration. Barth's view of the final eschaton as a universal manifestation of what has occurred on the cross is problematic if he wants to take seriously a resurrection of the dead, final judgment, and the releasing of creation from its bondage. Does not the eschatological redemption include further alteration of the situation between God and humanity even while it completes the salvation inaugurated on the cross?

58. One significant portion of the discussion is the following: "And the time will come when the created world as a whole will only have been. . . . Everything that

limited time of each creature is eternally preserved in God's life. While he rejects the necessary immortality of the creature, this does not mean the allotted time of the creature is lost to the eternal God. In the final eschaton and the completion of history, which occurs with the final and general revelation of Jesus Christ, the life of the creature is preserved by God's eternity. The creature, so it seems, has a place in eschatological existence.

Yet Barth also states that time and history will end. This includes not only time in general, "the totality of everything that was and is and will be will only have been" (III/3, 90), but also time as the *Existenzform* of the creature, time experienced as the succession of past, present, and future and allotted time. He states that the creature "will not need any continuance of temporal existence. And since the creature itself will not be there, time which is the form of existence of the creature will not be there" (III/3, 88). The reason he gives for this termination is the sufficiency of time and history as such. Barth rhetorically asks: "What need has it of more time and duration, of more reality and activity, when in the limits marked off for it God has already given to it all things, namely, Himself, in the person of His Son, when its end was to be manifested as the recipient of that gift?" (III/3, 89). Thus, the limited time of history and individuals is sufficient for God's work with the creature and the human response.

Nevertheless this end of history and time is not destruction but an eternal preservation: "this does not mean that its preservation by God is terminated" (III/3, 88). Barth notes a "recapitulation" of created existence and states that God's preservation of creation and the creature remains. He explains this in negative and positive terms. Negatively, the eternal preservation of the creature means that "its destruction is excluded." Though the creature is a "transitory speck of dust," God's love for it is the last word. Positively, then, the creature "can continue eternally before

---

happened in the course of that history will then take place together as a recapitulation of all individual events. It will be made definitive as the temporal end of the creature beyond which it cannot exist any more. Its life will then be over, its movement and development completed, its notes sounded, its colours revealed, its thinking thought, its words said, . . . the possibilities granted to it exploited and exhausted. And in all this it will somehow have a part in that which Jesus Christ has been and done as its Foundation and Deliverer and Head. And since the creature itself will not be there, time which is the form of its existence will not be there. Yet this does not mean that its preservation by God is terminated" (III/3, 87–88).

Him" (III/3, 89). No times will escape the eternal preservation of God (III/3, 90). For Barth, God's eternity as *simul* not only anticipates and is synchronic with all times but recapitulates all past times, even times beyond human experience. Barth reiterates this in relation to eternal preservation in III/3. Specifically in relation to posttemporality, God's eternity recapitulates all times—all that was, is, and will be. This includes not only human temporality but also the times of creation, even the history which is not observed by human experience but present to God's eternity: "no wing-beat of the day-fly in far-flung epochs of geological time" will be lost (III/3, 96).[59]

While one may appreciate Barth's view of maintaining the creature after death without resorting to the immortality of the soul, or his insistence that what is preserved is the particular allotted lives that were actually lived (there is no escapism here),[60] the termination of temporal-

---

59. He describes the eschatological recapitulation of times in this captivating passage: "And one day—to speak in temporal terms—when the totality of everything that was and is and will be will only have been, then in the totality of its temporal duration it will still be open and present to Him, and therefore preserved: eternally preserved; revealed in all its greatness and littleness; judged according to its rightness or wrongness, its value or lack of value; but revealed in its participation in the love which He Himself has directed towards it. Therefore nothing will escape Him: no aspect of the great game of creation; no moment of human life; no thinking thought; no word spoken . . . no suffering or joy . . . no wing-beat of the day-fly in far-flung epochs of geological time. Everything will be present to Him exactly as it was or is or will be, in all its reality, in the whole temporal course of its activity, in its strength or weakness, in its majesty or meanness. He will not allow anything to perish, but will hold it in the hollow of His hand as He has always done, and does, and will do. He will not be alone in eternity, but with the creature. He will allow it to partake of His own eternal life. And in this way the creature will continue to be, in its limitation, even in its limited temporal duration. . . . In all the unrest of its being in time it will be enfolded by the rest of God, and in Him it will itself be at rest in the rest of God. This is the eternal preservation of God. It is not a second preservation side by side with or at the back of the temporal. It is the secret of the temporal. It is the secret of the temporal which is already present in the fullness of truth, which is already in force. And yet it has still to be present in the fullness of truth; it has still to come into force; it has still to be revealed in all its clarity" (III/3, 89–90).

60. Jüngel explains this idea of the preservation of one's limited life in God's eternity: "Salvation then, can only mean that it is *the life man has lived* that is saved, not the man is saved *out* of this life. . . . It involves the participation of this earthly, limited life in God's eternity; the sharing of this temporally limited life in God's eternity; the participation of a life which has incurred guilt in the glory of God. To share in God's glory means that man is honourably acquitted of his guilt. It is as finite that man's finite life is *made eternal*. . . . He will make everything whole; everything, including what we have been. Our *person* will then be our *manifest history*" (*Death*, 120).

ity altogether is questionable—if that is in fact what Barth is suggesting. It is unclear how humans could exist, even in the state of glorification in the eschaton, without some form of temporality. Barth defines human nature as *imago dei*, ensouled bodies, and existence in time. How can humanity exist if this universal *Existenzform* is taken away? While allotted time, with its definite beginning and end is transformed, it is unclear what glorified existence in the eschaton, including resurrected embodiment, would look like without some form of temporality. The physicist and theologian John Polkinghorne, for example, calls into question eschatological views that atemporalize human existence. He first explains that time is an essential feature of the universe: "Just as it is intrinsic to humanity to be embodied, so it is surely intrinsic to our being that we are temporal creatures. General relativity has taught us that in this universe space, time and matter all belong together in a single indivisible theoretical embrace. . . . Matter curves spacetime and the geometry of spacetime curves the paths of matter, so together they constitute a package deal."[61] Furthermore, if eschatological existence is to be a new or transformed creation, and not the destruction of nature as such, then Polkinghorne argues that "human destiny beyond death will no more be atemporal than it will be disembodied, though, once again, there will also be a dimension of discontinuity, so that the 'time' of the world to come is not just a prolongation of the time of this world. . . . Rather, it is a new time altogether, possessing its own independent nature and integrity."[62] Though Polkinghorne does not elaborate, his hints can be taken to imply that the time of the eschaton will have a different quality. This would be commensurate with the interpretation of Barth thus far. The difference between created, fallen, and ecclesial time is not time's structure as past, present, and future, but whether time is filled with the encounter between God and humanity or with sinful human action. Barth could have extended such thinking to include time in the eschaton. That is, the successive nature of time would remain though it is "filled" with the activity of eternal life. The "quality" of time would result from the eschatological glorification of the creature and creation in the eternal fellowship with God.[63]

61. Polkinghorne, *Science and the Trinity*, 156.

62. Ibid., 156–157.

63. Polkinghorne points to remnants of Greek thinking behind this suspicion of temporality (ibid., 157). For a view of eschatological time which moves in this direction

There are perhaps different reasons for the eschatological cessation of temporality in Barth's view. Concerning internal dogmatic components, Edwin Chr. van Driel connects this ending of creaturely time and space to Barth's doctrine of Nothingness. *Das Nichtige*, the ominous and often ambiguous force arising from God's rejection (the other side of election), lends to the tendency in Barth of what van Driel terms "creational entropy," which implies that "creation in and by itself lapses into evil by ontological necessity."[64] And what "renders whether a being is subject to sin, evil and the threat of *das Nichtige*, depends on whether it is self-grounded or not.... For God to overcome *das Nichtige* is therefore to give it a 'share in his own life'—that is, to assume creation in the divine life."[65] Following this, there is a rejection of human agency, and thus time, in the eschaton. For such an existence "would imply an ontological 'overagainstness' between the Creator and the creature; but it is exactly such overagainstness which gives space for creation's entropy. Only if the creature exists no longer in its own being and agency, but is incorporated in the divine life, is it safe."[66] If van Driel is correct, Barth's doctrine of Nothingness leans toward a view of creation in which the creature must lose its agency, and thus time, if it is to have eternal life. This overrides temporality as a permanent feature of the creature's *Existenzform*.

As for external non-dogmatic components of Barth's construction, his failure to think more critically about the connection between subjective and objective time may be recalled.[67] As already noted in chapter 3, although Barth views human existence in general as embodied (soul and body, temporal existence), he does not fully integrate subjective time within the objective, especially the succession of past, present, and

---

see Moltmann, *The Coming of God*, 279–95; and *Science and Wisdom*, 98–110. Similarly, in a brief discussion of existence in the eschaton as pure hospitality, which incidentally draws on Irenaeus, see Hans Boersma, *Violence, Hospitality, and the Cross*, 257–61.

64. van Driel, *Incarnation Anyway*, 123. Similarly, Farrow notes the negative correlativity between God and creation evident in various places in the *CD* ("Karl Barth on the Ascension," 143–48). He suggests that there is a "false correlativity and opposition between God and man which appears (in spite of all that Barth has achieved to the contrary) to be a problematic feature of the *Dogmatics* at several levels" (ibid., 147). The origins of this are difficult to detect, perhaps in Barth's version of supralapsarian Christology, his doctrine of nothingness, or even Barth's actualism (ibid.).

65. Ibid., 124.

66. Ibid.

67. The reference to the "internal" and "external" components of Barth's comes from Dalferth; see the introduction below.

future within in the space-time continuum of the cosmos. The objective time of the cosmos is based on its movement, and the subjective time of human consciousness is a result of being embedded within this. But if time as the form of existence of the creature ceases to exist then it is also implied that the movement of the cosmos ceases as well. But to suggest that the cosmos and the creature will cease in all such movement seems too radical a discontinuity between present existence and the eschatological one. So while Barth does place human time within the cosmos he does not critically think this through.

Could it be that Barth is being misread here? In the same passage he does have some positive content concerning human existence in God's eternal preservation. Barth suggests, for example, that God "will not be alone in eternity, but with the creature. He will allow it to partake of His own eternal life. And in this way the creature will continue to be, in its limitation, even in its limited temporal duration" (III/3, 90).[68] Is this not a positive relation? In the end however this eternal relation is in contrast to existence in time. "In all the unrest of its being in time it will be enfolded by the rest of God, and in Him it will itself be at rest in the rest of God. This is the eternal preservation of God" (ibid.). Despite Barth's positive intentions then, the eternal life with God is an eternal rest, seeming to imply some form of static existence.

The thrust of my interpretation would lead to the idea that the filling and fulfilling of time by the Son, including his coming in glory to judge the living and the dead, would mean an eschatological existence in which the covenantal partnership between God and humanity is fulfilled and the relations between God, humanity, and creation are perfected.

---

68. We could also point to the earlier work *Credo*, published in German in 1935, where Barth briefly discussed eschatological existence, seeming to give human temporality more place: "Resurrection of the flesh means therefore that our existence as *carnal* existence, our heaven and earth as theatre of revolt, our time as time of Pontius Pilate, will be dissolved and changed into an existence, into a heaven and earth, into a time, of *peace* with God without conflict, of that peace which, hidden from our eyes in the flesh of Christ, is already a reality" (*Credo*, 169). Here Barth suggests an eschatological time of final peace. Yet he is quite cautious in describing what eternal life might look like: "we, who must do our thinking from this time that is known to us, have not the slightest idea what we are saying when we talk either positively or negatively about the time of that God with Whom we shall live in unbroken peace in eternal life. We can spare ourselves many unnecessary pains (for this is really enough to satisfy us) if we hold fast to what is the decisive feature of eternal life: that it is eternal in its being lived in the unveiled light of God and in so far participating in God's own life" (ibid., 171).

One would think that such an existence would mean the continuation of some form of temporality; after all, would not such an embodied existence of the creature be implied in the resurrection of the dead? Such a view appears problematic for Barth if all forms of time cease to exist in the eschaton, as seems to be his view.

CONCLUSION

Despite such problems, it should be clear that for Barth the fulfilling time by the Son is anticipated in pretemporal eternity and recapitulates all times by retrieving the purpose of created time and redirecting all times toward their fulfillment in the eschaton. In this way, Jesus-history is central and determinative for the full breadth of God's pretemporal, supratemporal, and posttemporal activity and life. Yet this history is only possible because within the eternal divine life the Father generates the Son, and with the Son gives the Spirit who is the bond between Father and Son, and because in pretemporality the Son was elected to be the reconciler between God and humanity. The fulfilling time of the Son is thus analogous to his role within the eternal Trinity and his election to become incarnate. This is the eternal intra-divine possibility before the temporal actualization. Yet the recapitulating of time by Jesus Christ also includes human participation by the Holy Spirit in ecclesial time. This is the concern of the next chapter.

FIVE

The *Vinculum* of Contemporaneity

The Holy Spirit and the Time of the Community

WHEN DESCRIBING HUMAN PARTICIPATION in eternity Barth once again rejects theological abstraction. Creaturely participation in eternity is not a matter of the mystical experience of timelessness or belief in the inevitable progress of history toward the Kingdom of God, but rather of believers participating in the reconciling history of Jesus Christ.[1] This occurs penultimately in the time of the church and ultimately in the eschaton. This is the third major loci of Barth's *analogia trinitaria temporis*, the Holy Spirit filling ecclesial time by gathering, building up, and sending the Christian community.[2]

This inclusion of human participation was articulated and presupposed in the previous chapters. In chapter 3 it was argued that God in his fatherly goodness and patience created and preserves human temporality for covenantal relations. The creature rejected this divine purpose however and lives in fallen time. The *Existenzform* of time remains though the content or quality of creaturely temporality is disrupted by sinful existence. Barth argues, nevertheless, that the human creatures in their allotted times may be filled with hope and promise given the

---

1. On the mystical experience of timelessness see Achtner, et al., *Dimensions of Time*, 103–8. They briefly discuss Plotinus, Augustine, Boethius, Meister Eckhart, Angelus Silesius, and Schleiermacher.

2. "Ecclesial time," "time of the community," and the "history of community" will be used synonymously. The terms "middle time" and "interim time" refer to the time between the forty days and the eschaton which may or may not be referring to the time of the community, since, for example, history in general exists in the middle time as well.

assumption and defeat of the second death by Jesus Christ on the cross. In this chapter human participation in Jesus-history will be put in its broader dogmatic context of ecclesial time, or, as Barth prefers, the time of the community.

Barth's rethinking of eternity along trinitarian and dynamic lines allowed him to define eternity not merely in its ontological distinction from time but to suggest that God creates and is present within time. This radical rethinking of the eternity-time relation should now be obvious, especially after the last chapter. But thinking of God's supratemporality at work in Jesus-history is incomplete without the work of the Holy Spirit who is activity present in the time of the church and individual lives. Here divine temporality is concretely at work in the "here and now," making actual in creaturely history what was elected and determined in pretemporal eternity. Before we explicate this, however, a few words on Barth's pneumatology are appropriate.

Barth's pneumatology incorporates basic features of the Christian tradition. Like Basil of Caesarea, the Spirit is the perfecting cause or end, since the Spirit subjectively imparts unto believers the reconciliation accomplished in Jesus Christ.[3] But like Augustine, within the triune life the Spirit is the bond between the Father and the Son.[4] In the first chapter some concerns were raised as to the compatibility of these two views of the Spirit. If the Holy Spirit is the third divine mode and perfecting cause in revelation then there should be a corresponding description of God *in se*, some alternative to the bond between the Father and Son. However, if we see the role of the Spirit as bond in dynamic terms there is coherence in Barth's view. Because the Spirit's mediation between the Father and Son in eternity is an eternal movement, the Spirit can mediate the relation between Jesus-history and the history of the community. The bonding work of the Spirit includes the *telos* of *koinōnia* or communion both *in se* and *ad extra*. As such the Spirit is the bond of contemporaneity. Following this, as pointed out in chapter 3, that the Spirit is the communion between Father and Son is also the intra-divine possibility for the existence of the creature as such (III/1, 56 ff). As David Guretzki

3. See Basil of Caesarea, *The Treatise on the Holy Spirit*, Chapter XVI, where this is expounded in relation to creation, reconciliation and redemption (in *Nicene and Post-Nicene Fathers*, Second Series, Vol 8). In speaking of creation he summarizes "bethink thee first, I pray thee, of the original cause of all things that are made, the Father; of the creative cause, the Son; of the perfecting cause, the Spirit" (XVI, 38).

4. See Augustine, *The Trinity*, Books VIII and IX.

states, the Spirit "is antecedently responsible for maintaining the unity and difference between Father and Son in the immanent Trinity and is therefore the ground by which the unity and difference between God and the temporal creature is maintained."[5] But the analogous relation between the Holy Spirit's eternal role *in se* and temporal work *ad extra* is evident back in *CD* II/1. When discussing the glorification of God by the creature, Barth summarizes:

> But the Holy Spirit is not only the unity of the Father and the Son in the eternal life of the Godhead. He is also, in God's activity in the world, the divine reality by which the creature has its heart opened to God and is made able and willing to receive Him. He is, then, the unity between the creature and God, the bond between eternity and time. If God is glorified through the creature, that is only because by the Holy Spirit the creature is baptized, and born again and called and gathered and enlightened and sanctified and kept close to Jesus Christ in true and genuine faith. There is no glorification of God by the creature that does not come about through this work of the Holy Spirit by which the Church is found and maintained, or that is not itself, even it its creatureliness, this work of the Holy Spirit (II/1, 669–70).[6]

Therefore, appropriating the time of the community to the Spirit follows the lead of Barth's doctrine of the Trinity in general. For Barth in *CD* IV the ascended Jesus Christ lives in his heavenly-*Existenzform*, while the church exists as his earthly-*Existenzform*. In this earthly form of existence the Spirit works the subjective realization of the objective justification, sanctification, and vocation of humanity accomplished in the reconciling history of Jesus Christ. The Spirit's particular activity includes the gathering, building up, and sending of the Christian community, as well as awakening faith, quickening love, and enlightening hope in individual believers. In these movements, moreover, I will suggest

---

5. Guretzki, "The *Filioque* in Karl Barth's *Church Dogmatics*," 226.

6. George Hunsinger also summarizes well the role of Holy Spirit for Barth: "The Holy Spirit is the communion between the Father and the Son within the Holy Trinity. This mediating activity is then paradigmatic for every aspect of the Spirit's work in relation to the world. In various ways the Spirit's operation in time reiterates his operation in eternity" ("The Mediator of Communion," 149–150). Hunsinger correctly summarizes Barth's pneumatology by stating that the Spirit is the mediator of diverse communion. He explicates the trinitarian ground, Christocentric focus, miraculous operation, communal content, eschatological form, diversified application, and universal scope of Barth's pneumatology (ibid., 151–184).

that the Holy Spirit's temporal work may be characterized as continuous, dynamic, particular, and unifying. The time of the community, ecclesial time, is the time "of" this particular activity of the Holy Spirit.[7]

Our exposition of ecclesial time will proceed under two parts. First, there is a general discussion of the relation between Jesus Christ, the Holy Spirit, and the community, which is foundational for understanding Barth's ecclesiology. Following this, second, the Holy Spirit and ecclesial time are examined under three subsections: ecclesial time in general world occurrence, the internal movement of the community; and the external movement of the community. While these sections will provide a coherent interpretation of Barth's view we will also ask critical questions concerning the adequacy of his exposition along the way. Such issues were hinted at in chapter 1 when suggesting that Barth held a non-agential description of the Holy Spirit's role and that he displayed a tendency toward a disembodied ecclesiology.

JESUS CHRIST, THE HOLY SPIRIT, AND THE COMMUNITY

As evident in the last chapter, for Barth if any word is to be spoken about the Church it must be grounded in Christology. So to understand how the internal and external movements of the community fill ecclesial time, the general relation of Jesus Christ, the Holy Spirit, and the community in *CD* IV needs to be noted. We will draw from both § 62, "The Holy Spirit and the Gathering of the Christian Community," and § 72.1, "The People of God in World Occurrence." Not only will Barth's christological focus be evident, but important characteristics of the Holy Spirit's bonding work will be noted.

Barth defines the Christian community as the "earthly-historical form of the existence of Jesus Christ," which corresponds to his "heavenly-historical form of existence."[8] Throughout his discussion Barth makes it clear that the being of the church exists "only as a definite history takes place," when it is gathered by Jesus Christ through the Spirit. At the

---

7. Since chapter 3 examined the time of individuals, especially how the cross relativizes the despair and fear of movement toward death, this chapter will not focus on the time of individuals in the church. (Individual allotted time could possibly be supplemented in *CD* IV with the discussion of the faith, love, and hope created in believers by the Holy Spirit.) This chapter, then, will focus on the collective time of the community.

8. The term *Existenzform* is the same term used in Barth's anthropology when describing creaturely temporality. It connotes the conditions of living in space and time, meant for covenantal relation with God and humanity.

beginning of the paragraph itself Barth states that "The one reality of the atonement has both an objective and a subjective side in so far as . . . it is both a divine act and offer and also an active human participation in it: the unique history of Jesus Christ; but enclosed and exemplified in this is the history of many other men of many other ages" (IV/1, 643).[9] He substantiates his actualistic view by suggesting that the terms ἐκκλησία and *communio* imply the being of an event (IV/1, 651–52). This actuality and historicity is evinced in his basic definition of the church:

> The community is the earthly-historical form of existence [*Existenzform*] of Jesus Christ Himself. . . . The Church is His body, created and continually renewed by the awakening power of the Holy Spirit. Jesus Christ also lives as the Crucified and Risen in a heavenly-historical form of existence; at the right hand of the Father, before whom He is the advocate and intercessor of all men as the Judge who was judged in their place, the One who was obedient for them all, their justification. But He does not live only and exclusively in this form, enclosed within it. . . . He Himself lives in a special element of this history created and controlled by Him. He therefore lives in an earthy-historical form of existence within it. This particular element of human history, this earthly-historical form of existence of Jesus Christ, is the Christian community. He is the Head of this body, the community. And it is the body which has its Head in Him (IV/1, 661).

The being of the community, then, is constituted by the reality of the crucified, risen, and ascended Lord. In his absence, or as Barth prefers "invisibility," the Son sends his Spirit to awaken and sustain humanity in this new existence. Moreover, since it exists from its living Lord and his Spirit, the community "can only follow the movement of His life;" it "can reflect and illustrate and that way attest in its own activity His activity" (IV/1, 662). This awakened humanity, his body, is his earthly-historical *Existenzform*.

Barth supports this definition of the church with an exposition of Paul's metaphor of the church as the Body of Christ. Like the term *Existenzform*, σῶμα has a definite temporal and historical meaning, referring to life and activity, whether positively or negatively. As used by

---

9. "To describe its being we must abandon the usual distinctions between being and act, status and dynamic, essence and existence. Its act is its being, its status its dynamic, its essence its existence. The Church *is* when it takes place that God lets certain men live as His servants, His friends, His children" (IV/1, 650).

Barth, σῶμα refers primarily to Jesus Christ, crucified and raised, and only secondarily to the followers of Jesus gathered by the Spirit. The first use, according to Barth, is a reference to the dead body of Jesus Christ on the cross, where he was the representative of all human bodies and their earthly existence (IV/1, 663). But following this is the resurrected body and Easter time.[10] Here the salvation of humanity accomplished with his representative death are known to those whom he encountered during this time. The mystery of the community, then, is first and foremost the mystery of Jesus Christ himself (IV/1, 644).[11] He founds, governs, and directs those in ecclesial community who by faith know the secret of historical existence.

This definition of the church as the earthly-historical *Existenzform* of Jesus Christ underlies the major discussions of ecclesiology in *CD* IV. It is the dogmatic foundation for the inclusion of the history of the community in Jesus-history. When the activity of the Holy Spirit in ecclesial time is noted, it is never abstracted from the being and activity of Jesus Christ. The Holy Spirit's creation of the community arises from the agency of the risen and ascended Lord.

While Barth takes great pains to ground the subjective realization of the atonement, or the "active participation of man in the divine act of reconciliation" (IV/1, 643), in the objective reality of Jesus-history, it is the Holy Spirit that ensures this enclosure of the many histories into the one.[12] With reference to Luther, Tertullian, and Augustine Barth explains the work of the Spirit:

> We speak of human experience and action when we speak of the community and faith, and therefore of the subjective realization of the atonement. Yet it is that human experience and action which is not of man's 'own reason and power' or in virtue of his own capacity, resolve or effort, but (Luther) 'the Holy Spirit has

---

10. Here he explains the resurrection as a work of the Spirit, a rare place in which the Spirit is agential and active toward Jesus Christ (IV/1, 664). Here is the connection that Dawson is looking for, though it is undeveloped; Dawson, *The Resurrection in Karl Barth*, 224–27.

11. "His mystery is theirs. Having been given life by the Spirit, and Himself a life-giving Spirit, He has made it known to them—His election and birth and calling and institution as their Head and the Head of all men, His earthly-historical existence as that of their Representative and Substitute and Advocate, and therefore as the truth of their own earthly-historical existence" (IV/1, 644).

12. Barth points to previous sections of the *CD* that dealt with the noetic complement: I/1 §§ 6 and 12, I/2 §§ 16–18, and II/2, § 25.

called me by the Gospel, enlightened me with His gifts, sanctified and maintained me in a right faith, as He calls and gathers and enlightens the whole of Christendom, keeping it to Jesus Christ in the true and only faith.' The Holy Spirit is the *doctor veritatis* (Tertullian), the *digitus Dei* (Augustine) by whom this takes place (IV/1, 645).[13]

Specific features of Barth's relating Christology and pneumatology need mentioning. In the first place, the Spirit's work within the community *is the self-attestation of Jesus Christ*. The Spirit is the form and power in which the Son makes his completed work manifest to humanity. Closely following this, the work of the Spirit is *confirmatory and secondary*: "There can be no doubt that the work of the Holy Spirit is merely to 'realise subjectively' the election of Jesus Christ and His work as done and proclaimed in time, to reveal and bring it to men and women. By the work of the Holy Spirit the body of Christ, as it is by God's decree from all eternity and as it has become in virtue of His act in time, acquires in all its hiddenness historical dimensions. The Holy Spirit awakens the 'poor praise on earth' appropriate to that eternal-temporal occurrence" (IV/1, 667). As suggested in chapter 1, while it cannot be denied that Jesus Christ sends the Spirit or that the Spirit attests to the history of Jesus Christ, drawing individual histories into his, it seems here that Barth dissolves the agency of the Spirit into the Son's, thereby limiting the role of the Spirit.[14]

Nevertheless, for Barth the Spirit is the bond of contemporaneity. As the history of Jesus Christ continues, so the Holy Spirit ensures his contemporaneity. "[The Spirit] is the form of [Jesus Christ's] action in which this action continues, in which it is made present to the man to whom He gives Himself and who receives Him as the action which in its

---

13. Or later, when Barth asks why the community is the body of Jesus Christ, his earthly-historical form of existence, the answer is decisively pneumatological; see IV/1, 666.

14. Pneumatology here is minimal: "It is strange but true that fundamentally and in general practice we cannot say more of the Holy Spirit and His work than that He is the power in which Jesus Christ attests himself, attests Himself effectively, creating in man response and obedience. We describe Him as His awakening power. Later we will have to describe Him as His quickening and enlightening power" (IV/1, 648). Barth even suggests that beyond the description of the Spirit's attestation and confirmation of Jesus Christ "there did not emerge any doctrine of the Holy Spirit and His work even in the secondary and later theology of the Church" (IV/1, 649). Perhaps it is not incidental that the *filioque* is reiterated throughout this discussion; see for example IV/1, 646.

singularity takes place today, in which as he is free to know and grasp it in faith, as he participates in it, it makes Him its contemporary. It is the form of His action in which this action hastens from His resurrection as its first revelation to a few to its final and general revelation to all" (IV/1, 648). These features of the relation of Jesus Christ, the Holy Spirit, and the community remain throughout *CD* IV. The relation between Jesus-history and the history of the community is generally couched in terms of the twofold *Existenzform* of Jesus Christ. And in all cases the mediating or bonding between these two histories is the work of the Holy Spirit: the self-attesting and confirming power of Jesus Christ.[15]

Further description of the Spirit's work in the community is tucked away at the end of § 72.1, "The People of God in World-Occurrence." At the end of this subsection Barth asks how it is that the community lives and persists in world-occurrence. In answering, he finally explicates the christological and pneumatological foundations of ecclesial time—which has in fact been assumed throughout the subsection.[16] The redirecting theme of recapitulation is evident here as Jesus Christ is the head of his body, his earthly-historical *Existenzform* (IV/3, 752–758).[17] The community acquires the movement and direction of its history from its head; it "exists as He, Jesus Christ, exists" (IV/3, 754). But the christological basis includes the pneumatological. As Christ's self-attesting creative and gracious power, the Spirit mediates the asymmetrical relation

---

15. Another theme worth noting in passing is the asymmetrical relation between the Holy Spirit and the Christian community. It follows for Barth that even while the Spirit creates faith and freedom in the community and the individual, they cannot "subjugate or possess or control Him, directing and overruling His work" (IV/1, 646). This means that the response to the Spirit "can only be one of obedience and of prayer for His new coming and witness and quickening: *Veni creator Spiritus*" (IV/1, 647). This founds Barth's rejection of liberal pneumatology. Barth emphases the point that, contra liberal ecclesiology, the eternal Spirit must not be confused with other spirits. He uses the *filioque* and the Augustinian view of the Spirit as the bond of love to do this (IV/1, 646). Rosato, in *The Spirit as Lord*, repeatedly points out Barth's distinguishing himself from his liberal predecessors.

16. On the continuous presence of Jesus Christ see IV/3, 686, 706, 707 and 716; for references to the Holy Spirit as the self-attestation of Jesus Christ see 686 and 706.

17. As mentioned, this is Barth's form of the *totus Christus*. In a brief small print section, however, Barth hints at a third form of Christ's existence as Lord of all the cosmos and world history: "His being as *Pantocrator* who already reigns, as the principle of lordship in world-occurrence?" (IV/3, 756). Barth leaves this brief note unexplained. Is he thinking of Christ as Lord who preserves creation in the middle time, or of the future eschatological unveiling of Christ's Lordship over creation? Perhaps it is both.

between Jesus Christ and the community (IV/3, 759). To explicate this work of the Holy Spirit, Barth begins with the role of the Holy Spirit in the eternal life of God and suggests that this corresponds to the Spirit's work within the community:

> Just as the Holy Spirit, as Himself an eternal divine 'person' or mode of being, as the Spirit of the Father and the Son (*qui ex Patre Filioque procedit*), is the bond of peace between the two, so in the historical work of reconciliation He is the One who constitutes and guarantees the unity of the *totus Christus*, i.e., of Jesus Christ in the heights and in the depths, in His transcendence and in His immanence. He is the One who constitutes and guarantees the unity in which He is at one and the same time the heavenly Head with God and the earthly body with his community. This co-ordination and unity is the work of the active grace of God" (IV/3, 760).

Clearly for Barth there is an analogical relation between the Spirit's role *in se* and his work *ad extra*; just as the Spirit is the bond between Father and Son, so too he is the bond between Jesus Christ and his body. The Holy Spirit is the power "of the co-ordination of the being of Jesus Christ and that of His community as distinct from and yet enclosed within it (ibid.).

In these few pages there is also some indication as to the character of the Spirit's work in the history of the community. In the first place, this work is *dynamic* and *historical*. The bonding or mediating work of the Spirit is ongoing in the history of the community. The "relationship of the being of Jesus Christ to that of His community is not static nor immobile, but mobile and dynamic, and therefore historical. As the act of the Holy Spirit which underlies the existence of the community takes place in the order of the being of Jesus Christ and His community, the latter existing as He exists" (IV/3, 759). Or, to put it otherwise, the community "is a history which takes place as Jesus Christ exercises His power, as this power is operative as the power of His calling Word, and therefore as the gracious power of the Holy Spirit" (IV/3, 761). But, second, this dynamic co-ordinating is *particular* in both time and place. His Word "does not only go out into all lands and even to the ends of the world (Ps 19:4), but here and now is heard by very human ears and received and understood by very human reason. . . . here and now in human faith and love and hope and knowledge, its echo in human confession at his specific time and place. In the work of the Holy Spirit it takes place that Jesus Christ is present and received in the life of His community of this or that century, land or place" (IV/3, 761). Following this, third, the Holy Spirit *unifies that which is different*. A correspondence occurs between the divine and human, protecting the being and freedom of both, without mixing.[18] The work of the Spirit "is to bring and to hold them together, not to identify, intermingle nor confound them, not to change the one into the other nor to merge the one into the other, but to co-ordinate them, to make them parallel, to bring them into harmony and therefore to bind them into a true unity" (IV/3, 761).

For Barth, then, the eternal Spirit, who is the bond between the Father and the Son, mediates between Jesus-history and the history of the community. The history of the community occurs when the Holy Spirit works continuously, dynamically, and particularly, unifying the history of the Son and temporal history of creatures. The Spirit *continuously* works within the community until the eschaton. This work is *dynamic* as the community itself is history, event, and act; it is *particular* in each here and now and in diverse places; and it *unifies* that which is different—Jesus Christ and the church, and believers with one another (IV/3, 762).

THE HOLY SPIRIT AND THE TIME OF THE COMMUNITY

Ecclesial time is the time of the being and activity of the Christian community between the forty days and the eschaton. This history of the community follows and corresponds to Jesus-history, as the witnessing community is the creation of Jesus Christ by the Holy Spirit. Barth's exposition of the activity of the community in the middle time may be summarized under the rubric of internal and external movements. Internally, the community is gathered and built up, externally it is sent into the world to witness to God's reconciling work.[19] This is the activity that "fills" the time of the community. But Jesus Christ by the Holy Spirit

---

18. This work is the "the divine working, being and action on the one side and the human on the other, the creative freedom and act on the one side and the creaturely on the other, the eternal reality and possibility on the one side and the temporal on the other" (IV/3, 761).

19. The use of "internal" and "external" to describe the activity of the community are appropriations. It will be obvious that the activities Barth lists under the sending of the community also build it up.

conducts these movements. In explicating ecclesial time I will argue that the Holy Spirit as the bond between Jesus-history and the history of the community ensures a correspondence in general history to the recapitulating history of the risen and ascended Lord. This work, moreover, as the *vinculum* of contemporaneity can be characterized as *continuous, dynamic, particular*, and *unifying*.

Discerning this interpretation however is not straightforward. Barth's discussion in § 62.3, "The Time of the Community," does not do full justice to the work of the Spirit in the ecclesial time. In that subsection Barth defines the "time of the community [as] the time between the first *parousia* of Jesus Christ and the second" (IV/1, 725).[20] The time of the community is the historical and eschatological existence of believers between the forty days and the final eschaton. This time has a pneumatological concentration: "[In] this movement by His Holy Spirit He Himself is invisibly present as the living Head in the midst of it as His body" (IV/1, 725). However, one might expect more detail here on the particular activity and work of the Spirit that constitutes ecclesial time. But what is found is Barth struggling with the nature and necessity of ecclesial time itself. He examines the community's strength and weakness, and lastly, answers the question as to why there is this time at all. Why didn't God usher in the eschaton with the resurrection of Jesus since he had already judged humanity on the cross?[21] Therefore,

---

20. The term *parousia* refers to "the immediate visible presence and action of the living Jesus Christ Himself" (IV/1, 725). The first occurrence of his visible presence and action took place with the resurrection and the forty days, while the second occurrence is "His final coming in His revelation as the Judge of the quick and the dead" (ibid). Later Barth will define a threefold *parousia* (IV/3, 293–96), the second being the *invisible* presence and action of Jesus Christ during ascension time, and the third being the final visible manifestation of the eschaton. Though the terminology is different, the substance is the same; the time of the community is the time of Christ's invisible presence and action by the Holy Spirit in and with the community during the middle time. We may also point out that the parallel with Barth's discussion of human temporality is again evident. Just as individual humans have a limited time with a definite beginning and end, so now the time of the church has a definite beginning and end.

21. The strength and weakness of the community centres on both its beginning with the resurrection and its ending in the eschaton. It is strong because it knows that the whole of history is moving toward an end. But the community only lives this in faith and not sight. Thus ecclesial time is also weak (IV/1, 725–34). Nevertheless, the community is strong in the final analysis because the Holy Spirit is the author of its faith (IV/1, 733). What is more, God does not usher history into eschatological completion because he desires a response from humanity to the completed work of reconciliation (IV/1, 737).

in order to substantiate the present trinitarian interpretation further analysis of *CD* IV is needed. If, as suggested, ecclesial time is the "time of" the Spirit's activity in and with the community, then this will need to be filled out elsewhere. The pneumatological interpretation of ecclesial time being offered here will be gleaned from § 67, "The Holy Spirit and the Upbuilding of the Christian Community" in IV/2 and § 72 "The Holy Spirit and the Sending of the Christian Community" in IV/3. The downside of this indirect approach to the time of the community is that Barth does not describe ecclesial time qualitatively. Because Barth in fact spends little time reflecting on the nature of ecclesial time, he does not substantiate the discussion of temporality as he did with subjective time in III/2.

Nevertheless, the following analysis and explication will have three parts. In the first there is an examination of the time of the community in relation to history in general. The history of the community is but one history in the multitude of histories that occur in general world-occurrence. In the two parts that follow, there is an exposition of the Holy Spirit's work in the internal movement of building up the community and the external movement of sending it into the world.[22] In each case, the work of the Spirit as the bond of contemporaneity is evident.

Ecclesial Time in General World-Occurrence

The trinitarian breadth of Barth's interpretation of time becomes obvious in the discussion of § 72.1 "The People of God in World-Occurrence."[23] Much attention has been given to subjective forms of time—rational-linear time and allotted time. Barth also briefly discusses time as a feature of the cosmos in general, namely as the place in which human time is embedded. A fourth form is the broad category of general world history or general world-occurrence: the history of the cosmos and humanity

---

22. This exposition does not by-pass the gathering of the community (§ 62) since this paragraph has been discussed in the previous section. Nevertheless, the focus of the internal movement of the community will be on § 67.

23. The context of IV/3, "Jesus Christ, the True Witness," is the prophetic work of the God-man. He has already established Jesus Christ as the Lord who became servant (*vere Deus*, High Priest) in IV/1, and the Servant who became Lord (*vere homo*, King) in IV/2. Now his concern is the declaration to the world of the accomplished reconciliation completed on the cross. The pneumatological sections of IV/3 are concerned, then, with the sending of the community to the world, § 72, and Christian hope, § 73.

in the widest possible sense; the history of creation itself and of multiple empires, nations, and cultures of human history (IV/3, 684).[24]

But, again, Barth understands this collective form of time in light of his trinitarian and covenantal ontology. He describes general world-occurrence as the history of *hominum confusione et Dei providentia regitur*. General world-occurrence takes place under God's fatherly providence, but is also the history and time of human confusion. On the one hand humanity lives in light of God's good creation (IV/3, 695), while on the other, "there is the reality and operation of the absurd, of nothingness, grounded in no possibility given by God, neither elected nor willed by God, but existing only *per nefas*" (IV/3, 696). In this confusion, Nothingness, "the negation of the good creation of God, becomes the master, controller and ruler of this creation, and the good creation of God is set in the service and under the control of its own negation" (IV/3, 697).[25]

But from the perspective of the Christian community time and history are not merely the dialectic between divine providence and human confusion. For Barth, there is a third term wherein the community may truly see itself. This is the work of God's grace in the person of Jesus Christ, the one mediator between God and humanity. Contra Hegel, Jesus Christ is not a third term in the sense of a human concept or product of human thought, but the event of God's gracious action (IV/3, 706–14).[26] It is the free and sovereign power of God actualized in the life, death, and resurrection of Jesus Christ who speaks by his Holy Spirit (IV/3, 709). But God's answer to the problem of the power of nothingness over his good creation will not be complete until the eschaton. Thus there is still time for the community: "*time for* the community to proclaim the Word of Jesus Christ and what has taken place in Him; *time*

---

24. This is similar to creation history (III/1, 65–71), though human history in general is included here.

25. Barth points to war as evidence of this, wherein even times of peace are "a continual preparation for war" (IV/3, 699). He mentions the atomic bomb of as an illustration of human confusion in the face of God's good creation (IV/3, 701).

26. Jesus-history as a third term is not a synthesis between thesis (God's good creation) and antithesis (human sin as a result of nothingness), but a term that is above them both (IV/3, 703-6). According to Barth, the difference in his own dialectic is that providence and confusion remain distinct and are not two stages on a third way (IV/3, 704). The third term, moreover, is not a human possibility. Humanity cannot "go beyond that twofold view in his own strength or by his own choice, finding and fixing a supposedly superior point in the void" (IV/3, 705).

for the world to receive this Word" (IV/3, 714, italics added). In faith the community awaits the final and universal revelation of Jesus Christ and so participates in world history in a different light (IV/3, 716). The time of the community, moreover, is time for proclaiming the reconciliation accomplished in Christ to the world, and time for the world to receive it, as all of history is moving toward its completion.[27]

Similar to the discussion of created, fallen, and gracious time in *CD* III, here the form of time is thus understood in light of Barth's trinitarian and covenantal ontology. Yet the form of time is different. In IV/3, Barth is thinking of time in larger collective forms. In the context of general world-occurrence, the time of the community is but one small history in the grand march of history itself. But these collective forms of time are understood theologically. General history is under the providential control of the Father but also the force of sin and nothingness. But God responds to this in the history of Jesus Christ and the community. Therefore, the time of the community, as a collective history, is simultaneous preserved, fallen, and gracious time. Much as the individual may experience allotted time in either anxiety or hope, so the community lives in history itself not merely in the face of confusion but in light of the final redemption that is to come.

The Internal Movement of the Community

The time of the community as the collective history of believers in general world-occurrence contains two simultaneous movements. The first is its internal movement of being gathered and established into a body, while the second is its being sent into the world to bear witness to the accomplished reconciliation between God and humanity. Within general world-occurrence, which is the preserving work of the Father, and corresponding to Jesus-history, the Holy Spirit creates this double movement of the community which fills ecclesial time. In this way, the time of the Spirit complements the times of the Father and Son. These movements will be the focus of the next two subsections.

To illustrate the internal movement of the community the focus will be on § 67, "The Holy Spirit and the Upbuilding of the Christian Community." Here Barth is turning to the effects of sanctification in

---

27. In this subsection Barth also asks how the people of God is to see itself in world-occurrence (IV/3, 721–62). This corresponds to the external movement of the community, which is given explication below, thus the topic can be bypassed.

humanity.²⁸ This is unfolded using the NT metaphor of the upbuilding (οἰκοδομή) of the community, which is described as both growth (αυξειν, αυξάνειν) and upholding, and illustrated with a discussion of church order and law. Throughout the discussion the continuous, dynamic, particular, and unifying work of the Spirit is evident.²⁹

The term "upbuilding" (οἰκοδομή) encapsulates what Barth aims to say about the community in this paragraph (IV/2, 626). The term is a reference to the Christian community and not individuals in isolation (IV/2, 627). The point of the term, moreover, is not the final construction of a building as such but "of the actual occurrence, the event, the fulfillment, the work of edification, and therefore the construction of a building" (IV/2, 627).³⁰ But the goal of the construction is integration and communion: "These men need to be brought together, to be constituted, established and maintained as a common being—one people capable of unanimous action" (IV/2, 635). As the community "allows the Holy Spirit to exercise it in self-integration, it is the true Church, prepared to look and move forward, to give this provisional representation, and thus to offer the witness which is the meaning and its existence in world-history" (IV/2, 636). For Barth, the building of the community is centred in its worship; the community is εκκλησία (IV/2, 638). In fact, common worship is the central event of the community wherein it is given direction for its movement in being built up (IV/2, 639). The building of the community necessarily includes divine agency. In regular construction there is a master builder with a definite plan and an ending, and with the community there is one Lord who "continually" gives directions (IV/2, 631). The triune God works to build the community:

---

28. Found in *CD* IV/2, this section follows the sanctification of humanity in the exaltation of Jesus Christ, the servant who is Lord. The sin overcome in the sanctification of humanity is sloth. The sanctifying activity of the risen and ascended Lord through his Spirit upon the community is the establishing of the community.

29. Indeed, the temporal work of Jesus Christ and the Spirit are evident throughout the paragraph. The time of the community is mentioned nine times and discussed more directly (IV/2, 695–698), while the continuous presence of Jesus Christ is directly examined (IV/2, 695–698 and 710–711) it is noted in thirteen other places. References to the work of the Holy Spirit in the community are found on fifteen occasions, while the Spirit as the power and activity of Jesus Christ is found in over twenty places.

30. This focus on the event nature of construction seems to prevent Barth from taking the building metaphor into a more Roman Catholic direction on the institutional church.

"It is in and through the man Jesus in the power of His Spirit that the one God is at work in the upbuilding of His community" (IV/2, 633).

Throughout the discussion the bonding work of the Spirit in the history of the community is evident. For example, Barth discusses the "True Church" with reference to the visible/invisible dialectic. Similar to the discussion in IV/1 (652–68), he argues that the church's visibility is only possible because of the invisible work of Jesus Christ and His Spirit. Here the continuous work of the Spirit is necessary to the being and existence of the community (IV/2, 616–17). For example, when the true church emerges from the sinful action of Christians, traditions, and institutions, the Spirit's continuous work makes this possible: "If it is also visible as a true Church, this means that the victory of the divine operation, the mighty act of the Holy Spirit in the face of the sinfulness of human action, finds further expression in a free emergence and outshining of the true Church from the concealment in which it is enveloped by the sinfulness of all human volition (and therefore of ecclesiastical), and in which it must continue to be enveloped apart from this continuation of the operation of the Holy Spirit" (IV/2, 619).

This section also contains discussion of the community as the provisional representation of the accomplished reconciliation between God and humanity. As a provisional representation, the community has both a final goal and a role to play in the interim time. The goal is the definitive and universal revelation of Jesus Christ as the saviour of all; while its role in the interim time is to be "a witness to all others, representing the sanctification which has already come upon them too in Jesus Christ" (IV/2, 620). Thus the "meaning and content of our time—the last time—is the fulfillment of this provisional representation as the task of the community of Jesus Christ" (IV/2, 621). The impetus and direction of ecclesial time, moreover, is found in Jesus-history, which necessarily includes continuing pneumatological intervention:

> Jesus the Lord, in the quickening power of His Holy Spirit, is the One who acts where this provisional representation takes place, and therefore where the true Church is an event. . . . We are speaking, therefore, of the history of this race in the sequence of its human thoughts and efforts and achievements. But we are speaking of the history in which it is unfit, but continually fitted, in and with its human thought and word and will and work to make this provisional representation. More precisely, we are speaking of the history in which God continually sets this people

on the way and in movement, continually indicating both the goal and the direction towards it (IV/2, 623).

The work of Jesus Christ by the Spirit continuously enables the church to fill its time. As Jesus Christ acts with his Spirit "to and with His people, *this people fills with His activity the time given to itself and the world*" (IV/2, 623, italics added). Here again the bonding activity of the Spirit is evident. It is dynamic since the community is act, event, and history; particular in "the sequence" of human thought, activity, and effort; unifying that which is different by making fit what is unfit; and continually directing the community to its goal.

Barth expands on the building of the community by discussing both its growth and its being upheld. First the growth (αυξειν, αυξάνειν) of the community is discussed both extensively and intensively. With the aid of Bonhoeffer, Barth begins with a brief exposition of the church as a communion of saints. The communion of saints is the event in which, by the Holy Spirit, the *sancti* (saints) are engaged in *sancta* (holy acts) (IV/2, 641–643).[31] The growth of the community is the saints engaged in these acts. The unifying activity of the Spirit is central for this work: "Communion is an action in which on the basis of an existing union (*unio*) many men are engaged in a common movement towards the same union. This takes place in the power and operation of the Holy Spirit, and the corresponding action of those who are assembled and quickened by Him. Communion takes place as this divine and human work is in train" (IV/2, 641, see 642 as well).

The extensive, or quantitative, growth of the community may be described numerically or geographically (IV/2, 645). But this extensive growth, which comes from within, is not a matter of the church perpetuating itself in some complete form since its final extension is an eschatological reality (IV/2, 648). It is the "intensive, vertical and spiritual growth," then, which is truly significant (IV/2, 650–51). The true growth of the community is the growth of Christians in a fellowship of activities.

The immanent power enabling this growth however is not merely the work of Christians in their holy activities; it is the ascended and exalted Jesus Christ working by His Spirit.[32] The unifying work of the

---

31. Barth gives a partial list of such acts: the community is a fellowship of knowledge, confession, worship, penitence, prayer, service, hope, prophesy, proclamation of the gospel, prayer, and liturgy (IV/2, 643).

32. The "community lives as the communion of saints because and as Jesus lives.

Holy Spirit is evident. Not only is the Holy Spirit "the self-attestation of the risen and living Lord Jesus . . . but also the particular, factual sanctification of Christians—their union with Him and therefore with one another" (IV/2, 651). It is in "the Holy Spirit as the self-attestation of Jesus they thus know themselves in and with Him; themselves in their union with Him, and also with one another, in the fellowship of faith and love in which they express themselves as His and find self-awareness as this people which has a common descent" (ibid.). Thus the "Holy Spirit achieves the *communio sanctorum* and causes it to grow (intensively and extensively). It lives by His power – from the very first and on all its way and ways in the realisation of the relationship of the *sancti* to the *sancta* right up to its goal at the end of all history when it will meet the *eschaton* which will be the *eschaton* of the cosmos" (IV/2, 652). The Holy Spirit as the self-attesting power of Jesus Christ is continuously active in the time of the church, creating union between Jesus Christ and believers and enabling the saints to grow as they participate in the holy activities of the community.

This growth of the community is also explained with reference to the definition of the church as the body of Christ, Barth's version of the *totus Christus*. To begin, Jesus Christ is remote and transcendent from the community.[33] But again this distance between the risen and ascended Lord and his body is mediated by His Holy Spirit: "If in spite of this He is still at work in earthly history, and in the community as it exists in it, by the quickening power of His Holy Spirit, we can certainly call this His operation at a distance. From the point to which there is no way . . . He overcomes that abyss in the Holy Spirit, operating here from that exalted status, working in time, in which the *communio sanctorum* is an event and has its history in many events, from the eternity of the life which He has in common with God" (IV/2, 652). Again, the earthly-historical *Existenzform* of Christ is a work of the Holy Spirit, creating unity and bringing together that which is different and particular, making the community one body.[34] The Spirit is the bond that ensures that

Jesus is the power of the life immanent within it" (IV/2, 651).

33. Here Barth comes close to a strong sense of absence or at least distance. In his heavenly form of existence at the right hand of the Father Jesus "is separated from [the community] by an abyss which cannot be bridged. He is even hidden from it in God (Col. 3:3)" (IV/2, 652).

34. "Similarly, His Holy Spirit is one. As the quickening power which accomplishes sanctification, He comes down with utter novelty and strangeness from above (as de-

that which is different, particular, and separate grows into the one history of the community. As such, the Spirit enables the community to be a provisional representation in this interim time (IV/2, 654).

Following the growth of the community, the concept of the upholding of the community suggests how it is that the community is preserved given its weakness in the world. That is, how it is that the community is maintained and preserved in the world given both outward and inward threats. The outward threats relate to the church's extensive growth, while inward threats relate to its intensive health, arising from the fact that believers are still sinners (IV/2, 665–66).[35] Despite these threats, the community "cannot and will not actually be destroyed. It is indestructible" (IV/2, 672). Barth argues that the preservation of the community against both internal and external threats occurs in its attention to the scriptures (IV/2, 673–674). But again this preserving function of the scriptures must be understood in light of the continuing work of the risen Lord. The Holy Spirit, moreover, mediates this hidden presence of the risen Lord through the scriptures. When the scriptures are read and heard within the church "there concretely His Holy Spirit comes and works and rules. It is thus true already that from there concretely the Church is upheld by the Holy Spirit" (IV/2, 675).

In the last subsection of § 67, "The Order of the Community," Barth examines the life of the community in terms of order and law. The growth and preservation of the community is not ad hoc or haphazard but orderly and with form. The centre of the community's order moreover is found in public worship (IV/2, 676–79). The bulk of the discussion centers on the presuppositions of true Church law: it is a law of service, a liturgical law, a living law, and an exemplary law.[36] These

---

scribed in the story of Pentecost) and thus constitutes an absolute basis and starting-point. But as the same power He also rules and works in these events, in the sequence and multiplicity, of the temporal history of the *communio sanctorum* which is still the *communio peccatorum*, in all the relativities of that which is called Christian and ecclesiastical and even theological life" (IV/2, 653).

35. Outward extensive threat may include either active pressure and even persecution, or passive toleration, ignoring, or relativizing (IV/2, 663–65). Inward intensive pressure comes in the form of alienation (secularization), when the community is directed away from its true being, or self-glorification (sacralization), when the church is concerned with its own self-preservation and power in relation to the world around it (IV/2, 667–670).

36. Before this, however, Barth mentions the basis of church law and the law of church and state. The basis of church law is found in the sanctification of humanity in

presuppositions "will always be normative for every true Church law" (IV/2, 689).

A few illustrations from this discussion will demonstrate that the orderly growth of the community is viewed within Jesus-history, and therefore is the bonding work of the Spirit. This is evident, for example, with the discussion of the second presupposition: church law is liturgical (IV/2, 695–710). Earlier Barth argued that the centre of upbuilding itself is worship. Here he reiterates this by suggesting that worship is the centre of order, where church law "has its original seat" (IV/2, 695). But even this central happening is derived from the christological agency: Jesus-history directs and controls the liturgy (IV/2, 695). Barth emphasizes the being of Jesus Christ as both *history* and a *particular* history.[37] The community expectedly corresponds to his historicity and particularity. This is a result of the Spirit's dynamic and particular work. "If His community then, created and ruled and upheld by His Holy Spirit in the time between His resurrection and His return in glory, is His body . . . it is inevitable that His particular history, both as history and in its particularity, should be actively and recognisably reflected and represented in its life" (IV/2, 696). Thus the community "is itself history. . . . It is an event. Otherwise it is not the Christian community" (ibid.). Moreover, while the church exists in the individual lives of Christians dispersed throughout society, wearing "working clothes of an anonymity," it comes together in its particularity in worship (IV/2, 697–698).[38] Thus the living

---

Jesus Christ, who directs his community in their corresponding obedience by listening to scripture (IV/2, 680–83). The law of church and state is recognition that the law of the state is a *ius circa sacra* and not *ius in sacra*. In fact, to be taken up later in the discussion, church law can be an example to state law.

37. As history, Jesus Christ "is the man who not only went but still goes and always will go the way from Bethlehem to Golgotha. The One who goes this way is manifested on Easter Day as the living Lord, and His Spirit, His quickening power, is the Holy Spirit, who has created and rules and upholds the Christian community. The being of the Head of the community is the event of the life of this man" (IV/2, 695). As a particular history, to use Lessing's phrase a "contingent fact of history," the "event of this life is indissolubly connected with His name. It is the event which exhausts itself in this name—concrete, limited in time and space, singular and unique. It is this event and not another" (IV/2, 696). It is only in this particular history that the God-man fulfills the covenant and establishes reconciliation between God and humanity (ibid.). For a critical discussion of Barth's appropriation of the descent and ascent theme noted here see Farrow, *Ascension and Ecclesia*, 243–54.

38. It is noteworthy that Barth's focus on worship here does not lead him to reflect on the sacraments. This is true even in the next section when the external movement of

The Vinculum *of Contemporaneity* 179

Lord gathers the community together by the Holy Spirit as a particular event and history focused in worship. The law and order of the community arises from this centre.

The third basic presupposition of church law is that it is living law (IV/2, 710-718). As living, Barth optimistically suggests that church law is changing from worse to better. This growth of the law is possible, moreover, because Jesus Christ is living and works by the Spirit in every movement of his life. In following this, the community maintains a posture of listening obedience to its Lord. As it listens to its Lord and is directed by the Holy Spirit church law must be open to new developments (IV/2, 710-713).[39] This growth of the law may also be understood under the constraints of time. The law of the past, since it arose out of obedience, was necessary. And, therefore, the church is to adhere today to the law of yesterday. But just as it is obedient to the law of yesterday it must also be ready to be obedient to new and developed law today. Thus, both the law of the past and present are provisional since they are seen under the work of the continuous presence of Jesus Christ (IV/2, 714-16). But this temporal transition is not a spinning of the tires. As it moves from the past to the future under His lordship in the Holy Spirit, the community moves from worse to better canon law. "It will always have to move away from the worse and move forward to the better. If it were not somewhere engaged in this movement, it would be a sure sign that the Holy Spirit had left it and it had lost the attitude of obedience to its Lord" (IV/2, 716). In this transition, moreover, it will legitimately assume very different forms "at different times and places" (IV/2, 717). The Spirit, therefore, continually works as the community listens to its Lord, in each particular time and space.[40]

the community is summarized with the various forms of ministry in speech and action.

39. For where "there is the genuine dynamic from above, the power of the Holy Spirit (who is obviously no sceptic), the community cannot refuse this venture" (IV/2, 711).

40. The continual work of Jesus Christ by his Spirit is hinted at in the last presupposition as well. The fourth and last presupposition of all church law is that it is exemplary. Since the church is a provisional representation of humanity sanctified in Jesus Christ, its law "is a pattern for the formation and administration of human law generally, and therefore of the law of other political, economic, cultural and other human societies" (IV/2, 719). This exemplification consists in being a witness and "a reminder of the law of the kingdom of God already set up on earth in Jesus Christ, and a promise of its future manifestation," toward which both the church and the world are moving (IV/2, 721). Barth even suggests a final eschatological law (IV/2, 720). This exemplary role

The External Movement of the Community

The internal movement of being gathered and built up is incomplete for Barth without its external movement of being sent. The community, as a provisional representation, is sent into the world to witness to the reconciliation established in Jesus Christ. This external movement is the subject of § 72, "The Holy Spirit and the Sending of the Christian Community" in IV/3. Barth expounds this external movement by first making the argument that the community's responsibility to the world is essential to its being the body of Christ. He then describes the task of the community as confessing Jesus Christ as God's "Yes" to humanity, while finally Barth examines the actual forms of ministry in their witnessing to the world. At important junctures of the discussion Barth reiterates the basis of the community's being sent into the world with reference to the work of Jesus Christ and his Spirit.[41] Again the bonding work of the Spirit can be characterized as continuous, dynamic, particular, and unifying.

Barth argues that the community is for the world not merely because it is creaturely itself but also because its being follows that of God's work under the Lordship of Jesus Christ in the power of the Holy Spirit. In fact, the Holy Spirit's sending of the community is fundamental to its being, for its being called-out-of is also its being called-into the world (IV/3, 763-64). But this being-for-the-world needs the foundation and direction of divine agency. Barth explains this with four points.

In the first place, the origin and continuation of the mission of the church to the world is achieved by the continuous power of the Holy Spirit (IV/3, 786-87). The Holy Spirit enables the church "to give its own corresponding, and to that extent appropriate, and to that extent

---

implies a twofold function. First, it has the critical task of reminding other forms of law of their limitations, of their not being the last word (IV/2, 721). But second, this provisional representation of God's law in the law of the church may in fact serve the positive function of changing other forms of law from worse to better (IV/2, 722).

41. As in IV/2, the discussion of the church in IV/3 affirms that it is act, event, and history. Thus the temporal nature of the church and the work of Jesus Christ and the Spirit in it underlie all discussions. Jesus Christ's continuous presence is noted at least fourteen times, the work of the Holy Spirit in and with the community nearly thirty times, and the Holy Spirit as the meditation between Jesus Christ and the community twenty times. While explicit reference to "the time of the community" (714, 755, 757, 815, 840, and 883) is less frequent, it is clear throughout that the history and time of the community as the work of Jesus Christ and His Spirit is presupposed in all that Barth takes up.

obedient answer to the Word of God spoken to and reasonably received by it" (IV/3, 786; see 787 as well). Second, this work of the Holy Spirit in human spontaneity and freedom consists in its confession of Jesus Christ (IV/3, 787-90). And third, Jesus Christ, as the risen and ascended Lord, is the continuous and active agent in the community by the Spirit (IV/3, 790). In arguing the fourth point, that the community is the likeness or image of Jesus Christ, Barth argues that the community participates in the prophecy of Jesus Christ and calls the world to him (IV/3, 793-94). This calling activity, empowered by the Holy Spirit, fills ecclesial time in the interim.

> The ongoing of this calling of the world to the service of God takes place in the likeness of the community founded, maintained and guided by the power of His Holy Spirit, between the *terminus a quo* of its history and its *terminus ad quem*, here and now, in every hour of our time which is the time between the times. This time is not, therefore, a vacuum between the other two. It is the time of the *parousia* of Jesus Christ in its second and middle form, in the power of His Holy Spirit; and therefore it is especially the time of the community (CD IV/1, § 62.3). This time is given the community in order that it may be to the world an indication, representation and likeness of its calling in Jesus Christ to the service of God as it proceeds in this time between (IV/3, 794-795).

Next Barth describes what the community in the world is to do. He explicates the task of the community in reference to its content, to whom it is directed, and its purity (IV/3, 797-824). In short, the content of the task is to confess Jesus Christ as the "Yes" of God to humanity. This Yes of God is God with humanity, and thus humanity as the object of God's goodness (IV/3, 800). Following this, the Yes of God is directed to humanity. Not humanity as understood in other forms of knowledge, but humanity that is loved by God and addressed in the gospel (IV/3, 809-10). As for the purity of the content, Barth suggests that there are two basic dangers toward which the church may drift. It can either fail to see that the Word addressed to humanity is a living word, thus failing in its prophetic witness by sliding into neutrality, or it can fail to see the Word as constant, thus accommodating the gospel for other religious or philosophical messages which appear more relevant.

Here Barth makes it clear, especially in discussing the livingness of the Word, that the risen and ascended Lord is constantly present by the Holy Spirit and thereby maintains the purity of Christian witness. The Spirit's work in this purifying is particular and continuous. Barth rhetorically asks, is "there really any *hic et nunc* in which it may maintain with good conscience that it cannot hear the living Word of its living Lord spoken to this *hic et nunc*?" (IV/3, 815). In fact, "there can be no doubt that, when its relevance to specific times and situations is taken from it, intentionally or unintentionally the Gospel is no longer preached as the declaration of the risen Jesus Christ who rules at the right hand of the Father Almighty but who also by His Holy Spirit lives and acts and speaks in the ongoing earthly and temporal history of the world and the Church" (IV/3, 816). Thus the mediating Spirit ensures that the prophetic Word of Jesus Christ is continuously heard and thus maintains the purity of the message.

Barth finally comes to the actual forms of the ministry in the last subsection of § 72. While previous sections have dealt with the being and message of the church as it is sent into the world, Barth is concerned here with what the church actually practices in the interim time. These forms of ministry fill the time of the church in its external movement into the world. The forms are divided between forms of speech and forms of action—with the understanding that each category is contained in the other. The forms of speech include praise of God, preaching, teaching, evangelism, missions, and theology (IV/3, 865–882). The forms of action include prayer, curing of souls, personal examples, the diaconate, prophetic action, and establishing fellowship (IV/3, 882–901). These forms will not be rehearsed in detail since our concern is to describe how the forms are mediated by the Holy Spirit in ecclesial time.[42] Yet even though the Spirit fills ecclesial time in this way, Barth does not move toward any reflection on how these activities qualitatively transform the experience of time for the community.

42. Barth first discusses the character and nature of ministry before the forms (IV/3, 830–854). In both of these discussions Barth presumes the continuing presence of Jesus Christ by his Spirit in the time of the community. For example, when discussing the definite character of ministry he states: "As the living Word of God in the calling, enlightening and awakening power of the Holy Spirit, He marches through the history of humanity which hastens to its goal and end, continually moving from our yesterday, through our today into our tomorrow. Yet he does not do so alone. He is accompanied by the community gathered, built up and sent by His attestation. He is surrounded by the people established and characterized by the ministry laid upon it. Thus the ministry of this people also takes place in the course, in the constantly changing stages and situations, of ongoing human history" (IV/3, 831).

Nevertheless, that Barth is thinking of the Spirit's temporal work is evinced in the preamble (of sorts) to discussing the forms. Here he gives a brief exposition of the difference and unity of the forms of ministry. The forms of ministry are integrated and manifold, there is a unity in witness but a differentiation in form. Within this dialectic the role of the Holy Spirit as the *vinculum* of contemporaneity is central. In this case, the Holy Spirit's unifying action ensures that the diversity, variety, and particularity of the forms are united to the one purpose of witnessing to the work of Jesus Christ.[43] Thus again, the Holy Spirit is the bond not only between Christ and his body but also between the many members in the body.

Barth supports the Holy Spirit's work in the diversity and unity of ministry with a reflection on a few Pauline passages.[44] Barth takes the terms χαρίσματα (spiritual gifts), διακονίαι (services), and ενεργήματα (activities) as synonymous. In fact, all the forms of ministry in which the church is a witness are united in purpose and united under its Lord by the work of the Holy Spirit. This is expounded with three points. First, the one body has many members. This is recognition of the plurality of gifts, ministries and works as not a "necessary evil, but right and good and inwardly necessary" (IV/3, 857). In fact the diversity and particularity of gifts is not accidental but are "works of God, of Jesus Christ, of the Holy Spirit. As χαρίσματα, they are forms of the one χάρις addressed to the community as such and operative in it. The very unity of the ministry of the community demands and creates its multiplicity" (ibid.). Second, the many are one body. This diversity of gifts, ministries, and works is right and necessary because they "do not arise or exist for themselves but for all, for the totality of the life and work of the community" (IV/3, 857). What is more, "all these groups with their particular tendencies must keep rigidly to the rule that they have not to exist or act for themselves . . . but with the selfless desire to serve and with openness on every side to all others and to the whole" (IV/3, 858).

---

43. These gifts are particular, specific, and diverse: "Their divine calling and endowment are as such manifold. They are always new and different. There are specific in each and every case. They demand of each and all specific attention, specific obedience and specific faithfulness. And the more openly they are received by each and all, the more will the ministry and witness of the community necessarily display *de facto* as well as *de iure* an integrated multiplicity" (IV/3, 855–856).

44. These include 1 Cor 12:4–31, Rom 12:3–8, and Eph 4:1–16.

The unity and multiplicity of the forms in one body, however, is only found in the "one ministry and witness of the one Son of God and Son of Man" (IV/3, 858). Thus it is as Paul "looks up to this Head that he understands as he does the community, the unity and plurality of its ministry and witness, and the relation of the fellowship to the fellowships, and that he is so certain of the one Spirit and yet also of the multiplicity of His gifts" (IV/3, 859). But the Holy Spirit ensures that the unity of the diverse gifts within the community corresponds to the unity of its head, Jesus Christ. "The Holy Spirit of χάρις with the unity and integration of His χαρίσματα is the Spirit, and only the Spirit, in whom it is known and confessed that Jesus is the *Kyrios* (1 Cor. 12:3). Where this Spirit is and works, there the union arises in which as such freedom rules, and there freedom rules which as such creates union" (IV/3, 859). All that follows, then, in Barth's discussion of the forms of ministry is work of the Holy Spirit enabling the diverse gifts, services, and activities to witness to the reconciliation found in Jesus Christ.[45] This unifying action of the Spirit, bringing together the diversity of gifts, continually fills the time of the church on the way to the eschaton.

CONCLUSION

The creating and preserving of time by the Father and the recapitulating of time by the Son would be incomplete without the ecclesial time of the Spirit. Whereas the Father's work establishes time and history as the place in which the covenant may be enacted, the times of Jesus Christ and His Spirit fill and fulfill creaturely time by rescuing humanity from sinful time and directing the community toward the eschaton. What is more, the times of the Father, Son, and Spirit correspond or are analogous to the life and roles of the triune persons *in se*. In this way, Barth's view of the eternity-time relation may be termed an *analogia trinitaria temporis*.

In this trinitarian narration of time the Holy Spirit is the *vinculum* of contemporaneity, creating the history of the community to correspond and thus participate in Jesus-history. The Holy Spirit, as the self-attestation of Jesus Christ, is the divine power that gathers, builds, and sends the community. The activity that fills the time of the community

---

45. There is occasional mention of the Spirit's work in the discussion of the forms; see IV/3, 861, 871, 888, and 898.

can be summarized as internal and external movements. The internal movement of the community, its being built up, includes its extensive and intensive growth and upholding, illustrated in its being an orderly community. The external movement of the community, its being sent into the world, is also essential to its being. Its task is to proclaim the gospel, God's "Yes" to humanity in Jesus Christ, in a diversity of forms. This diversity of forms are united in their purpose to witness to Jesus Christ, to participate in his prophetic office. The focus for Barth in both internal and external movements is the living Lord who operates in the history of the community by his Holy Spirit. The Holy Spirit continually and dynamically works in each particular time uniting Jesus-history with the history of the community. This action of the Spirit fills ecclesial on the way to the eschaton.

One may be of two minds, however, in judging Barth's view of ecclesial time. First, critically, we can follow up on the concerns discussed in chapter 1. There it was suggested that Barth has an underdeveloped view of the Holy Spirit's agency and he tends toward a disembodied ecclesiology. These issues manifest themselves when gleaning the Spirit's work in ecclesial time. For example, in the subsection "The Time of the Community" there is actually little mention of the Spirit's mediating role, though it is under the rubric of pneumatology. In fact, the central argument of this chapter is most clearly explicated in IV/3, almost hidden way at the end of 72.1, "The People of God in World Occurrence," and the bulk of the material used in this chapter arises from pneumatological sections in IV/2 and IV/3. What this indirect route to Barth's view suggests is that ecclesial time as the time of the Spirit is not a major concern of Barth and therefore is insufficiently developed. What is more, the qualitative character of narrative time seems to be missing. For example, in III/2 Barth provides a sustained discussion of the phenomenon of subjective temporality with both ancient and modern concerns in view. He rethinks the fleetingness of the present and the movement toward death in light of God's preserving of time and the work of the cross. This sort of sustained reflection on ecclesial time is not found in *CD* IV. Perhaps we might say, then, that Barth provides a minimal dogmatic outline of ecclesial time.[46]

46. This lack of a phenomenology of ecclesial time could be a result of Barth's preference for the "invisible presence" over "absence" to describe the heavenly session. It may be argued that with invisible presence there is less need for ecclesial mediation and

Second, despite these concerns, explicating pneumatological time displays the radical contribution that Barth is making in redefining eternity and time. There is much continuity with his previous discussions. As usual, eternity and time are ontologically distinct though asymmetrically and analogically related. And we also see Barth's dynamic view of eternity as the Holy Spirit continuously works to bring communion to that which is different, creating the history of the community corresponding to Jesus-history. This is no abstract philosophical description of eternity but serious attention to the concrete work of God who is not immune to time. So while there is a general argument that Barth's view is incomplete, it seems to be moving the right direction.

---

thus Barth's lack of reflection on the quality of ecclesial time on the way to the eschaton. For a critique of Barth's preference see Farrow, *Ascension and Ecclesia*, 250–54.

Conclusion

WE BEGAN WITH BARTH'S claim that the "theological concept of eternity must be set free from the Babylonian captivity of an abstract opposite to the concept of time" (II/1, 611). This statement captures Barth's basic desire to define the perfection of eternity with reference to the content of the Christian faith. That Barth made strides towards fulfilling this should now be obvious. But how far does Barth take the discussion forward? What, if the basic contours of his thought are followed, remains to be done? What criticisms might be made? In view of what he set out to do, it could be argued that Barth remained faithful to his insights, even adding to them, but still did not fulfill the inherent potential found in the turn to central Christian doctrines for relating eternity and time. Barth's achievements first need to be reviewed, however.

BARTH'S CONTRIBUTIONS

Barth's contribution to the discussion of eternity and time in the western tradition begins with his definition of eternity and follows with the narrative relation between eternity and time. Both of these features suggest the analogical relation of eternity and time. This is to be expected, for as noted in the introduction, there is no proper Christian view of the God-world relation without evidence of analogy in one form of another.[1] Barth identifies eternity as the life of Father, Son, and Spirit. Eternity is not motionless or timeless, but rather divine motion and divine time. This allows Barth to construct a positive relation between eternity and

---

1. Of course, it is not that analogy is an overarching concept that is valid in its own right, but that it is a useful tool in explaining the Christian view of things.

time evinced in the trinitarian pattern of created, recapitulated, and ecclesial time.

The major thinkers in the Christian tradition defined eternity with use of the *via negativa*. For them eternity is defined in its difference from time and nearly always thought of in a negative relation to time. The theological value of the traditional approach, however, is the insistence on maintaining the *ontological distinction* between eternity and time. Eternity is not time, and God is not under the control of time, he does not succumb to the decay and fragility of human temporality. Though he does not end here, Barth in fact affirms this aspect of the traditional discussion. He can state the following, for example: "Time can have nothing to do with God. . . . It is quite correct, as in older theology, to understand the idea of eternity and therefore God Himself in this clear antithesis. In the sense mentioned, it is in fact non-temporality" (II/1, 608). Following this, there is also found in the traditional discussion a notion of the *asymmetrical relation* between eternity and time. Eternity creates and controls time; eternity is the prototype and time the type. There is an element then of a *via positiva* (or *via causalitatus*) in which there is a creative and preserving relation between eternity and time. Again Barth affirms this. Eternity "decides and conditions all beginning, succession and end. It controls them. It is itself that which begins in all beginnings, continues in all successions and ends in all endings" (II/1, 610). But this is where the basic similarities end and the limits of the traditional approach arise. How is there to be a positive relation between eternity and time if eternity is motionless? Is it really coherent to suggest that the living God of Christian scriptures, who creates and acts within time, is timeless?[2]

The advantage of Barth's position is that he actually follows through with the *via triplex*. Not simply content with the ontological distinction (*via negativa*) and the asymmetrical relation (*via positiva*), Barth defines eternity as its own divine time (*via eminentiae*). Eternity, as the ordered, moving, and electing life of Father, Son, and Spirit, is supremely temporal. "And God does not first create multiplicity and movement, but He is one and simple, He is constant, in such a way that all multiplicity and movement have their prototype and pre-existence in Himself. Time, too, pre-exists in this way in Him, in His eternity, as His creation" (II/1, 612). Because of this, there is a positive and truly analogous relation

---

2. See Heron, "The Time of God," 231–239.

between eternity and time.³ Traditional views, under the influence of Greek thought, did not follow through by defining eternity in such a way. For Barth eternity is the true prototype of the succession and movement of created time—and thus the analogous relation between eternity and time. Demonstrating Barth's struggle for and articulation of this was one of the main aims of Part I of the book.

Yet the varied discussions throughout the *Church Dogmatics* move beyond this merely formal depiction of the eternity-time relation. Barth not only defines eternity as pure duration—the simultaneity of beginning, middle, and end—but also assimilates temporality within the contours of his dogmatic concerns. Thus the discussion of time takes on more of a material or narrative form as the *CD* proceeds along the creedal lines of creation, reconciliation, and redemption. With the help of Ricoeur it was argued that time is best understood in relation to narrative, time is "for" or "of" particular activity that is directed toward an end. Time is not merely understood quantitatively but also qualitatively since the experience of time changes depending on the relations and ends occurring within it. Similarly for Barth, created time is not simply the flow of past, present, and future but the opportunity for covenantal relation with God and fellow humanity. And despite the fact that created time becomes fallen time, God faithfully preserves the creature in their time in order to provide an opportunity to respond to fulfilled or gracious time. This fulfilled or gracious time, as it is termed in III/1, is expanded in later discussions to include the recapitulation of time by the Son and the work of the Holy Spirit in the time of the community.

That Barth had in mind such a full narrative, even in *CD* II/1, is evinced in his description of eternity as pretemporality, supratemporality, and posttemporality (619–40). The breadth of this threefold division suggests that time and history are enclosed within eternity, as God lives before time, accompanies time, and will live after time has run its course. God prepares for time, especially in the election of Jesus Christ

---

3. The distinction between univocal, equivocal, and analogous language and relations corresponds to the distinction between the *via positiva, via negativa,* and *via eminentiae*. In Thomas Aquinas, for example, the *via positiva* undergirds the discussion of univocity, the *via negativa* the equivocal, and the *via eminentiae* the final defense of analogy. Because God's being contains a divine temporality as eternity (*via eminentiae*) then the relation between eternity and time is analogous. The concerns of the ontological distinction (equivocacy, *via negativa*) and asymmetrical relation (univocity, *via positiva*) are maintained and strengthened.

to become incarnate, enacts his will by creating and preserving time, enters time in Jesus Christ, and will complete time in the eschaton. Although not expounded in II/1, there is also brief mention of the idea that general world history finds its meaning in Israel and the Church (II/1, 623–25).

This threefold division, moreover, is decisively christocentric. In the discussion of pretemporality the election of Jesus Christ to become incarnate is the true purpose of God's "pre-time": "For this pre-time is the pure time of the Father and the Son in the fellowship of the Holy Spirit. And in this pure divine time there took place the appointment of the eternal Son for the temporal world, there occurred the readiness of the Son to do the will of the eternal Father, and there ruled the peace of the eternal Spirit—the very thing later revealed at the heart of created time in Jesus Christ. In this pure divine time there took place that free display of the divine grace and mercy and patience, that free resolve to which time owes its existence, its content and its goal" (II/1, 622). What is more, when supratemporality is discussed the focus is on Jesus Christ as the turning point between the past and the future, between sin and salvation. In him the past of death and sin is overcome, while the future of life and salvation is open (II/1, 626–629). Here Barth seems to be thinking of the fleetingness of the present in the flux of time and not history itself—as becomes the case in III/2 and IV/1. Nevertheless, the contemporaneity of Jesus Christ is the focal point.[4] This Christological focus remains in the highly developed discussions of later volumes, which has been illustrated under the rubric of anticipation and recapitulation.

What is missing in *CD* II/1, however, is mention of the Holy Spirit and time and any substantial discussion of posttemporality. In discussing posttemporality, for example, there is little content to indicate what Barth actually means by this; the small print section, for example, is a discussion of the historical relation between pre, supra, and posttemporality from the Reformers, through Protestant Liberalism, into the modern focus on eschatology—including Barth's own work in *Romans*. The point Barth is making is that the three forms of God's eternity need to be thought of together, as one is not to be favored over another (II/1, 640). As noted in chapter 4, minimal content is given to posttemporality later in the *Dogmatics*, though this is not without problems. This, along with the neglect of the Holy Spirit, will be discussed below. Nevertheless,

---

4. See Hunsinger, "*Mysterium Trinitatis*," 203–5.

at the end of his discussion of eternity in *CD* II/1 Barth states that in "the future course of dogmatics we shall often have occasion to think of both the distinction and the unity in God's eternity" (II/1, 640). The return to the theme of eternity and time throughout *CD* III and IV was the focus of Part II of the book "Barth's *Analogia Trinitaria Temporis*."

The first locus of this interpretation is the Father's work in creating and preserving time. Examining pertinent sections of III/1–III/3, chapter 3 outlined Barth's view of time as the theatre for covenantal activity and relations. Time is a fundamental structure of human existence, a gift meant to enable covenantal relations with God and other humans. Barth's favorite forms of time, rational-linear time and allotted time, are understood in this way. There is also evidence in his exegesis of Genesis 1 that Barth understood human temporality within the context of cosmic and natural times, though this is not thoroughly explicated. In the doctrine of providence Barth takes care to articulate God's preserving of time in order that covenantal activity may take place. The creating and preserving of time are analogous to the Father's role as origin in the divine life and reflect his goodness and patience. Humanity rejects the true purpose of time, however, and the forms of time are filled anew with sinful activity. Following Augustine, Barth expresses the fleetingness of the present "now" as a source of anxiety rather than opportunity, and, following Heidegger, the movement toward death elicits fear and not the hope of eternal life. Despite this sinful time, God preserves creatures in their time and the passage of time may become a possibility for fellowship and the movement toward death may be filled with hope. This is only possible, however, since God responds to fallen time with fulfilled or gracious time, begun in Israel and revealed in Jesus Christ and the church. There is, then, a new time of reconciliation. This fulfilled or gracious time is examined in the following two chapters.

The second and central locus of Barth's analogy between eternity and time is Christology. Within the triune life the Father generates the Son, and with the Son gives the Spirit. In God's pretemporality, moreover, the Son was elected to be the reconciler between God and humanity. Thus the fulfilling of time by the Son is analogous to his role within the immanent Trinity and his election to become incarnate. The relation of Jesus Christ and time was expounded with the conceptual use of anticipation and recapitulation. For Barth, the fulfillment of time by the Son is anticipated in pretemporal eternity, created time, and the history of Israel. It also recapitulates all times by retrieving the true purpose of created time and by redirecting all times toward their eschatological fulfillment. The redirecting of time includes the various episodes of Jesus-history: pre-Easter life, resurrection and forty days, ascension and intercession, and the final return in glory. There was concern expressed in reference to Easter time, since Barth's description of it sometimes suggests the fulfillment of eternity in time—though this becomes tempered throughout his discussion. There were also some questions concerning eschatology and time, which are addressed below. What becomes clear, however, is that Jesus-history is definitive for the full breadth of God's pretemporal, supratemporal, and posttemporal activity and life.

The third locus of this interpretation is the ecclesial time of the Holy Spirit. The work of the eternal Spirit in time and history complements the creation of time by the Father and the recapitulating of time by the incarnate Son. Ecclesial time, the history of believers in the middle time, beginning with the ascension and ending with the eschaton, is the time of the Holy Spirit awakening believers to the new reality found in Jesus-history. As the self-attestation of the Son, the Spirit awakens believers to the fact that their histories are enclosed within and correspond to the history of Jesus Christ and that he is their contemporary. The Spirit's work in ecclesial time was summarized with reference to the internal and external movements of the community. Internally, the Spirit gathers and builds up the community, while externally sends it into the world. Within these movements the Holy Spirit's temporal work was characterized as continuous, dynamic, particular, and unifying. In this way, Barth presents the eternal Spirit as the bond of contemporaneity. The Spirit's work in ecclesial time is analogous to his eternal role as the bond between the Father and the Son. Just as he is the mediator and bond of eternal life so he is the mediator and bond of salvific contemporaneity. The appropriation of ecclesial time to the Holy Spirit, however, is the most contentious appropriation that the present interpretation makes. As will be discussed below, this locus of the interpretation is least explicit in Barth and leaves one wanting more in terms of describing ecclesial time.

Nevertheless, Barth's *analogia trinitaria temporis* can be summarized as follows. God's triune being is the perichoretic, differentiating, and electing life of Father, Son, and Spirit. This life contains its own movement, its own time, which is eternity. This dynamic eternity is the primary analogate of created time, which is the secondary analogate.

Eternity's creation of and work within time reiterates or corresponds to this triune life. This is reflected in the creation of time by the Father, the recapitulating of time by the incarnate Son, and the creation of ecclesial time by the Spirit. In this way, there is an analogy between eternity and time in Barth's theology.

This trinitarian interpretation of the analogy between eternity and time supplements well studies of eternity that have noted the importance of Barth's trinitarianism and christocentrism. Given the focus on *CD* III and IV, this project seems to have uncovered something of the full breadth of Barth's conceptualization of this important theme; this is the main contribution of the project. While it does not examine all the discussions of temporality in the *CD* it does provide a stable hypothesis that may be tested in other places of Barth's *oeuvre*.[5] It seems fair to conclude that he does not reintroduce atemporality into his theological construction; both the triune movement of God *in se* and his gracious movement toward the creature *ad extra* are central for his view of eternity. It is safe to say, then, that in Barth there is no "grin of the timeless cat,"[6] and certainly no "cancerous *Doppelgänger* ... perfecting in exquisite form what could be seen as the most profound and systematically consistent theological alienation [sic] of the natural order ever achieved."[7] Rather, for Barth, God creates and sustains the creature in time, while reconciling humanity to himself in the recapitulating time of Jesus Christ, which includes human participation by the Spirit in the time of the community.

Given the parameters of this study, moreover, there are still historical and genetic questions that may be more fully examined. In the first place, the relation of Barth's view in the *CD* to his earlier work in *Romans*, *The Göttingen Dogmatics*, and *Die christliche Dogmatik im Entwurf*, may be more fully explored as some of these connections were only briefly noted. This would also help discern Barth's connection to his theological predecessors on this issue. For example, in the small print discussion under posttemporality in II/1 (631–38) Barth gives something of biographical reflection on his relation to eschatological thought since the Reformation. He suggests, for example, his eschatological turn

---

5. Various discussions have been passed over, for example: I/2, 45–121; III/4, 372–73, 569–94; and IV/3.1, 165–274.

6. Jenson, *God after God*, 154.

7. Roberts, "Karl Barth's Doctrine of Time: Its Nature and Implications," 124.

in connection with the elder Blumhardt and Franz Overbeck (634–38). A full genealogy of eternity and time in Barth would have to take these and other sources into consideration, even while noting Barth's attempt for a more balanced treatment of pretemporality, supratemporality, and posttemporality in the *CD*.

Another avenue worth exploring is comparing Barth with predecessors he does not mention as influencing him. Take Hegel for example.[8] A key element in Barth's view of eternity is God's livingness and self-movement. How does this conceptually relate to the idea of movement in Hegel's philosophy and philosophy of religion? Barth states at the end of his chapter on Hegel in *Protestant Theology in the Nineteenth Century* that in Hegel there is "a great problem and a great disappointment, but perhaps also a great promise."[9] The problem and disappointment for Barth centers on Hegel's failure to recognize the freedom of God, which led to the collapsing of God into human reason and reducing doctrines such as sin and reconciliation into necessary stages of the dialectical movement of human thinking toward truth.[10] Yet wherein lays the promise? Surely it is not within Hegel's view of humanity's confidence in reason, the subject of the first two points of Barth's chapter. But perhaps it is that Hegel viewed God as *living*. While Hegel's living God was in fact "the living man," Barth also argues that Hegel "saw God's aliveness well, and saw it better than many theologians."[11] How is the livingness of God found in Barth related to similar ideas in Hegel, despite the obvious differences? This seems to be worthy of further exploration.

TOWARD A TRINITARIAN THEOLOGY OF ETERNITY AND TIME: LACUNAE AND CRITICISM

It should be obvious that the basic contours of Barth's *analogia trinitaria temporis* provide a fertile ground from which to construct a theology of eternity and time. This much should be clear from the interpretation that has been presented. Yet despite the possibilities arising from Barth's discussions, there are still lacunae to fill and problems to be overcome if a fuller theology of eternity and time is to be realized. Two lacunae and

---

8. One may also include Hegel's university roommate Friedrich Schelling, who also articulated a trinitarian pattern of times; see Jüngel, *God's Being is in Becoming*, 29 nt57.

9. Barth, *Protestant Theology in the Nineteenth Century*, 407.

10. Ibid., 403–5.

11. Ibid., 405.

two basic criticisms will be noted. Of course, the constructive opinions that follow remain on the level of suggestions and conjectures.

The benefits of Barth's view for a contemporary theology of eternity and time deserve brief summary. In the first place, Barth defines eternity, even when using formal categories such as pure duration and *simul*, with reference to the triunity of God. The perfection of eternity, like all of the perfections, is commentary on the living God and is not merely defined in abstraction from time. Second, a Christian theology of time ought to evince some form of the trinitarian pattern of times. For Barth, this includes the Father's creating and preserving of time, the incarnate Son's entering time, and the Spirit's work among and in humanity as they come to participate in salvation. This takes account of the appropriations necessary to God's trinitarian work.[12] Third, Barth understands time to be for covenantal relations. He does not merely describe time as the flow of past, present, and future or as allotted time, but understands these *Existenzformen* as foundational for relations with God and fellow humanity. This understanding of time falls within what Paul Ricoeur describes as narrative time. In Barth's view, the narrative of God's creating, reconciling, and redeeming the creature dictates how time is understood. Following Barth, a Christian theology of eternity and time would reject a merely quantitative and formal description of time since God creates time with a distinct purpose. Fourth, within Barth's view non-theological forms of time are incorporated. While Barth has sometimes been criticized for not dialoging with other disciplines it ought to be clear that his theology of time incorporates both ancient and modern discussions of time with a fair degree of ease and creativity. As noted in the introduction, Ingolf Dalferth argues that Barth includes both internal (theological) and external (non-theological) components in his dogmatic construction, while the former always takes priority.[13] One strength of Barth's approach is the ability to read different views of time within his theological ontology.

Fifth, underlying these positive contributions of Barth is a methodological shift. Barth may be compared with analytical philosophy of religion on this point. In the past few decades the debate in this field has centered on whether or not God is atemporal. Some continue to defend

---

12. Welker makes suggestions along these lines in "God's Eternity, God's Temporality, and Trinitarian Theology."

13. Dalferth, *Theology and Philosophy*, 121–24.

a view of eternity as timelessness, while the majority of scholars seek to articulate some form of temporality. Within the latter group, this ranges from those who seem to collapse eternity into time to those who support some form of interventionism—God is timeless but occasionally acts within time. While a fuller engagement with this range of opinion is well beyond this project, the following methodological difference should be noted. From what can be gathered, the search for a coherent view of eternity and time in analytical philosophy has not sufficiently taken account of the fecundity of Christian belief. That is, the doctrines of the Trinity and incarnation, for example, are not given the centrality they deserve. There is often a basic assumption by those defending some form of divine temporality that God acts in history and thus is not atemporal, but the dynamic movement of the triune life *in se* is not exploited. It is even suggested that eternity cannot be measured.[14] It may be argued, however, that the best platform from which to develop an argument for divine temporality is the life and movement of the divine persons *in se* and *ad extra*. While eternity is not the movement of created time itself and is ontologically distinct from time, such a dynamic definition of eternity can be viewed as the true basis of created time. God's eternity can be "measured" if described in trinitarian terms.[15] It seems that the contemporary analytical discussion has not moved from the *via positiva* and *via negativa* into a *via eminentiae*. While there are analytical defenses of God's creation of and action within time (*via positiva*), there is less discussion of how God's being contains it own time (*via eminentiae*). Christian philosophers working on this theme might take note of this methodological distinction in Barth's view.

Despite these positive contributions, there are still concerns with Barth's position that need to be addressed. These issues are not concerned with the fundamental method or outline of Barth's position but seek to correct his position from within. Taking heed of these concerns could aid in moving toward a fuller theology of eternity and time. There are two lacunae and two points of criticism that need mention.

---

14. As Padgett states, God's "time (eternity) is infinite and immeasurable," *God, Eternity and the Nature of Time*, 2; see 126–127 as well.

15. See Heron, "The Time of God." Analytical philosopher of religion Brian Lefthow notes the applicability of temporal predicates to God's eternity as well; see "Response to 'Mysterium Trinitatis,'" 196–201.

The first lacuna is the failure of Barth to explicitly reflect on the nature of time as such. While Barth takes temporality as a major preoccupation in the *CD*, he more or less assumes popular notions of time without critically reflecting on them. For example, as pointed out in chapters 3 and 4, while Barth suggests that human temporality is embedded within the time of the cosmos he does not systematically reflect on this. It has been suggested that Barth's ambiguity toward eschatological time may have been avoided by reflecting on the relation of subjective and objective times more systematically.[16] In Barth's defense, it may be noted that the discussions of temporality in *CD* III and IV are located within larger dogmatic concerns, thus temporality is not always the direction subject of investigation. Nevertheless, anyone wishing to theologize on eternity and time would do well to reflect on the nature and plurality of time, even while subjugating such reflection to dogmatic concerns.[17]

Closely following this, a second lacuna is incorporating notions of time from modern science. If non-theological forms of time are readily incorporated by Barth, then it would be reasonable to follow this through with the inclusion of scientific views of time. For, as Barth wrote on the relation of theology and science in the preface of III/1, "future workers in the field of the Christian doctrine of creation will find many

---

16. Although not without problems, Achtner, et al., in *Dimensions of Time* make an attempt to integrate endogenous and exogenous times, though they do not set the discussions of time under an overarching narrative of God's work to the degree Barth does.

17. Not surprisingly, theologians incorporate discussions of time into theological ontology in differing degrees. Welker calls for a trinitarian pattern in understanding time, though he makes less use of the immanent Trinity to define eternity than does Barth; see "God's Eternity, God's Temporality, and Trinitarian Theology." Moltmann understands well the fulfilling of time in eschatological existence (see *The Coming of God*, 279–95, and *Science and Wisdom*, 98–110), but is less inclined to speak of God's eternal life *in se* as temporal, though he does suggest that God is spacious in his perichoretic life (*Science and Wisdom*, 117–18). Moltmann also seems to favour posttemporality over pretemporality and supratemporality. Polkinghorne was also positively cited for his articulation of an eschatological understanding of time. Yet his view of eternity is dipolar (similar to process theology), in that God is both atemporal and temporal (*Science and the Trinity*, 104–10). This fails to take up God's trinitarian life *in se* to the degree necessary. In her wide-ranging work *Time & Eternity*, Jackelén summarizes well various discussions of time, recognizing the importance of narrative, relationality, and eschatology. Yet there is no controlling theological ontology or narrative to guide the discussion. Thus the need of placing various understandings of time into a theological framework is evident in contemporary theology.

problems worth pondering in defining the point and manner of this twofold boundary"(x).[18] There are two basic discussions that could be taken up.

First, there is the deep time of cosmic and biological evolution. It is standard scientific opinion that the universe is over 13 billion years old, our planet around 4.5 billion years old, and life itself around 3.8 billion. It is assumed that creation and its creatures have gradually evolved over this time. A Christian theology of time could incorporate these developments.[19] In the first place, as noted in chapter 3, Barth views the Genesis narratives of creation as saga. They are neither timeless myth nor are they literal descriptions of what occurred with creation. Though they do refer to the actual creation of the universe and time by God, they do not provide a scientific description of the time of creation in the modern sense. In other words, they suggest *that* God created the world with and in time and not *how* he did so. Following this, it may be argued that notions of deep time can be subjugated within a doctrine of creation and preservation. For Barth, creation is the initial direct act of God to bring the world and time into existence, while in providence God indirectly preserves that which has been created. While a Christian doctrine of creation and providence would need to critique materialist presuppositions found in evolutionary theory, there is room to subsume basic claims of evolutionary theory. For example, evolutionary science

18. There seem to be a number of reasons for Barth's hesitancy in dealing with the natural sciences. In the first place, Barth admitted that he did not possess the training and skill in mathematics in order to dialogue with science. (He admitted this to Torrance in their last conversation; see Torrance, *Karl Barth*, 135). Second, methodologically, he assumes the autonomy and neutrality of academic disciplines. Each discipline has an object of its own and there is no apparent need for dialogue with other disciplines (see III/2, 198–202). Barth's point is that biology, ethics, existentialism, and theistic anthropology do not have knowledge of real humanity, as known through Jesus Christ—though he does insist these disciplines have their own genuine knowledge). Third, Barth assumes the supremacy of theology in relation to other disciplines. Theology goes beyond any other science because it provides the true meaning for human existence—this is the thrust of § 44 (III/2). It may be argued, however, that these concerns may be insufficient since Barth in fact does incorporate non-theological thought into his *Dogmatics*—though giving them secondary importance in relation to theological loci.

19. For examples of how theists have incorporated deep time see Peters and Hewlett, *Evolution from Creation to New Creation*, especially chapters 6 and 7. Unfortunately, there is a tendency in the dialogue between theology and science to displace the dogmatic distinctions of creation and preservation that would help place deep time theologically.

has demonstrated that time began at a distinct and distant point in the past and that life has gradually evolved over long periods of time. Such claims are commensurate with *creatio ex nihilo* and God's preserving of time, and may be subsumed under these doctrines. The major break that would have to be made with Barth's view is that there needs to be some form of continuing creation to account for evolution, whereas Barth only views creation as the initial and direct act of God.[20]

A second issue with time in modern science is the discovery of the space-time continuum in relativity theory. Here there is a move away from the Newtonian view of absolute space and time to a relative view in which space, time, energy, and matter are fundamentally related.[21] This discovery of time may seem to be less a threat than notions of deep time, which challenged traditional opinions on the age of the cosmos and life. Yet it may also be argued that different notions of time are more commensurate with Christian theology than others. In other words, neutrality in relation to scientific notions of space and time is not favorable to critical dialogue.

The work of one of Barth's ablest students illustrates this. Like Barth, Thomas Torrance argues that the purpose of Christian theology, like any other science, is rational engagement with the object of its inquiry: the revelation of God in Jesus Christ. For this reason it is improper both for theology to take up the rational methods of other disciplines and for other disciplines to critique theology from the "outside."[22] Unlike Barth,

---

20. For an example of such an attempt see Pannenberg, *Systematic Theology*, Vol 2, esp. 118–36.

21. It might be noted that some traditional assumptions about time are still applicable in relation to relative time. The time of relativity is still unidirectional and thus the modes of past, present, and future are still applicable—not only in a particular frame of reference but also in comparing different frames of reference. The major difference is that there is no universal "now" of absolute time which all times relate to. The reference point in comparing different time frames is the constant of the speed of light as opposed to an absolute now. In everyday experience, moreover, the relativity of time is not observable as it can only be noticed when approaching the speed of light. What is more, the notions of endogenous and exogenous time are still relevant as well as the rational-linear and duration definitions.

22. This is a focus of *Theological Science*, where he compares theological method with that of other academic disciplines. Torrance argues that all scientific activity is committed to the object of its inquiry and that the methods of each discipline are tied to their respective objects. On the independence of each science he writes: "A dogmatic science of this kind, whether it be in physics or theology, will not allow another department of knowledge working in quite a different field to dictate to it on its own

however, Torrance makes a significant attempt to draw out the methodological and epistemological similarities and dissimilarities between theology and the other disciplines.[23] This posture also enables him to critically engage with scientific discussions of space and time. His first major attempt at this was *Space, Time and Incarnation*.[24] In this brief work, which actually focuses more on the concept of space, Torrance argues that the central doctrines of creation and incarnation are more commensurate with a relational view of the space-time continuum than with receptacle notions of space.[25] In fact, he argues that the receptacle concept of space, from Aristotle to Newton, has led to dualistic thinking on the God-world relation, thus making a doctrine such as the incarnation difficult to articulate. Christian theology, then, must think of the incarnation as the central place to construct the God-world relation and thus reject the receptacle notion of space in favor for a relational view. In *Divine and Contingent Order* he takes up again space-time concepts and makes a similar argument. In particular, he finds Newton's concept of absolute space and time wanting in that it gives rise to a dualist separation of God and creation. This basic deism with its closed mechanistic view of space and time contributed, in Torrance's opinion, to Newton's own Arianism.[26] Yet Torrance reserves a positive assessment for the work of

---

ground, either in prescribing its methods or in predetermining its results—that would be the bad sort of dogmatizing which unfortunately theology encounters today not infrequently from the side of 'scientism' and from some philosophical empiricists" (*Theological Science*, 341).

23. *Theological Science* not only dialogues with the philosophy of science and western philosophy but is also indebted to Karl Barth's theological epistemology as found in *CD* II/1. *Theological Science*, unfortunately, was published in 1969, one year after the death of Barth, thus Barth himself was not able to comment on the work. Torrance does recall from their last conversation, however, that Barth did allow for parallels between his method and other sciences; see *Karl Barth*, 129–130.

24. The follow-up to this work, *Space, Time and Resurrection*, was originally intended to take up the concept of time in scientific and philosophic discourse and relate it to the resurrection of Jesus Christ. *Space, Time and Resurrection*, however, discusses the resurrection in biblical and theological terms.

25. The receptacle notion of space refers to the idea that space is a container that controls matter within it. Often space is considered closed and finite. The relational notion of space, however, suggests that space, time, and matter are interrelated and affect one another, as in modern relativity theory.

26. Torrance summarizes the effects of Newton's views in the following way: "Behind all that development, however, and fostering it, lay a contradiction in Newton's theology, between his concept of God as an inertial power, detached in his absoluteness,

Einstein and modern physics.[27] What this implies is that the movement from an absolute view of space and time to the relative and relational view is commensurate with Christian belief: "the basic ideas of classical Christian theology as to the relation between God and the universe are emancipated, as it were, from the constrictions of a dualistic outlook in which a god of inertial motion and a determinate universe governed by necessary relations are correlated with each other."[28]

The point here is not whether Torrance's reading of classical and contemporary physics is correct,[29] but to suggest that in contrast to Barth Torrance advances a critical and constructive stance toward scientific views of space and time. Torrance argues that time in relativity theory is more commensurate with central Christian doctrines than classical notions. Following such a procedure, it would seem quite possible for

and his concept of God's role within the mechanistic or causal system of the world. The fall away of the latter left Western thought geared to a massive deism, in which God cannot be thought of as interacting with the universe he has made without interfering in its natural operations, which ruled out any idea of miracle as some unacceptable suspension of natural law" (*Divine and Contingent Order*, 10).

27. He summarizes the difference in contemporary physics with the following: "Everything changes, however, when space is no longer regarded as empty but filled with matter and energy, and when time enters effectively into the equation as an inalienable ingredient in the intervening relations between particles or events affecting their configuration—that is, when all absolutes fall away, and space and time are no longer regarded as empty of unvarying containers but as relations intrinsic to the ongoing contingent processes of the universe, so that particles or events are to be regarded as spatially and temporally extended and not as simply contained in space and time. And the change is deeper still when the concept of space-time is introduced, and thus the continuous, dynamic metrical field, with a reciprocal action between it and the constituent matter and energy of the universe, unifying and ordering everything within it.... [This view eliminated] the damaging dualism in Newtonian physics, replacing its rigid absolutes in the foundations of science with a more profoundly objective, unitary dynamic relatedness inherent in the structure of the universe, invariant for any and every observer, but which cannot be constructed in terms of a closed axiomatic framework" (ibid., 13, see 14 and 35 as well).

28. Ibid., 21.

29. For an appreciative exposition of Torrance's view of natural theology and dialogue with science see Part Two of McGrath, *Thomas F. Torrance*, esp. chapters 8 and 9. For some criticism of Torrance's scientific appropriations see Polkinghorne, *Faith, Science and Understanding*, 173–80. It should be noted however that Polkinghorne applauds Torrance's assumption that theology and the other sciences are to be methodologically and epistemologically controlled by their particular objects, Torrance's emphasis on relational space-time, and the focus on the incarnation as the place for Christian theology to begin the dialogue with scientific cosmologies (181–85).

theologians to dialogue with scientific notions of time—whether from cosmology, biology, or physics. The strength of Torrance's method is the ability to prioritize dogmatic concerns and subjugate scientific notions of time to these. Thus, if one keeps in mind the specifically theological definition of eternity, with reference to the triune God, and the full breadth of God's work within the economy of salvation, then dialogue with time in modern science turns out to be quite fruitful, even necessary.

As for more direct criticisms of what Barth actually presents, the issues of pneumatology and time and eschatological time need to be noted. A fuller trinitarian view of the eternity-time relation ought to develop these themes more fully than what Barth himself presents. It should be clear from the last chapter that Barth has a pneumatologically underdeveloped view of time. While the discussions of eternity and time in CD II/1, as well as CD III and IV, are christologically concentrated they do not contain a robust explication of the Holy Spirit and time. For example, Barth scarcely mentions the work of the Spirit in 62.3, "The Time of the Community" (IV/1), though in fact this subsection is found under pneumatology. Therefore, in the last chapter other pneumatological sections of CD IV had to be mined in order to piece together the connection between the Holy Spirit and ecclesial time. If one locus of the present interpretation can be accused of "reading into" or of being overly favorable to Barth it would be the last chapter.

What Barth actually does say on the Spirit and time seems to be a fruitful dogmatic basis from which to begin reflections, however. For example, in III/2 Barth presents a sustained phenomenological discussion on human temporality that accounts for the anxiety experienced in light of time's fleetingness and the movement toward death. This experience is recast in light of God's preserving presence and his work on the cross so that time is experienced as a possibility for fellowship and the movement toward death with hope. There is a full description of how the subjective experience of time may be transformed from anxiety and fear to hope and possibility. As for ecclesial time, Barth has been interpreted as saying that the Holy Spirit is the bond between Jesus-history and the history of the community, as the Spirit continuously mediates Christ's presence to the particular and diverse times of believers. While this is a solid beginning, the discussions in CD IV do not suggest how the fragility and weakness of the time of the community is transformed by the work of the Spirit into stability and strength. While Barth does this earlier in the *Dogmatics* for the time of individual, this is not followed through with the time of the community. But this may have been a possibility. Barth, for example, provides a comprehensive list of the activities that fill the time of the community, which are the work of the Holy Spirit in contemporizing the presence of the ascended and risen Lord. These include forms of speech and forms of action (IV/3, 865–901). But the next step is to ask how the experience of time within the community is transformed through these practices. It has been argued throughout that a proper understanding of time suggests that time is for covenantal relations. Following this, the activity and relations that occur within time dictate and control the *quality* of time. As Michael Welker suggests, a pneumatological view of time is not merely a time filled with spiritual and liturgical practices but a time that transforms human life through these practices.[30] It is not that Barth views the time of the community as void of the Spirit's work in ecclesial practice, but that the connection between these practices and the transformative and qualitative nature of ecclesial time is neglected. Therefore, a trinitarian account of the relation of eternity and time ought to include a more robust account of the Spirit's work in ecclesial time.[31]

---

30. Drawing on the work of biblical scholar Miller, Welker describes this time of the Spirit with reference to spiritual practice, worship, and liturgy: "God does not simply want to dispose of and dominate creatures. God looks for a living relation to the creatures, a relation in which God is again and again invoked, persuaded, assailed and praised, asked in prayer, and glorified. In searching for and asking for God's living presence, but also in the experience of this presence, we come up with a third form of time, which, however, does not gain clear religious forms of expression without historical memory and cultic continuity. I would like to term this temporal form *the complex of salvific kairological times*" (Welker, "God's Eternity, God's Temporality, and Trinitarian Theology," 326). On this as a transformative time of the Spirit he writes: "Through the activity of the Spirit, certain constellations of creatures are again and again torn from certain constancies and historical processes of development in corrective and healing manners. Through the Spirit, the historical times do not only become *kairoi*, fruitful and fulfilled times. Through the Spirit, God's creative powers are mediated and become known as saving and renewing powers that, without interruption, act upon and through creatures. Life, which seemed destined to perish, is renewed.... Through the *overcoming power of the renewing and reviving times* of the Spirit, creatures participate in God's eternal life; they are drawn into and become involved in this life" (ibid.).

31. For example, how does ecclesial time give hope to believers? How does ecclesial time become a time of strength through spiritual practise and liturgy? How does ecclesial time alter the posture of the church in relation to the world in the middle time? How is the time of the community an anticipation of final eschatological time? Such questions could be asked and attempts to answer them could be made within a

It might be noted that this deeper connection between the Holy Spirit and time was not found at the beginning of Barth's discussion in *CD* II/1 either. While Barth was able to supplement the discussion of II/1 by adding the creation and preservation of time by the Father, there is less development on the Holy Spirit and time. It is difficult to assess why this is left underdeveloped. Perhaps Barth did not see the importance of thinking of ecclesial time in such a transformative way. Yet the fact that Barth spent such effort with phenomenological description in *CD* III/2 suggests he was aware that time takes on qualitative dimensions. It is more likely that the problem is symptomatic of Barth's pneumatology in general. It was noted in chapter 1 that the problems of Barth's pneumatology might not necessarily arise from the *filioque* but from a lack of exegesis and consideration of the Spirit in general. It may simply be the case that Barth's pneumatology suffers from what Colin Gunton described as "the under-determination of the person of the Holy Spirit in almost all areas of dogmatics," which he suggested is endemic to western theology in general.[32] Whatever the answer, it is still the case that Barth's pneumatology provides a basic dogmatic outline from which a fuller account of ecclesial time may begin.

Lastly, there were also some questions concerning Barth's brief treatment of time in the eschaton. In *CD* III/3, he seems to suggest that time as the *Existenzform* of the creature is done away with. It was argued that this might be a result of his tendency toward "creational entropy." It was also suggested that if Barth had thought through more thoroughly the relation of subjective and objective time (his focus is nearly always on creaturely temporality) then the dissolution of creaturely time in the eschaton would have implied too much discontinuity between the present state of creation and the new creation to come. A fuller account of the eternity-time relation would need to include an account of eschatological temporality. If eschatological existence is eternal *life* then this must include some form of activity and thus some form of time. If relations and activity only occur in and with time, as Barth suggests, then

---

more robust view of ecclesial time. For some of these connections, especially in relation to public time, see Rashkover and Pecknold eds. *Liturgy, Time, and the Politics of Redemption*. See for example Bader-Saye, "Figuring Time: Providence and Politics"; and Pecknold, "Liturgy, Time, and the Politics of Redemption."

32. Gunton, *Theology through the Theologians*, 86.

the eschatological fulfillment of God's relationship with his creatures ought to include some form of temporality.

Nevertheless, these criticisms aside, Barth's theology of eternity and time provides excellent moorings from which to construct a contemporary view. He allows the central doctrines of the Trinity and incarnation to guide the definition of eternity and its relation to time. In God's pre-temporal life the Son was elected to take up his particular history. Jesus-history and its fulfilling of time is the true basis of the initial creating and preserving of time by the Father and the foundation for the Spirit's work in ecclesial time. The Son's fulfilling of time is the true purpose of all time and history as they will be completed in the eschaton. Thinking about the nature of time itself, including important notions of time in modern science, as well as a more robust reflection on the Spirit's work in ecclesial time and corrections to eschatological time could only add to the strengths of Barth's foundations. The basic strength of Barth's view is that he has a *Christian* doctrine of eternity and its relation to time. He insists that one must think and speak of this important attribute only on the basis of who God has revealed himself to be in the gospel of Jesus Christ: the electing, perichoretic, and differentiated life of Father, Son, and Spirit. Such a thoroughly *theological* perspective would definitely aid a contemporary articulation of eternity and its relation to time.

Bibliography

Achtner, Wolfgang, Stephan Kunz and Thomas Walter. *Dimensions of Time: The Structures of the Time of Humans, of the World, and of God.* Grand Rapids: Eerdmans, 2002.
Aquinas, Thomas. *Summa Contra Gentiles.* Translated with introduction and notes by Anton Pegis. London and Notre Dame: University of Notre Dame Press, 1975.
———. *Summa Theologica.* Trans. by the Fathers of the English Dominican Province. London: Burns, Oats & Washbourne, 1941.
Aristotle. *The Basic Works of Aristotle.* Edited with an introduction by Richard McKeon. New York: Random House, 1941.
Augustine. *The Confessions of Saint Augustine.* Translated with an introduction and notes by John K. Ryan. New York: Doubleday, 1960.
———. *Concerning the The City of God against the Pagans.* Translated by Henry Bettenson. London and New York: Penguin Books, 1972.
———. *The Trinity.* Translation with an introduction and notes by Edmund Hill. New York: New City Press, 1991.
Badcock, Gary. *Light of Truth and Fire of Love: A Theology of the Holy Spirit.* Grand Rapids: Eerdmans, 1997.
Bader-Saye, Scott. "Figuring Time: Providence and Politics" in *Liturgy, Time, and the Politics of Redemption.* Editors Randi Rashkover and C.C. Pecknold. Grand Rapids and Cambridge: Eerdmans, 2006: 91–111.
Balthasar, Hans Urs von. *The Theology of Karl Barth: Exposition and Interpretation.* Translated by Edward Oakes. San Francisco: Ignatius Press, 1992.
Barth, Karl. *Church Dogmatics,* volumes 1-14. Eds. Geoffrey Bromiley and Thomas Torrance. Trans. by Geoffrey Bromiley et al. Edinburgh: T & T Clark, 1956–1975.
———. *Dogmatics in Outline.* Trans. by G. T. Thompson. New York: Harper & Row, 1959.
———. *Credo.* Trans. with a foreword by Robert McAfee Brown. New York: Charles Scribner's Sons, 1962.
———. *The Epistle to the Romans.* Trans. from the 6th Edition by Edwyn Hoskyns. Oxford and New York: Oxford University Press, 1968.
———. *The Göttingen Dogmatics: Instruction in the Christian Religion, Vol 1.* Edited by Hannelotte Reiffen. Trans. Geoffrey Bromiley. Grand Rapids: Eerdmanns, 1991.
———. *Protestant Theology in the Nineteenth Century.* New Edition. Trans. Brian Cozens and John Bowden. Grand Rapids: Eerdmans, 2002.
Basil of Caesarea. *The Treatise on the Holy Spirit* in *Nicene and Post-Nicene Fathers,* Second Series, Vol 8. Eds. Philip Schaff and Henry Wace. Peabody: Hendrickson Publishers, 1994.

Berkoff, Hendrikus. *The Doctrine of the Holy Spirit*. Atlanta: John Knox Press, 1964.
Berkouwer, G.C. *The Triumph of Grace in the Theology of Karl Barth*. Trans. Harry Boer. Grand Rapids: Eerdmans, 1956.
Betz, John. "Beyond the Sublime: The Aesthetics of the Analogy of Being," *Modern Theology* 21:3 (July) 2005: 367–411 and *Modern Theology* 22:1 (January) 2006: 1–50.
Boersma, Hans. *Violence, Hospitality, and the Cross: Reappropriating the Atonement Tradition*. Grand Rapids: Baker Academic, 2004.
Boethius. "Philosophiae Consolationis" in *Boethius: The Theological Tractates and the Consolation of Philosophy*. Trans. H. F. Steward and E.K. Rand. London and Cambridge, Mass: William Heinmann Ltd and Harvard University Press, 1913.
———. *The Consolation of Philosophy*. Translated with an introduction by V.E. Watts. Middlesex: Penguin Books, 1969.
Brandenburg, Albert. "Der Zeit – und Geschichtsbegriff bei Karl Barth," *Theologie und Glaube* 45 (1955): 357–78.
Buckley, James. "A Field of Living Fire: Karl Barth on the Spirit and the Church," *Modern Theology* 10:1 (January 1994): 81–102.
Bultmann, Rudolf, et al. *Kerygma and Myth: A Theological Debate*. Edited by Hans Werner Bartsch. New York: Harper and Row, 1961.
Burgess, Andrew. *The Ascension in Karl Barth*. Aldershot: Ashgate, 2004.
Busch, Eberhard. *Karl Barth: His Life from Letters and Autobiographical Texts*. Trans. John Bowden. Grand Rapids: Eerdmans, 1994.
Cochrane, Arthur. "Karl Barth's Doctrine of the Covenant" in *Major Themes in the Reformed Tradition*. Ed. Donald K. McKim. Grand Rapids: Eerdmans, 1992: 108–16.
Colwell, John. *Actuality and Provisionality: Eternity and Election in the Theology of Karl Barth*. Edinburgh: Rutherford House, 1989.
Craig, William. *The Problem of Divine Foreknowledge and Future Contingents From Aristotle to Suarez*. Brill's Studies in Intellectual History, 7. Leiden: Brill Academic Publishers, 1997.
———. *God, Time and Eternity: The Coherence of Theism II: Eternity*. Dordrecht: Kluwer Academic Publishers, 2001.
Dalferth, Ingolf. *Theology and Philosophy*. Basil Blackwell, 1988. Reprinted by Wipf and Stock Publishers, Eugene OR, 2001.
Daniel, Randolf. "The Double Procession of the Spirit in Joachim of Fiore's Understanding of History," *Speculum* 55:3 (July 1980): 469–83.
Davies, Paul. *About Time: Einstein's Unfinished Revolution*. London: Orion, 1995; New York: Simon and Schuster, 2005.
Dawson, Dale. *The Resurrection in Karl Barth*. Aldershot: Ashgate, 2007.
Deddo, Gary. *Karl Barth's Theology of Relations: Trinitarian, Christological, and Human: Towards an Ethic of the Family*. Issues in Systematic Theology Vol. 4. New York: Peter Lang, 1999.
DeWeese, Garrett. *God and the Nature of Time*. Aldershot: Ashgate Publishers, 2004.
Dillion, John. "Plotinus: An Introduction" in Plotinus, *Enneads*. Trans. Stephen MacKenna. London: Penguin Books, 1991: lxxxiv–ci.
Dostal, Robert. "Time and phenomenology in Husserl and Heidegger" in *The Cambridge Companion to Heidegger*. Ed. Charles Guignon. Cambridge and New York: Cambridge University Press, 1993: 141–169.

Farrow, Douglas. *Ascension and Ecclesia: On the Significance of the Doctrine of the Ascension for Ecclesiology and Christian Cosmology.* Edinburgh: T & T Clark/Grand Rapids: Eerdmans, 1999.

———. "Karl Barth on the Ascension: An Appreciation and Critique," *International Journal of Systematic Theology* 2:3 (July 2000): 127–150.

———. "Ascension and Atonement" in *The Theology of Reconciliation.* Ed. Colin Gunton. London: T&T Clark, 2003: 67-91.

Farrow, Douglas, David Demson, J. Augustine Di Noia. "Robert Jenson's *Systematic Theology*: Three Responses," *International Journal of Systematic Theology* 1:1 (March 1999): 89–104.

Ford, David. *Barth and God's Story: Biblical Narrative and the Theological Method of Karl Barth in the* Church Dogmatics. New York: Peter Lang, 1985.

Freyer, Thomas. *Zeit – Continuität und Unterbrechung: Studien zu Karl Barth, Wolfhart Pannenberg und Karl Rahner.* Bonner Dogmatische Studien 13. Echter, 1993.

Gabriel, Andrew. "A Trinitarian Doctrine of Creation?: Considering Barth as a Guide," *McMaster Journal of Theology and Ministry* 6 (2003–2006): 36–48.

Gathercole, Simon. "Pre-existence, and the Freedom of the Son in Creation and Redemption: An Exposition in Dialogue with Robert Jenson," *IJST* 7:1 (January 2005): 38–51.

Gockel, Matthias. *Barth and Schleiermacher on the Doctrine of Election: A Systematic-Theological Comparison.* New York: Oxford University Press, 2007.

Grant, Robert. *Irenaeus of Lyons.* London and New York: Routledge, 1997.

Griffiths, Paul J. "Is there a Doctrine of the Descent into Hell?," *Pro Ecclesia* 17:3(2008): 257–180.

Gunton, Colin. *The Triune Creator: A Historical and Systematic Study.* Edinburgh Studies in Constructive Theology. Grand Rapids and Cambridge: Eerdmans, 1998.

———. *Christ and Creation.* The Didsbury Lectures, 1990. Carlisle and Grand Rapids: Paternoster and Eerdmans, 1992.

———. *A Brief Theology of Revelation: The 1993 Warfield Lectures.* London: T&T Clark, 1995.

———. *Theology through the Theologians: Selected Essays, 1972–1995.* London and New York: T&T Clark, 1996.

———. *Becoming and Being: The Doctrine of God in Charles Hartshorne and Karl Barth.* 2nd Edition. London: SCM Press, 2001.

———. "The Spirit Moved Over the face of the Waters: The Holy Spirit and the Created Order," *International Journal of Systematic Theology* 4:2 (July 2002): 190–204.

Guretzki, David. "The Genesis and Systematic Function of the *Filioque* in Karl Barth's *Church Dogmatics*." PhD diss., McGill University, 2006.

Harink, Douglas. "The Time of the Gospel and the History of the World," Society of Biblical Literature, San Diego, November, 2007.

Hart, Trevor. "Irenaeus, Recapitulation and Physical Redemption" in *Christ in our Place: The Humanity of God in Christ for the Reconciliation of the World. Essays Presented to Professor James Torrance.* Eds. Trevor Hart and Daniel Thimell. Exeter and Allison Park: Paternoster Press and Pickwick Publications, 1989: 152–81.

———. "Revelation" in *The Cambridge Companion to Karl Barth.* Ed. John Webster. Cambridge: Cambridge University Press, 2000: 37–56.

Hasker, William. *God, Time, and Knowledge.* Cornell Studies in Philosophy of Religion. Ithaca, NY: Cornell University Press, 1989.

Healy, Nicholas. "The Logic of Karl Barth's Ecclesiology: Analysis, Assessment and Proposed Modifications," *Modern Theology* 10:3 (July 1994): 254–55.

———. "Karl Barth's ecclesiology reconsidered," *SJT* 57:3 (2004): 287–299.

Henry, Paul. "The Place of Plotinus in the History of Thought" in Plotinus, *Enneads*. Translated by Stephen MacKenna, abridged with an introduction and notes by John Dillion. London: Penguin Books, 1991: xliii–lxx.

Heron, Alasdair. "The Time of God" in *Gottes Zukunft - Zukunft der Welt: Festschrift für Jürgen Moltmann zum 60. Geburtstag*. Eds. Hermann Deuser, Gerhard Marcel Martin, Konrad Stock and Michael Welker. München: Chr. Kaiser Verlag, 1986: 231–239.

Hilary of Poitiers. *On the Trinity* in *Nicene and Post-Nicene Fathers*, 2nd Series, Vol. 9. Eds. Philip Schaff and Henry Wace. Peabody: Hendrickson Publishers, 1994.

Hoffman, Piotr. "Death, time, history: Division II of *Being and Time*" in *The Cambridge Companion to Heidegger*. Ed. Charles Guignon. Cambridge and New York: Cambridge University Press, 1993: 195–214.

Holmes, Christopher. "Eberhard Jüngel and Wolf Krötke: Recent Contributions toward a Trinitarian Doctrine of God's Attributes," *Toronto Journal of Theology* 22:2 (2006): 159–180.

Hunsinger, George. *How to Read Karl Barth*. Oxford: Oxford University Press, 1991.

———. "The Mediator of Communion: Karl Barth's doctrine of the Holy Spirit" in *Disruptive Grace: Studies in the Theology of Karl Barth*. Grand Rapids: Eerdmans, 2000: 148–185.

———. "*Mysterium Trinitatis*: Karl Barth's Conception of Eternity" in *Disruptive Grace: Studies in the Theology of Karl Barth*. Grand Rapids: Eerdmans, 2000: 186–209.

———. "Hellfire and Damnation: Four Ancient and Modern Views" in *Disruptive Grace: Studies in the Theology of Karl Barth*. Grand Rapids: Eerdmans, 2000: 226–249.

Hütter, Reinhard. "Karl Barth's 'Dialectical Catholicity': Sic et Non," *Modern Theology* 16:2 (April 2000): 137–157.

Irenaeus. *Against Heresies* in *Ante-Nicene Fathers*, Vol 1. Eds. Alexander Roberts and James Donaldson. Peabody: Hendrickson Publishers, 1994.

Jackelén, Antje. *Time and Eternity: The Question of Time in Church, Science and Theology*. Trans. Barbara Harshaw. Philadelphia and London: Templeton Foundation Press, 2005.

Jenson, Robert. *God after God: The God of the Past and the God of the Future, Seen in the Work of Karl Barth*. Indianapolis and New York: The Bobbs-Merrill Company, 1969.

———. *The Triune Identity*. Minneapolis, MN: Fortress Press, 1982.

———. "Karl Barth" in David Ford, ed., *The Modern Theologians: An Introduction to Christian Theology in the Twentieth Century*, Vol. 1. Oxford: Blackwell, 1989: 23–49.

———. "You Wonder Where the Spirit Went," *Pro Ecclesia* 2:3 (1993): 296–304.

———. *Systematic Theology, Vol. 1, The Triune God*. Oxford and New York: Oxford University Press, 1997.

Johnson, Keith J. *Karl Barth and the* Analogia Entis. London: T&T Clark, 2010.

Johnson, William Stacy. *The Mystery of God: Karl Barth and the Postmodern Foundations of Theology*. Louisville: Westminster John Knox Press, 1997.

Jüngel, Eberhard. *Death: the riddle and the mystery*. Trans. Iain and Ute Nicol. Philadelphia: The Westminster Press, 1974.

———. *God's Being is in Becoming: The Trinitarian Being of God in the Theology of Karl Barth. A Paraphrase*. Trans. John Webster. Grand Rapids: Eerdmans, 2001.

———. "Theses on the Eternality of Eternal Life," trans. Christopher Holmes in "Eberhard Jüngel and Wolf Krötke: Recent Contributions toward a Trinitarian Doctrine of God's Attributes," *Toronto Journal of Theology* 22:2 (2006): 163–169 of 159–180.

Kim, Eunsoo. "Time, Eternity, and the Trinity: A Trinitarian Analogical understanding of Time and Eternity." Ph.D. diss., Trinity Evangelical Divinity School, 2006.

Kirby, W.J. Torrance. "Praise as the Soul's overcoming of Time in the *Confessions* of Augustine," *Pro Ecclesia* 6:3 (1997): 333–350.

Kneale, William. "Time and Eternity in Theology," *Proceedings of the Aristotelian Society* 61 (1961): 87–108.

Knuuttila, Simo. "Time and Creation in Augustine" in *The Cambridge Companion to Augustine*. Eds. Eleonore Strump and Norman Kretzmann. Cambridge, UK: Cambridge University Press, 2001: 103–115.

Krotke, Wolfe. "The humanity of the human person in Karl Barth's anthropology," trans. Philip G. Ziegler, in *The Cambridge Companion to Karl Barth*. Ed. John Webster. Cambridge University Press, 2000: 159–176.

Langdon, Adrian. "Confessing Eternity: Karl Barth and the Western Tradition," *Pro Ecclesia* 21:2(2012): 125–144.

Lauber, David. *Barth on the Descent into Hell: God, Atonement and the Christian Life*. Aldershot: Ashgate, 2004.

Lawson, John. *The Biblical Theology of Saint Irenaeus*. London: Epworth Press, 1948.

Leftow, Brian. "Response to 'Mysterium Trinitatis'" in *For the Sake of the World: Karl Barth and the Future of Ecclesial Theology*. Ed. George Hunsinger. Grand Rapids: Eerdmans, 2004: 191–201.

———. "Eternity and Immutability" in *The Blackwell Guide to the Philosophy of Religion*. Ed. William E. Mann. Oxford: Blackwell Publishing, 2005: 48–77.

Lewis, Alan. *Between Cross and Resurrection: A Theology of Holy Saturday*. Grand Rapids and Cambridge: Eerdmans, 2001.

Lyttkens, Hampus. *The Analogy between God and the World: An Investigation of its Background and Interpretation of its Use by Thomas of Aquino*. Uppsala: Almquist & Wiksells, 1953.

May, Gerhald. *Creatio ex Nihilo: The Doctrine of 'Creation out of Nothing' in Early Christian Thought*. Trans. A. S. Worrall. Edinburgh: T & T Clark, 1994.

McCormack, Bruce. *Barth's Critically Realistic Dialectical Theology: Its Genesis and Development 1909-1936*. Oxford: Clarendon Press, 1995.

———. *Orthodox and Modern: Studies in the Theology of Karl Barth*. Grand Rapids: Baker Academic, 2008.

———. "Grace and being: the role of God's gracious election in Karl Barth's theological ontology" in *The Cambridge Companion to Karl Barth*. Ed. John Webster. Cambridge: Cambridge University Press, 2000: 92–110.

———. "Barth, Karl" in *The Oxford Companion to Christian Thought*. Ed. Adrian Hastings. Oxford: Oxford University Press, 2000: 64–67.

———. "The Ontological Presuppositions of Barth's Doctrine of the Atonement" in *The Glory of the Atonement: Biblical, Theological, and Practical Perspectives*. Eds. Charles Hill and Frank James III. Downers Grove: InterVarsity Press, 2004: 346–366.

———. "*Justitia aliena*: Karl Barth in Conversation with the Evangelical Doctrine of Imputed Righteousness" in *Justification in Perspective: Historical Developments and Contemporary Challenges*. Ed. Bruce McCormack. Grand Rapids: Baker Academic, 2006: 167–196.

———. "Divine Impassibility or Simply Divine Constancy? Implications of Karl Barth's Later Christology of Debates over Impassibililty" in *Divine Impassibility and the Mystery of Human Suffering*. Eds. James Keating and Thomas Joseph White. Grand Rapids: Eerdmans, 2009: 150–186.

McGinn, Bernard. *The Calabrian Abbot: Joachim of Fiore in the History of Western Thought*. New York: Macmillan Publishing Co., 1985.

McGrath, Alister. *Thomas F. Torrance: An Intellectual Biography*. T&T Clark: Edinburgh, 1999.

McInerny, Ralph. *Aquinas and Analogy*. Washington: The Catholic University of America Press, 1992.

McLean, Stuart. "Creation and Anthropology" in *Theology beyond Christendom*. Ed. John Thompson, Princeton Theological Monograph Series, ed. Dikran Y. Hadidian, no. 6. Allison Park, Penn: Pickwick Publications, 1986.

Merleau-Ponty, Maurice. "What is Phenomenology?" in *Phenomenology of Religion: Eight Modern Descriptions of the Essence of Religion*. Ed. Joseph Dabney Bettis. New York and Evanston: Harper and Row, 1969: 13–30.

Metzger, Paul L. *The Word of Christ and the World of Culture: Sacred and Secular through the Theology of Karl Barth*. Grand Rapids: Eerdmans, 2003.

Migliore, Daniel. "Karl Barth's First Lectures in Dogmatics: *Instruction in the Christian Religion*" in Karl Barth, *The Göttingen Dogmatics: Instruction in the Christian Religion*, Volume One. Ed. Hannelotte Reiffen. Trans. Geoffrey Bromiley. Grand Rapids: Eerdmans, 1991: xv–lxii.

Molnar, Paul. *Divine Freedom and the Doctrine of the Trinity: In dialogue with Karl Barth and contemporary theology*. London and New York: T & T Clark, 2002.

Moltmann, Jürgen. *Theology of Hope*. Trans. Margaret Kohl. Minneapolis: Fortress, 1993.

———. *God in Creation: A New Theology of Creation and the Spirit of God*. Trans. Margaret Kohl. Minneapolis: Fortress, 1993.

———. *The Coming of God: Christian Eschatology*. Trans. Margaret Kohl. Minneapolis: Fortress Press, 1996.

———. *Science and Wisdom*. Trans. Margaret Kohl. Minneapolis: Fortress, 2003.

Mondin, Battista. *The Principle of Analogy in Protestant and Catholics Theology*. 2nd Edition. The Hague: Martinus Nijhoff, 1968.

Mostert, Christiaan. *God and the Future: Wolfhart Pannenberg's Eschatological Doctrine of God*. London and New York: T & T Clark, 2002.

Myers, Benjamin. Review of "Andrew Burgess: The Ascension in Karl Barth," http://faith-theology.blogspot.com/2007/01/andrew-burgess-ascension-in-karl-barth.html (accessed January 27, 2008).

Neilsen, Brent Flemming. "Karl Barth—a brief introduction, Eternity and Time," http://www.teol.ku.dk/ast/Ansatte/Pdf-filer/timeandeternity.pdf (accessed November 20, 2006).

Nimmo, Paul. *Being in Action: The Theological Shape of Barth's Ethical Vision*. London: T&T Clark, 2007.

Oakes, Kenneth. "The Question of Nature and Grace in Karl Barth: Humanity as Creature and as Covenant-Partner," *Modern Theology* 23:4 (October 2007): 595–616.

O'Donnell, John. *Trinity and Temporality: The Christian Doctrine of God in the Light of Process Theology and the Theology of Hope*. Oxford: Oxford University Press, 1983.

Oh, Peter S. *Karl Barth's Trinitarian Theology: A Study in Karl Barth's Analogical use of the Trinitarian Relation*. T & T Clark: London and New York, 2007.

Padgett, Alan. *God, Eternity and the Nature of Time*. London: Macmillan, 1992.

Palakeel, Joseph. *The Use of Analogy in Theological Discourse: An Investigation in Ecumenical Perspective*. Tesi Gregoriana, Serie Teologia 4. Rome: Editrice Pontificia Universita Gregoriana, 1995.

Pannenberg, Wolfhart. *Jesus—God and Man*. Trans. L. Wilkins and D. Priebe. 2nd Ed. Philadelphia: The Westminster Press, 1977.

———. *Systematic Theology*, Vols. 1-3. Translated by Geoffrey Bromiley (Grand Rapids and Edinburgh: Eerdmans T & T Clark, 1991-1998.

———. "The Doctrine of the Spirit and the Task of a Theology of Nature" in *Toward a Theology of Nature: Essays on Science and Faith*. Edited by Ted Peters. Louisville: Westminster/John Knox Press, 1993: 123-137.

Parmenides. *The Fragments of Parmenides: A Critical text with introduction, translation, the ancient testimonia and a commentary* by A. H. Coxon. Assen/Maastricht: Van Gorcum, 1986.

Pecknold, C.C. "Liturgy, Time, and the Politics of Redemption: Concluding Unscientific Postscript" in *Liturgy, Time, and the Politics of Redemption*. Eds. Randi Rashkover and C.C. Pecknold. Grand Rapids and Cambridge: Eerdmans, 2006: 229-244.

Peters, Ted and Martinez Hewlett. *Evolution from Creation to New Creation: Conflict, Conversation, and Convergence*. Nashville: Abington Press, 2003.

Pitstick, Alyssa. *Light in Darkness: Hans Urs von Balthasar and the Catholic Doctrine of Christ's Decent into Hell*. Grand Rapids: Eerdmans, 2007.

Pitstick. Alyssa and Edward Oaks, "Balthasar, Hell, and Heresy: An Exchange," *First Things* 168 (December 2006): 25-32; and "More on Balthasar, Hell, and Heresy," *First Things* 169 (January 2007): 16-19.

Placher, William. *Narratives of a Vulnerable God: Christ, Theology, and Scripture*. Louisville: WJK Press, 1994.

Plato. "Timaeus." Trans. Benjamin Jowett in *The Collected Dialogues of Plato, Including the Letters*. Edited by Edith Hamilton and Huntington Cairns. Princeton: Princeton University Press, 1961: 151-211.

Polkinghorne, John. *Faith, Science and Understanding*. New Haven and London: Yale University Press, 2000.

———. *Science and the Trinity: The Christian Encounter with Reality*. New Haven and London: Yale University Press, 2004.

Rashkover, Randi and C.C. Pecknold eds. *Liturgy, Time, and the Politics of Redemption*. Grand Rapids and Cambridge: Eerdmans, 2006.

Reeves, Majorie. *The Influence of Prophecy in the Latter Middle Ages: A Study of Joachimism*. Oxford: University of Oxford Press, 1969.

Ricoeur, Paul. "Narrative Time," *Critical Inquiry* 7:1 (Autumn 1980): 169-190.

———. "The Time of the Soul and the Time of the World: The Dispute between Augustine and Aristotle" in *Time and Narrative*, Vol. 3. Translated by Kathleen Blamey and David Pellauer. Chicago and London: University of Chicago Press, 1988: 12-22.

Roberts, Richard H. "Karl Barth's Doctrine of Time: Its Nature and Implications" in *Karl Barth: Studies in his Theological Method*. Ed. Stephen W. Sykes. Oxford: Clarendon Press, 1979: 88–146.

Rosato, Philip. *The Spirit as Lord: The Pneumatology of Karl Barth*. Edinburgh: T&T Clark, 1981.

Rowe, William. "Myth and Counter-Myth: Irenaeus' Story of Salvation" in *Interpreting Tradition: The Art of Theological Reflection*. Ed. Jane Kopas. Cico, California: Scholars Press, 1989: 39–54.

Sanders, Fred. *The Image of the Immanent Trinity: Rahner's Rule and the Theological Interpretation of Scripture*. Frankfurt am Main and New York: Peter Lang, 2005.

Schmitt, Richard. "Phenomenology" in *Encyclopedia of Philosophy, Vol. 6*. Editor in Chief Paul Edwards. New York and London: Macmillan Publishing Company and The Free Press, 1967: 135–151.

Schwöbel, Christoph. Forward to Peter S. Oh, *Karl Barth's Trinitarian Theology: A Study in Karl Barth's Analogical use of the Trinitarian Relation*. T & T Clark: London and New York, 2007: ix–xii.

Sorabji, Richard. *Time, Creation and the Continuum: theories in antiquity and the early middles Ages*. Ithaca, NY: Cornell University Press, 1983.

Stump, Elenore and Norman Kretzmann. "Eternity," *The Journal of Philosophy* 78:8 (1981): 429–458.

Tanner, Kathryn. *God and Creation in Christian Theology: Tyranny or Empowerment?* Oxford: Basil Blackwell, 1988.

———. *Jesus, Humanity and the Trinity: A Brief Systematic Theology*. Minneapolis: Fortress Press, 2001.

———. "Creation and Providence" in *The Cambridge Companion to Karl Barth*. Ed. John Webster. Cambridge: Cambridge University Press, 2000: 111–126.

Theophilus of Antioch. *Theophilus to Autolycus* in *Ante-Nicene Fathers*, Vol 2. Eds. Alexander Roberts and James Donaldson. Peabody, MASS: Hendrickson Publishers, 1994.

Thompson, John. *The Holy Spirit in the Theology of Karl Barth*. Allison Park: Pickwick, 1991.

Torrance, Alan. *Persons in Communion: Trinitarian Description and Human Participation*. Edinburgh: T&T Clark, 1996.

Torrance, Thomas F. *Theological Science*. New York and Toronto: Oxford University Press, 1969.

———. *Space, Time and Incarnation*. New York and Toronto: Oxford University Press, 1969.

———. *Space, Time and Resurrection*. Edinburgh: Handsel Press, 1976.

———. *Divine and Contingent Order*. Oxford and New York: Oxford University Press, 1981.

———. *Karl Barth, Biblical and Evangelical Theologian*. Edinburgh: T&T Clark, 1991.

Van Driel, Edwin Chr. *Incarnation Anyway: Arguments for Supralapsarian Christology*. New York: Oxford University Press, 2008.

———. "Karl Barth on the Eternal Existence of Jesus Christ," *Scottish Journal of Theology* 60:1 (2007): 45–51.

Vondey, Wolfgang. "The Holy Spirit in contemporary Catholic and Protestant theology," *Scottish Journal of Theology* 58:4(2005): 393–409.

Wagner, Falk. "Analogy" in *The Encyclopedia of Christianity*, Vol. 1 A-D. Eds. Erwin Fahlbusch, et al. Grand Rapids and Leiden: Eerdmans and Brill, 1999: 48–49.
Webster, John. *Barth*. Outstanding Christian Thinkers. London and New York: Continuum, 2000.
———. *Holy Scripture: A Dogmatic Sketch*. Cambridge: Cambridge University Press, 2003.
———. "Karl Barth" in *Reading Romans through the Centuries: From the Early Church to Karl Barth*. Eds. Jeffrey Greenman and Timothy Larsen. Grand Rapids: Brazos Press, 2005: 205–23.
Webster, John. Ed. *The Cambridge Companion to Karl Barth*. Cambridge: Cambridge University Press, 2000.
Weinandy, Thomas. *The Father's Spirit of Sonship*. Edinburgh: T&T Clark, 1995.
———. *Does God Suffer?* Notre Dame: University of Notre Dame Press, 2000.
———. "Easter Saturday and the Suffering of God: The Theology of Alan E. Lewis," *International Journal of Systematic Theology* 5:1 (March 2003): 62–76.
Welker, Michael. "God's Eternity, God's Temporality, and Trinitarian Theology," *Theology Today* 55:3 (Oct 1998): 317–328.
Wenham, Gordon J. *Genesis 1–15*. Word Publishing: London, 1987.
Whitehouse, W. A. "Election and Covenant" in *Theology Beyond Christendom: Essays on the Centenary of the Birth of Karl Barth*. Ed. John Thompson. Allison Park, PA: Pickwick Publications, 1986: 63–86.
Williams, Rowan. "Barth on the Triune God" in S.W. Sykes ed. *Karl Barth: Studies of his Theological Method*. Oxford: Clarendon Press, 1979: 147–193.
Wright, N. T. *Surprised by Hope: Rethinking Heaven, the Resurrection, and the Mission of the Church*. New York: HarperOne, 2008.
Zagzebski, Linda. "Omniscience, Time, and Freedom" in *The Blackwell Guide to the Philosophy of Religion*. Ed. William E. Mann. Oxford: Blackwell Publishing, 2005: 3–25.
Zeitz, James. *Spirituality and Analogia Entis according to Erich Przywara, S.J.* Washington, D.C.: University Press of America, 1982.

Index of Names and Subjects

Achtner, Wolfgang, 4–5, 93–94, 159, 197
actualism, actualistic ontology, 29, 42–43, 49, 75–76, 79–81, 91–92, 100–101, 103–5, 129, 163, 167, 173–76. *See* event *as well*.
analogy, 9–16, 23, 45, 89, 92, 110, 124, 161, 187–93; *analogia entis*, 10–11; *analogia fidei*, 11–12; *analogia relationis*, 12–13, 88; *analogia trinitaria temporis* or *analogia temporis*, 3, 14–16, 82, 123–24, 159, 184–85, 192–94
analytical philosophy of religion, 85, 195–96,
Anselm, 68–69
anthropocentricity, 107–8
anthropology, 37, 86, 93, 153–56; *imago dei*, 37; soul-body relation, 37, 116
anticipation, divine, 30, 77, 79, 125–129, 191
anticipation, human, 109, 112–13, 124
'anticipation, synchronicity, and recapitulation', 34–35, 52, 110–113. *See* eternity as simultaneity *as well*.
anxiety, 115–17, 120–21
appropriations, doctrine of. *See* Trinity.
Aquinas, Thomas. *See* Thomas Aquinas
Aristotle, 1, 5, 6, 200
atemporality. *See* eternity as atemporality.

Augustine, Saint, 67–69, 94, 107, 109, 113, 118, 160, 191

Badcock, Gary, 44
Balthasar, Han Urs von, 13, 120
Basil, Saint, 160
being. *See* ontology.
Berkouwer, G.C., 40
Betz, John, 11–12
binitarianism, 45
Blumhardt, Johann Christoph, 74
Boersma, Hans, 135, 156
Boethius, 31–35, 52, 65, 67–69, 100, 159
Bonhoeffer, Dietrich, 175
Brandenburg, Albert, 36–37, 121
Buckley, James, 45
Bultmann, Rudolph, 26–27, 113, 136–37, 140, 145, 149
Burgess, Andrew, 49, 144, 149
Busch, Eberhard, 163

Calvin, John, 88
Chalcedon, Chalcedonian, 36, 40, 124, 137–39, 143, 148
Christian community. *See* Church
christocentrism, 36–37, 43–44, 123, 125, 133, 190, 193
christology, see Jesus Christ
Church, 46–49, 146–47, 152; and ascension time, 146–47; as body of Christ, 47, 49, 163–65, 176–77; and Christology, 46; as communion of saints, 175–77; ecclesial practices, 46, 48–49, 143, 182–84; as event, 46–48,

217

163, 173–76, 178–79; as *existenzform* of Jesus Christ, 162–64, 166, 176; growth of, 175–77; law of, 177–80; mission of, 48, 180–84; as object of faith, 46; sacraments, 146; *Scheinkirche*, 47; upholding of, 177; *wirkliche Kirche*, 47, 174; worship, 177–78
Cochrane, Arthur, 90
Colwell, John, 101
contemporaneity, 16, 39, 102, 123, 125, 132–34, 136, 140–43, 146–48, 160, 165–68, 190, 192, 203; pseudo-contemporaneity, 140, 142
correlativity of God and creation, 40–43, 156
correspondence, 48, 168–169
cosmology, 96, 98–99
covenant, 88, 90–91
Craig, William, 32, 85
creatio ex nihilo, 94, 199
creation, 17, 87–93, 94–100, 128
crucicentrism, 38–43, 152

Dalferth, Ingolf, 7, 156, 195
Davies, Paul, 4–5
Dawson, Dale, 40, 42, 55, 135, 137, 165
death, 17, 107–8, 112–121; second death, 113–114, 116, 118–19, 120; as sign of judgment, 117, 121
Deddo, Gary, 13, 89
deism, 9, 200
Dostal, Robert, 107
Driel, Edwin Chr. van, 78, 93, 145, 156

ecclesiology. See Church
election, 30, 43, 48, 51, 75–81, 88, 90, 104–5, 124–126, 191
equivocy, 9–10
eschatology, 26–28; and recapitulation, 152–154; and time, 150–158, 204; Jesus Christ and, 150–158
eschaton, 28, 39, 48, 52, 58–59, 73–74, 92, 100, 103, 105, 118, 120, 124–25, 133, 145–46, 171, 176, 184, 190, 192, 204–5

eternity, 1–3; as atemporality, 3, 21–36, 66–71, 95, 97, 155, 193, 195–96; Boethius on, 31–34, 52, 65, 67–69; in *CD* II, 66–75; diastasis of eternity and time, 58–60, 62; as divine temporality, 2–3, 14, 23, 26, 31–32, 50–51, 52, 66, 85, 94–96, 188, 192–95; as 'eternal Now', 26–27, 29, 33, 56, 57, 72; in *Göttingen Dogmatics*, 61–62; Jenson on, 24–26; ontological distinction from time, 2, 31–32, 34, 53–54, 57, 70, 123–24, 160, 186, 196; as posttemporality, 28, 52, 54, 66, 71–74, 124–25, 129, 150–58, 189–90, 193–94; predication of, 50–51; as pretemporality, 25, 28, 30, 43, 52, 54, 66, 71–74, 76–79, 104, 124, 160, 189, 191–92; as pure duration, 29, 31, 33–34, 54, 62, 66, 68–70, 102, 195; in *Romans*, 56–61; as simultaneity (anticipation, synchronicity, recapitulation), 15, 24, 31–35, 42, 55, 62, 66, 69–70, 80–81, 110–113, 129, 154, 195; as supratemporality, 28, 30, 52, 54, 66, 71–74, 124, 160, 189–90; Thomas Aquinas on, 1; as timelessness, *see* atemporality
event, 23, 30–32, 46, 48, 50, 75–76, 100–101, 103–5, 173–76; as encounter, 100–101, 103–5; resurrection as event, 136–37, 151. See actualism *as well*.
evolution, 198–199

faith and history, modern problem of. *See* history.
Farrow, Douglas, 38–43, 48–49, 123–24, 129, 131, 133, 143, 145, 152, 156
filioque. *See* Holy Spirit
Ford, David, 37–38, 48–49, 133, 138, 152
foreknowledge and future contingents, 17, 87, 100, 103–5

freedom, divine and human, 80, 92, 100–101
Freyer, Thomas, 26, 41
futurity, 27–28, 52–53, 58

Gabriel, Andrew, 90
Gathercole, Simon, 25
Genesis, 96–98
Gockel, Matthias, 76
Göttingen Dogmatics, 28–29, 60–62, 193
Grant, Robert, 130
Griffiths, Paul, 120
Gunton, Colin, 30–32, 43, 49, 87, 90, 138–39, 204
Guretzki, David, 45–46, 160–61

Harink, Douglas, 8
Hart, Trevor, 130, 138
Hasker, William, 100
Healy, Nicholas, 46–47
heaven, 145
Hegel, G.W.F., 171, 194
Heidegger, Martin, 107, 113, 118–19, 191
Heron, Alasdair, 188, 196
Herrmann, Wilhelm, 140
Hewlett, Martinez, 198
Hilary of Poitiers, 101
historicity, human, 96–100
history, 36–37, 170–72; of covenant, 91, 93, 96; of creation, 128; eschatological view of, 28; 'first' and 'second' history of Jesus Christ, 127–28, 136, 143; of Israel, 124–28; Jesus-history, *see* Jesus Christ; modern problem of faith and, 17, 125, 136, 140–42, 147–49; primal, 128; world, 92. See time *as well*.
Hoffman, Piotr, 107, 113
Holy Spirit, 43–46, 146; agency of, 45–46, 162, 165, 160–68, 180–81; and ascension time, 146–47; *filioque*, 44–46, 204; Jesus Christ and, 162–68; as mediator, 146–50; outpouring of, 63–64; 'Pentecostally-centered', Barth's view as, 45; subordination of, 45–46; time of, 161–62, 168–84, 202–4. *See* ecclesial time, noetic participation *and* Trinity *as well*.
Hunsinger, George, 29, 34, 44–45, 49, 53–55, 66, 118, 161, 190
Hütter, Reinhard, 47–49

immortality, 102, 114–15, 153–54
incarnandus, 77–78
Irenaeus, 101, 124, 130–31, 135, 156

Jackelén, Antje, 197
Jenson, Robert, 21–22, 26, 32, 43–45, 49, 51, 54, 193
Jesus Christ: anhypostatic-enhypostatic union, 60; ascension of, 36, 38–39, 41–42, 124–25, 133, 143–50, 163; ascension of Jesus Christ as event, 143–46; ascension of Jesus Christ as sign, 143; cross, 27, 43, 63, 72–73, 117–19, 139–43, 148 (*see* crucicentrism *as well*); and election, 76–79; and eschaton, 150–51; forty days, 32, 36–38, 41–43, 124–25, 127, 133, 135–43, 149, 164; 'Jesus-history', 38–43, 123–24, 128–29, 132–58, 160, 164, 168, 171, 178, 185, 192, 205; *parousia* of, *see parousia*; preexistence of, 25 (*see* election *as well*); and recapitulation, 124, 129–58, 166; resurrection of, 37–39, 41, 60, 63, 72–73, 119–20, 124–25, 133–43, 149–50; resurrection of Jesus Christ as event, 136–37; historicity of resurrection of Jesus Christ, 136–37; and revelation, 63; second coming of, 119–20, 125 (*see* eschaton *and* eschatology *as well*); and time, 7–8, 22–23, 70, 72–73, 109, 123–58, 191–92; *totus Christus*, 76; two natures of, 40–41; two states of, 40–41. *See* Jesus Christ and time *as well*.
Johnson, Keith, 10–12
Johnson, William Stacy, 62

Index of Names and Subjects

judgment, final, 118, 151
Jüngel, Eberhard, 50–51, 54, 154

Kim, Eunsoo, 14
Kirby, W.J. Torrance, 109, 113
knowledge of God, 11–12, 58, 60. See revelation as well.
Knuuttila, Simo, 95

Lauber, David, 41, 117
Lawson, John, 130–31
Leftow, Brian, 35
Lessing, G.E., 125, 140
Lewis, Alan, 120
logos asarkos, 25, 77–78, 128–29
Lyttkens, Hampus, 9

May, Gerhald, 94
McCormack, Bruce, 13, 16, 34, 49, 59–62, 71, 75–78, 80, 90–91, 138
McGrath, Alister, 201
McInerny, Ralph, 9
McLean, Stuart, 93
memory, 109–113, 116
Merleau-Ponty, Maurice, 108
Metzger, Paul, 13
Molnar, Paul, 62, 78
Moltmann, Jürgen, 7, 22, 26–29, 51, 120, 156, 197
Mondin, Battista, 9
Mostert, Christiaan, 51
Myers, Benjamin, 144–45
myth, 96

natural order, 30
natural theology, 30, 60
Neo-Protestantism, 47–48, 74
Newton, Issac, and Newtonian, 145, 199–201
Nielsen, Bent Flemming, 102, 108, 114
Nimmo, Paul, 76
noetic participation, 39–40, 41–42, 44, 59–60. See participation *as well*.
nothingness (*Das Nichtige*), 156, 171–72

Oakes, Kenneth, 12
Oaks, Edward, 120

occasionalism, 46
O'Donnell, John, 28
Oh, Peter S, 12–13
ontology, 11–13, 49, 171, 195. See actualism *and* event *as well*.
Overbeck, Franz, 194

Padgett, Alan, 30, 32–35, 85, 196
Palakeel, Joseph, 10–13
Pannenberg, Wolfhart, 49, 51–53, 90, 199
panentheism, 101
pantheism, 9
Parmenides, 27
parousia, 16, 36, 37–38, 41–42, 52, 145, 148, 151–52; twofold *parousia*, 141, 169; threefold *parousia*, 38–39, 181 See eschaton *as well*.
Pecknold, C.C., 204
perichoresis. See Trinity
Peters, Ted, 198
phenomenology, 107–8, 202
Pitstick, Alyssa, 120
Plato, Platonic tradition, 23, 26, 28, 32, 50, 85
Plotinus, 52
pneumatology. See Holy Spirit
Polkinghorne, John, 7, 155–56, 197, 201
postemporality. See eternity as postemporality.
predestination. See election
pretemporality. See eternity as pretemporality.
providence, 100–106, 113, 171–72; *concursus*, 101, 103; *conservatio*, 101; *gubernatio*, 101; 'noncompetitive relation', 103

Rashkover, Randi, 204
recapitulation. See 'anticipation, synchronicity, and recapitulation' *and* Jesus Christ and recapitulation.
reconciliation. See soteriology.
redemption. See eschatology.
Reformation, Reformers, 74
regeneration, 49

resurrection. *See* Jesus Christ.
revelation, self-revelation, 12, 26–28, 30, 32, 44–45, 50–51, 62–64, 76–77
Ricoeur, Paul, 4–7, 189, 195
Roberts, Richard, 21–22, 28–30, 121, 129, 193
Romans (Barth's commentary), 3, 26–29, 35, 56–61, 74, 190
Rosato, Philip, 45, 166
Rowe, William, 130

saga, 96, 137, 198; *Genesis* as, 96, 198; resurrection of Jesus Christ and, 137
Sanders, Fred, 25
Schleiermacher, Friedrich, 74, 149
Schwöbel, Christoph, 12
self-alienation of God, 40
self-communication of God. *See* revelation
self-humiliation of God, 40
self-revelation. *See* revelation.
simultaneity (*simul*). *See* eternity as simultaneity.
Sorabji, Richard, 5
soteriology, 41–43
subjectivity of God, 26–28
supratemporality. *See* eternity as supratemporality.

Tanner, Kathryn, 87, 91, 103
theocentrism, 37
theological method, 7, 30, 55, 62–63, 67, 85–86, 107–9, 195–96, 200–201, 205
Theophilus of Antioch, 101
Thomas Aquinas, 1–2, 9–10, 67, 69, 91, 135, 189
time, 4–9; allotted time, 8, 16, 93, 102, 106, 114–121, 126, 153–55, 159–61, 191, 195; Aristotle on, 5; Augustine on, 4 (*see* Augustine as well); Christology and, *see* Jesus Christ and time; created, 3, 15, 42, 86–87, 93–100, 124–26, 128, 131–32, 155, 189, 191; ecclesial, 3, 15, 16, 36, 39, 41, 43, 46–47, 59, 124, 147–49, 159–62, 166–84, 189, 192, 195, 202–4; fallen, 16, 24, 37, 42, 73, 125–26, 128, 131–32, 134, 189, 191–91; fulfilled, 3, 15–16, 27–28, 36–43, 43, 73; as gift, 109, 115; human, 36–37, 86–87, 202–3; narrative, 4, 5–7, 87, 187–93 (*see* trinitarian pattern of time as well); and non-human creation, 99; objective, 4, 8, 37, 87, 93, 96–100, 102, 156–57, 191, 199, 204; preserved, 15, 86–87, 100–106, 124, 152–54, 189, 191, 195; qualitative dimension of, 6–7, 9, 14, 16, 43, 86–87, 106, 128, 146, 155, 157–58, 162, 168–69, 170–72, 182, 185, 189, 195, 203; rational-linear view of (succession of past, present, future), 4–5, 8, 15, 24, 33, 54, 68, 73, 106–13, 126, 155–57, 191, 195, 199; Ricoeur on, *see* Paul Ricoeur; in science, 4, 8, 197–202; subjective, 4, 98–100, 102, 106–121, 156–57, 199, 204 (*see* rational-linear view as well); Thomas Aquinas on, 1 (*see* Thomas Aquinas *as well*); trinitarian pattern of, 3, 66, 122, 150, 169, 172, 184, 187–93, 195, 205
Torrance, Alan, 44
Torrance, Thomas, 64, 87, 90, 148, 198–202
Trinity, 49–55, 62–66; agency of Son and Holy Spirit, 90–91; appropriations, doctrine of, 14–16, 24, 50, 64–65, 88–90; economic, 25, 31, 50, 64–65, 160–61; and election, 77–78; genetic relations, 64–66; *hypostases*, 53–54; immanent, 23–26, 31–32, 50, 64–65, 160–61, 191; modes of being (*seinsweisen*), 64; perichoresis, 50, 53–54, 65–66, 89–90
triplex mundus, 40, 148

univocity, 9–10

veiling-unveiling dialectic, 27–28, 32, 42, 44, 59, 60–61, 135, 137, 141, 149–40, 150–52. *See* revelation as well.
via triplex, 14, 61, 67, 188–89, 196; *via eminentiae*, 14, 67–70, 188–89, 186; *via negativa*, 14, 33, 35, 67, 85, 188–89, 196; *via positiva*, 14, 67–69, 188–89, 196
visible-invisible dialectic, 143, 145, 163, 174, 185
Vondey, Wolfgang, 43

Wagner, Falk, 13
Webster, John, 57, 62, 91, 107, 149
Weinandy, Thomas, 45, 120
Welker, Michael, 195, 197, 203
Wenham, Gordon, 96
Whitehouse, W. A., 90–91
Williams, Rowan, 44–45
Wright, N. T., 145

Zagzebski, Linda, 100
Zeitz, James, 10

www.ingramcontent.com/pod-product-compliance
Lightning Source LLC
Chambersburg PA
CBHW070338230426
43663CB00011B/2373